Jia Zhangke
on
Jia Zhangke

SINOTHEORY A series edited by Carlos Rojas and Eileen Cheng-yin Chow

Jia Zhangke on Jia Zhangke

MICHAEL BERRY

afterword by DAI JINHUA

DUKE UNIVERSITY PRESS   Durham and London   2022

© 2022 MICHAEL BERRY

This work is licensed under a Creative Commons Attribution-NonCommercial-NoDerivatives 4.0 International License available at https:// creativecommons.org/licenses/by-nc-nd/4.0/.
Designed by Aimee C. Harrison
Typeset in Minion Pro and Trade Gothic LT Std
by Westchester Publishing Services

Library of Congress Cataloging-in-Publication Data
Names: Berry, Michael, [date] author, interviewer.
Title: Jia Zhangke on Jia Zhangke/ Michael Berry ; afterword by Dai Jinhua.
Other titles: Sinotheory.
Description: Durham : Duke University Press, 2022. | Series: Sinotheory | Includes bibliographical references and index.
Identifiers: LCCN 2021027356 (print)
LCCN 2021027357 (ebook)
ISBN 9781478015499 (hardcover)
ISBN 9781478018124 (paperback)
ISBN 9781478022732 (ebook)
ISBN 9781478092605 (ebook other)
Subjects: LCSH: Jia, Zhangke, 1970- —Interviews. | Jia, Zhangke, 1970- —Criticism and interpretation. | Motion picture producers and directors—China. | BISAC: PERFORMING ARTS / Film / History & Criticism
Classification: LCC PN1998.3.J523 B477 2022 (print) | LCC PN1998.3.J523 (ebook) | DDC 791.4302/33092—dc23/eng/20211021
LC record available at https:// lccn.loc.gov/2021027356
LC ebook rec ord available at https:// lccn.loc.gov/2021027357

Cover art: Photo by Wang Jing, courtesy of Xstream Pictures.

THIS book is freely available in an open access edition thanks to TOME (Toward an Open Monograph Ecosystem)—a collaboration of the Association of American Universities, the Association of University Presses, and the Association of Research Libraries—and the generous support of Arcadia, a charitable fund of Lisbet Rausing and Peter Baldwin, and the UCLA Library. Learn more at the TOME website, available at: openmonographs.org.

for Naima,
wishing her a life filled with music, dance, and beautiful images

Contents

Series Editor's Preface CARLOS ROJAS ix
Acknowledgments xiii

Introduction From Fenyang to the World 1
One A Portrait of an Artist as a Young Man 19
Two The Hometown Trilogy 46
Three Documenting Destruction and Building Worlds 87
Four Film as Social Justice 113
Five Return to Jianghu 133
Six Toward an Accented Cinema 157
Coda To the Sea 182

Afterword DAI JINHUA 193
Notes 197
Jia Zhangke Filmography 205
Bibliography 207
Index 211

Series Editor's Preface

CARLOS ROJAS

WHEN JIA ZHANGKE, in one of his conversations with Michael Berry that compose this volume, remarks that "good films come in all shapes and sizes, but bad films all have a common feature," he is inverting the principle famously articulated in the first line of Leo Tolstoy's *Anna Karenina*: "All happy families are alike; each unhappy family is unhappy in its own way." The irony in Tolstoy's original formulation, of course, is that even as *Anna Karenina* focuses on several radically unhappy families, the novel itself has come to be regarded as an apogee of nineteenth-century literary realism. Even so, Tolstoy's work simultaneously heralded a wave of modernist developments in Euro-American literature and the arts, which in turn helped to reconfigure the standards for what might be considered an exemplary (or "happy") work of art. In contemporary China, meanwhile, Jia Zhangke has played a similarly decisive role in helping to expand assumptions of what constitutes a "good" film in the first place.

Almost precisely a century after the 1877 publication of *Anna Karenina*, the 1978 debut of post-Mao China's reform and opening-up campaign marked the beginning of a far-reaching reassessment of the standards of realism and of aesthetic value that had characterized cultural production under Mao. For the first quarter of a century following the establishment of the People's Republic of China in 1949, there was an expectation that cultural production would conform to the strictures of socialist realism, wherein art was viewed primarily as a vehicle for disseminating Communist values. The result was a relative homogeneity of cultural production that was disrupted during the post-1978 Reform Era, when a relaxation of China's censorship apparatus, an influx of European and American cultural works, and a rapidly growing economy helped facilitate the emergence of a more openly experimental, and even iconoclastic, art scene.

These developments had a particularly notable impact on domestic film production. During the Cultural Revolution (1966–76), China's flagship film school, the Beijing Film Academy, was shuttered, and it was not until 1978 that a new cohort of aspiring filmmakers (who came to be known as the Fifth Generation) was able to enroll in the recently reopened academy. After graduating in 1982, members of this cohort, which included figures such as Chen Kaige, Zhang Yimou, and Tian Zhuangzhuang, began producing films that diverged dramatically from the aesthetic and technical standards of earlier Maoist-era works, and in turn provided a new set of standards for what might be considered a "good" film.

Meanwhile, Jia Zhangke, who was born in 1970, describes how in 1991 he finally had a chance to watch Chen Kaige's classic *Yellow Earth* (1984), which he says changed his life and helped inspire him to become a filmmaker in his own right. In 1993, accordingly, Jia enrolled in the Beijing Film Academy, and after graduation he came to be recognized as one of the leading representatives of a rather eclectic group of young filmmakers sometimes referred to as the Sixth Generation. Unlike the Fifth Generation, this later cohort produced films that were often set in the contemporary post-Mao period, and they tended to favor an aesthetic that took inspiration from documentary cinema verité. To this end, these younger filmmakers often pursued a comparatively unpolished feel that not only sought to make a virtue of necessity (many of these early Sixth Generation films were produced on a low budget and without official permission) but also attempted to generate a more realistic sensibility.

Jia Zhangke's second feature-length film, *Platform* (2000), for instance, is set in Jia's hometown of Fenyang, in Shanxi Province, and explores how the cultural transformations that characterized the Reform Era gradually impacted not only China's urban areas but even relatively isolated communities like his hometown. Produced on a low budget with nonprofessional actors, the film spans the "long decade" of the 1980s, from 1978 to 1990, focusing on youngsters in a small song-and-dance troupe that shifts from performing canonical revolutionary works to more pop works inspired by international figures like the contemporary Taiwanese singer Teresa Teng (Deng Lijun) and the 1984 American break-dancing film *Breakin'*. The result is a moving exploration of not only the historical conditions under which Jia himself came of age but also some of the tectonic shifts in China's cultural and aesthetic orientation during this same period.

Three years after Jia Zhangke released *Platform*, China's Film Bureau organized a symposium at the Beijing Film Academy for filmmakers who, like Jia, were producing works without previously obtaining approval through official channels. Jia recalls that more than fifty "underground" directors showed up at the meeting, and that it was as a result of this event that he decided to submit his recently completed screenplay for official approval. The result was *The World* (2004), which was Jia's first film to be officially approved for domestic screening, though it still retained many of the documentary-style qualities that had distinguished *Platform* and his other underground productions.

Meanwhile, even as Jia's subsequent body of feature films, documentaries, and shorts has continued to extend his cinematic vision in new directions, his oeuvre continues to be driven by a concern that has shaped it from the beginning—namely, an attempt to reexamine and expand conventional assumptions about what constitutes a "good" film.

Acknowledgments

THERE ARE MANY PEOPLE I need to thank for helping to make this book a reality. I would like to begin by extending my sincere appreciation to Jia Zhangke for his friendship, generosity, and artistic spirit. He has given us some of the most remarkable Chinese-language films ever produced, and I am deeply moved by his willingness to share his thoughts and reflections on those films. Thanks to Jia Zhangke's staff, especially the team that accompanied him to Los Angeles in 2018, Casper Leung and Yang Xiuzhi. When I learned that Jia Zhangke's artist-in-residence program in Los Angeles conflicted with my jury duties for the Golden Horse Film Festival, it took some acrobatic feats of scheduling to arrange two separate trips to Taipei, sandwiched between a week of Jia Zhangke screenings in LA. Thanks to Ang Lee, Wen Tien-hsiang, and Mr. Luo Hai for accommodating my complicated schedule. Special thanks to my UCLA team of collaborators, Susan Jain, Paul Malcolm, and Cheng-Sim Lim. It was truly a pleasure to work with all of them on this unforgettable program. I especially appreciate Cheng-Sim and Berenice Reynaud, who traveled to Beijing to personally invite Jia to Los Angeles for our UCLA program. Thanks to Jonathan Karp, Charlie Coker, and Li Huang from the Asia Society Southern California and Susan Oxtoby from Berkeley Art Museum and Pacific Film Archive (BAMPFA) for inviting me to host further dialogues with Jia on *Ash Is Purest White* and *Swimming Out Till the Sea Turns Blue*. Many campus partners helped sponsor

Jia Zhangke's visit, thereby also making this book possible; they include the China Onscreen Biennial, the UCLA Confucius Institute, the Department of Asian Languages and Cultures, the Department of Film and Media Studies, and the Division of the Humanities. Appreciation is also due to the staff at the Hammer Theater and the Bridges Theater, where the dialogues were held. My deep appreciation to Eugene Suen, who provided interpretation for the majority of the screenings. I am grateful to my doctoral students, especially Lin Du and Yiyang Hou, who helped with Chinese transcription of a portion of the dialogues, and to all of the students, colleagues, and audience members who attended the various events and screenings, especially those whose questions made it into the book. Thanks to the legendary Peter Sellars (who attended every screening and dialogue!), Robert Rosen, Barbara Robinson, David Schaberg, Stanley Rosen, and Janet Yang for their support of this project. For more than twenty years, Professor Dai Jinhua has been one of my academic role models, and I am honored and humbled that she agreed to write an afterword for this book. It was a pleasure to be able to work with my old friends and Sinotheory series editors Carlos Rojas and Eileen Cheng-yin Chow on this project; they offered unwavering support from the first moment I reached out to them to pitch the idea. I have also been a beneficiary of the support and editorial wisdom of Elizabeth Ault, Liz Smith, Susan Ecklund, and Aimee C. Harrison at Duke University Press, who saw the book through the publication process. I want to also express my gratitude to Jason McGrath and an anonymous external reviewer, who offered valuable suggestions on two early versions of the manuscript. Finally, thanks to my family—my wife, Suk-Young Kim, and our children, Miles Berry and Naima Berry. Like many of the protagonists of Jia's films, Naima loves music, dance, and fashion, and it is to her that I dedicate this book.

Introduction
From Fenyang to the World

WHEN WE LOOK BACK ON the cinema of the People's Republic of China (PRC) from 1949 to the present, one can divide this period of film history into three phases: the socialist period, the Chinese New Wave, and the era of commercial cinema. From the early 1950s through the late 1970s, virtually all of PRC film history was dominated by government-sponsored propaganda films. This was socialist realist cinema that projected what an ideal world *should* look like—a world filled with utopian socialist visions, Maoist thought, images of patriotism and martyrdom, and clearly delineated lines between "heroes" and "villains." During this period, the war film—often depicting the Korean War, the War of Resistance against Japan, and the Chinese Civil War—and later the eight model opera films from the Cultural Revolution would dominate the Chinese screen.

With the reform policies initiated by Deng Xiaoping in 1978, a new cultural space opened up in China, and the 1980s saw the beginning of what would be called the "Culture Fever." Suddenly a vibrant combination of influences began to flood into China from the outside: rock and roll, the English pop duo Wham!, Western classical music, Nietzsche, Schopenhauer, magic realism, Milan Kundera, Umberto Eco. These examples of European culture combined with a rediscovery of traditional Chinese religion, thought, and cultural practices—Buddhism, Daoism, Confucianism, tai chi, qigong—to create a cultural renaissance in China. One by one, all the various arts saw radical movements that revolutionized the Chinese cultural landscape—the Stars (Xingxing huahui) collective in art; the Misty Poetry (Menglong shi) movement and the *Today* (Jintian) group that opened up a new space for cultural and poetic discourse; the Scar (Shanghen) movement that presented traumatic remembrances of the Cultural Revolution through poetry, oil painting, literature, and film; and the early origins of contemporary Chinese rock and pop music from artists like Cui Jian.

Eventually, this "Culture Fever" would give rise to China's first New Wave cinematic movement—the Fifth Generation. Dominated by a core group of filmmakers who graduated from the Beijing Film Academy in 1982, the Fifth Generation was fueled equally by the experience of growing up during the radicalism of the Cultural Revolution and reaching early adulthood during the vibrant early days of the Reform Era. They would go on to make films that challenged the very definition of Chinese cinema. Films like Chen Kaige's *Yellow Earth* (*Huang tudi*, 1984) represented a new page in Chinese cinema history. While the film presented peasants and soldiers—familiar subjects in socialist Chinese cinema—the method of representation was completely different from anything that had appeared previously on the Chinese screen. Instead of black-and-white heroes and villains, *Yellow Earth* featured morally ambiguous characters, a probing and brooding existential tone, an open-ended conclusion, and a bold new visual language that employed unorthodox horizon lines and extensive use of montage, metaphor, and symbolism. Starting around 1983, the Chinese New Wave would mark the beginning of the second major phase in PRC cinema history as *One and Eight* (*Yige he bage*, 1983), *Yellow Earth*, and other early films of the Fifth Generation began to establish a new aesthetic and narrative language for Chinese film. And while many Fifth Generation filmmakers would eventually turn toward more commercial cinematic pursuits, the experimental edge of their early work would be picked up and continued by the Sixth Generation in the early 1990s.

As the Sixth Generation evolved and the movement they represented began to develop a collective voice, fundamental differences between this group and its predecessors emerged. Early representative filmmakers of the Sixth Generation like Wang Xiaoshuai and Zhang Yuan eschewed epic narratives in favor of depictions of the everyday, heroes were replaced by characters from the margins of society, aestheticized mise-en-scène was abandoned in favor of a gritty documentary-esque style, and adaptations of contemporary literary classics were tossed aside in order to adapt original, autobiographical, and real-life stories set mostly in contemporary urban China. These differences aside, on some level, both the Fifth and the Sixth Generation can be seen as distinct phases of a second stage in Chinese film history that was very much dominated by aesthetics and principles of New Wave art cinema.

Born in 1970, Jia Zhangke was several years younger than filmmakers like Wang Xiaoshuai and Zhang Yuan, but he would eventually come to be regarded as the leading voice of the Sixth Generation. Jia grew up in Fenyang, a town in Shanxi Province. He would spend his first years during the latter phases of the Cultural Revolution, through which he was exposed to the socialist realist cinema of that era. But by the time Jia was six years old, the cultural thaw had begun, and a much broader tapestry of cultural influences would slowly become available throughout Jia's adolescence. He fell in love with the voice of Taiwanese songstress Teresa Teng (Deng Lijun) through shortwave radio broadcasts and imitated moves from the US break-dancing movie *Breakin'* (1984). He would study painting in the county seat of Taiyuan and eventually had his own artistic epiphany after attending a screening of Chen Kaige's *Yellow Earth*. Jia would later recall the dramatic impact this film had on him: "That film changed my life. It was at that moment, after watching *Yellow Earth*, that I decided I wanted to become a director and my passion for film was born. . . . Before [that], virtually all of the other Chinese films I had seen were basically state-sponsored works laden with propaganda, all made in a very conservative mold. So my cinematic imagination was always very limited; I never realized there were other possibilities for film. But all of that changed after watching *Yellow Earth*. Suddenly I was struck with a new paradigm for cinematic expression" (chapter 1). That fateful experience led Jia down a path to become a filmmaker. He went on to study film at the Beijing Film Academy, where he was active in several student film groups and began to make a series of short films. It was through that series of early short films—*One Day in Beijing*, *Du Du*, and *Xiao Shan Going Home*—that Jia started to develop his signature cinematic style.

Xiao Shan Going Home traces a few days in the life of a migrant worker in Beijing. As the Chinese New Year draws near, Xiao Shan (Wang Hongwei), an out-of-work restaurant cook, decides to return home to visit his family for the holiday. The entire fifty-eight-minute film traces Xiao Shan's journey—not as he returns home but as he traverses Beijing calling on a variety of characters, including a university student, a ticket scalper, and a prostitute, in hopes of finding someone willing to accompany him back to his hometown. The "Going Home" in the film's English title hints at an action eternally suspended; Xiao Shan never actually makes it to his destination, and "home" proves to be an ever-elusive site just out of grasp. This detail would prove to be a powerful metaphor for what was to come in Jia Zhangke's cinematic oeuvre, a world in which characters face an environment pregnant with possibilities that never come to fruition. *Xiao Shan Going Home* was actually a student film shot during Jia's days at the Beijing Film Academy; it would help establish his stylistic direction and attention to the everyday. *Xiao Shan Going Home* was also the first film to star Wang Hongwei, who would become one of Jia's most frequent collaborators. When Jia brought *Xiao Shan Going Home* to Hong Kong in 1997 for the Hong Kong Independent Short Film and Video Awards, it also set in motion the formation of his early core creative team—cinematographer Nelson Yu Lik-Wai (Yu Liwei) and producers Chow Keung (Zhou Qiang) and Lee Kit-Ming (Li Jieming). With the help of this team and its production company Hu Tong Productions, Jia would make a series of films that would rewrite the rules for Chinese independent cinema. Together they would go on to create some of Jia's most important films—*Xiao Wu, Platform, Unknown Pleasures, Still Life*, and *24 City*. Over the course of making these films—and all of his subsequent work—Jia would continually navigate the space between China's socialist past and its new identity as a global superpower. While the vast majority of China's filmmakers have wholeheartedly embraced the latter identity—making big-budget, blockbuster-style films that seem to complement China's political and economic rise—Jia has remained fairly consistent in making smaller-scale, art house–style films that ask difficult questions about one's place in society, alienation, technology, exploitation, the environment, and the disorientation one faces when living through moments of radical social change.

Jia's first major cinematic statement was a series of films that would come to be referred to as the "Hometown Trilogy" (*Guxiang sanbuqu*). *Xiao Wu, Platform*, and *Unknown Pleasures* constituted a remarkable group of films that broke new ground in terms of their sophisticated use of film language, documentary film–style aesthetics, realist tone, employment of nonprofessional actors, and complex, layered story lines. Each of the three films was shot in a different format (16mm, 35mm, and digital) and spanned a different time period (1996, the 1980s, and 2002, respectively), yet collectively they created one of the most consistent and powerful cinematic statements to come out of the contemporary Chinese film scene. All three eschewed portrayals of both the "backward" countryside and the "modern" big city usually seen in Chinese cinema in favor of "small-town," everyday China. The trilogy also focused not on traditional "heroes" but on everyday marginalized protagonists (dancers, pickpockets, and delinquents) in an attempt to reveal the texture of Chinese reality.

Highlighting a few days in the life of a small-time pickpocket in Fenyang, *Xiao Wu* revealed the breakdown of interpersonal relationships in Xiao Wu's world. The film utilized a documentary-like approach, yet woven into the handheld camerawork and gritty style was a carefully designed structure that traced the tragic destruction of Xiao Wu's relationships with his former best friend, a would-be girlfriend, and his soon-to-be-estranged parents. Playing out against Xiao Wu's story is the larger story of mass-scale demolition and forced relocation being carried out in his (and the director's) hometown of Fenyang. More ambitious, *Platform* unfolds in more epic time, spanning the entire decade of the 1980s, from the early days of the Reform Era in the late 1970s up until the time of the Tiananmen crackdown in 1989. Playing out against this canvas of massive social change is a more quotidian story of a group of young dreamers who are members of a song-and-dance troupe who attempt to navigate the changing world around them. *Unknown Pleasures* continued Jia's exploration and updated his take on China's transformation to 2002, portraying two lost teenagers whose coming-of-age story is plagued by a series of misfortunes and missteps. Shot entirely in digital, the film was also an important early example of digital filmmaking in China. *Platform* and *Unknown Pleasures* were also notable for introducing Zhao Tao. Trained in classical Chinese dance and a graduate of the Beijing Dance Academy, Zhao Tao would succeed Wang Hongwei as Jia's most important on-screen collaborator, starring in almost all of his subsequent dramatic features and eventually becoming his wife.

While Jia's Hometown Trilogy established the filmmaker internationally, in China his films were limited to small screenings in film clubs, universities, and independent film festivals and were available as underground DVDs. It was not until the release of *The World* (2004) that Jia Zhangke's films were commercially screened in China. *The World* also marked a turning point in Jia's film aesthetic. Its protagonists find themselves in Beijing working at World Park, a theme park modeled after Disney's Epcot Center where all the great tourist sites of the world are collected in miniature. There, migrant workers from Fenyang and beyond can have lunch atop the Eiffel Tower, stroll over London Bridge, and gaze at the World Trade Center towers, which, as one character observes, here are still standing. The cast features Zhao Tao as Tao, a dancer/performer who struggles with her relationship with her boyfriend Taisheng (Cheng Taishen), a security guard at the park. At the heart of the film is the deep disconnect between the glossy and glamorous global tourist destination sites, which are "fake," and the isolated, exploited lives of the workers and performers who inhabit the park, which are all too "real." Through this radical juxtaposition of opulent spaces and disenfranchised workers, *The World* unveils its scathing critique of globalism, its meditation on the place of the simulacrum in postmodern society, and a desperate vision of alienation in postsocialist China.

The film highlighted the director's trademark techniques and themes, but this time Jia surprised viewers with a thumping electronic music soundtrack by Lim Qiong, dreamlike Flash animation vignettes, and touches of what could almost be described as magic realism. In *Still Life* (2006), Jia again tested the boundaries between fiction film and documentary, while simultaneously pushing his magic realist tendency even further with painted Peking Opera actors, tightrope walkers, and spaceships all intermittently appearing among the ruins of a soon-to-be-submerged city. The film seemed to take Jia's politics of demolition and destruction, first introduced in *Xiao Wu*, to their ultimate destination, with an entire city slated to be "relocated" in anticipation of the rising level of the Yangtze River due to the Three Gorges Dam project. *Still Life* would go on to win Jia widespread critical acclaim, including a Golden Lion at the Venice Film Festival. As film scholar Dai Jinhua has pointed out, the film was also crucial for its inversion of long-ingrained cinematic themes:

> The visual space of *Still Life* has become a "site" in the narrow sense, a temporal appearance of a spatial form. Clearly, within the range of Chinese art cinema, or rather in the tradition of post-Mao film, *Still Life* is the first to accomplish the inversion of cultural and visual themes of fifth-generation Chinese cinema (or rather fifth-generation style film). No longer is space given priority over time, and no longer is the time of progress, reform, and life swallowed by Chinese historical and geographical space. Rather, it is temporality, that is to say development or progress, that sweeps away historical and natural spaces like a hurricane and rewrites them, as if once again corroborating a compressed experience of time: contemporary China experienced four hundred years of European capitalist history, from the Enlightenment to the critique of modernity in the thirty years leading up to the turn of this century.[1]

Besides its important intervention into temporality, *Still Life* also continued the director's complex investigation into the relationship between documentary film and narrative film storytelling. In *Still Life*, this was demonstrated not only through the use of real locations and nonprofessional actors but also through the film's connection with a companion documentary film, *Dong*, part of which focused on painter Liu Xiaodong's portraits of workers and residents in the same city.

Continuing to alternate between feature films and documentaries, Jia made two more feature-length documentary films, *Useless* in 2007 and *I Wish I Knew*, which was produced in cooperation with the 2010 Shanghai Expo. His film *24 City* (2008) again played with the line between documentary and fictional filmmaking, casting professional actors like Joan Chen and Zhao Tao alongside retired factory workers, who were the real-life interview subjects whose stories inspired the film. Jia's *24 City* was a nostalgic look back at the factory system of socialist China and the fate of the workers whose lives were once entirely bound by the structure of the factory work unit. Like *Still Life*, which depicted the literal drowning of the entire city of Fengjie, *24 City* is a portrait of disappearance. As Corey Kai Nelson Schultz observes: "The film creates 'portraits in performance' and 'memories in performance' which use history, memory, and emotion to construct a felt history of the worker class on the eve of its extinction. This creates a structure of feeling that ultimately commemorates and elegizes this group's irrevocable decline and disappearance in the Reform era, and mourns the class by placing it in the past."[2] In 2013, Jia Zhangke released what was perhaps his most controversial film, testing his sometimes-tenuous relationship with China's film censors. Inspired by a series of real-life news reports, *A Touch of Sin* documented a group of loosely intertwined stories about individuals frustrated, abused, exploited, or otherwise disenfranchised by society. In each of the stories, individuals pushed to the limit explode—or implode—triggering a series of violent acts that captured the disenchantment and frustrations lurking just beneath the surface of economic prosperity.

Mountains May Depart saw Jia return again to his hometown of Fenyang, but rather than a nostalgic vision of the past, Jia presented—for the first time in his body of work—a vision of the future. Like *Platform* fifteen years earlier, *Mountains May Depart* provided a sweeping narrative perspective from which to meditate on loss and change. These would also be some of the themes that Jia would pick up again in 2018 with *Ash Is Purest White*, which followed two self-styled gangsters as they navigate prison, illness, aging, and the loss of central values like brotherhood and loyalty in favor of a social economy that runs on money. Literally called "Sons and Daughters of Jianghu" in Chinese, *Ash Is Purest White* directly references *jianghu*, a concept that has been important throughout Jia's body of work. The term traditionally refers to the realm outside mainstream society where heroes and villains operate according to their own codes of righteousness and loyalty, which has been the setting for countless stories from *The Water Margin* (*Shuihu zhuan*) to the modern martial arts novels of Jin Yong. But jianghu can also point to a form of social bonding centered around notions of brotherhood and often displayed in modern martial arts and gangster films. While inspired by the 1980s gangster films of John Woo, Jia's reinterpretation of the jianghu genre is devoid of MTV-style editing, two-handed gun battles, white doves, and other melodramatic flourishes; instead, *Ash Is Purest White* offers what can almost be thought of as a deconstruction of the gangster genre. Chases and gunfights are replaced by searching and waiting; slow-motion action set pieces are replaced by slow cinema aesthetics; the male-centered bonding and misogynist undercurrent of many jianghu films are displaced by a strong central female character; and, by the time the surveillance cameras go up at the end of the film, we know that, under the watchful eye of the state, there is no longer space for this jianghu to survive.

From the martial arts extravaganzas *Hero* (*Yingxiong*, 2002), *House of Flying Daggers* (*Shimian maifu*, 2004), and *The Promise* (*Wuji*, 2005), to aestheticized visions of urban consumption in *Tiny Times* (*Xiao shidai*, 2013), to escapist fantasy films like *Monster Hunt* (*Zhuoyao ji*, 2015) and *The Mermaid* (*Meirenyu*, 2016) or even nationalist-fueled action cinema like *Wolf Warrior II* (*Zhanlang II*, 2017), Chinese cinema today has largely turned its back on the more experimental roots of the Fifth Generation and the Sixth Generation in the 1980s and 1990s. Today the Chinese film industry finds itself deeply entrenched in a third phase that is utterly dominated by the juggernaut of commercial cinema. But while the industry bulldozes forward into commercial cinematic forms and genres, Jia and his collaborators have homed in on that space between socialism and capitalism, destruction and revitalization. This liminal space is inhabited by marginal characters—dancers and drifters, prostitutes and pickpockets. Feeling a disconnect between the protagonists depicted in most Chinese-language films, Jia set out to create a world populated by figures he could relate to. As Jia explains: "I increasingly feel that the single most difficult thing in film is to create a new image of what a protagonist should be. That is where the absolute heart of cinematic innovation lies. You need to create a new type of person and capture that new character on film" (chapter 2).

Over the course of his films to date, Jia has indeed created some of the most recognizable characters in the history of Chinese cinema—Xiao Wu, the naive pickpocket who stubbornly lives by his own code of ethics even as he is swallowed up by a still larger world of swindlers and thieves; Cui Mingliang, whose youthful fire and idealism of the early 1980s gradually die off as he settles into middle age; Han Sanming, who silently searches the ruins of a doomed city in search of his long-lost wife; or Shen Tao, who struggles to navigate the complex web of relationships with the men in her life and later her son. Jia's creation of these and other characters—often those left behind amid China's economic revolution—can be seen as an active stance in his cinematic project to refocus the story of China's transformation.

The protagonists highlighted in Jia's films function as a revisionist intervention into both socialist soldier heroes like Dong Cunrui and Lei Feng, whose image dominated the cinematic imagination during the period when Jia was still a small child, and lead-actor tropes from both Hollywood and mainstream Chinese commercial cinema. Instead, Jia's characters reflect a sense of rootlessness, displacement, and wandering; they struggle to find their place in society; relationships are riddled with miscommunication, lies, and disappointment; and textbook cinematic devices often used to provide characters with "closure," "happy endings," and "resolution" are almost always withheld. This intervention, which has played out across his films over twenty-five years, has had a pervasive impact on the collective imagination of what on-screen representation looks like in Chinese cinema. These are voices from the subaltern that Jia's films have rendered visible, identifiable, and human.[3] Part of the director's insistence on highlighting perspectives that had been rendered invisible over the course of much of China's cinematic history comes from Jia's self-identification as a "folk director," a "grassroots director," or, as Li Yang and others have described him, a "migrant filmmaker."[4] At the same time, Jia Zhangke himself has spoken eloquently about how refocusing our attention on a different set of protagonists on-screen can almost be thought of as an intervention that attempts to retrain audience conceptions about the very notion of "marginality": "I don't agree with the claim that our films are about 'marginal' figures in society. . . . I feel these issues actually concern the majority of Chinese. These characters, therefore, are ordinary, not 'marginal.' The notion of marginality refers to something alienated from the center and the mainstream. Out of the city, however, what is the mainstream of Chinese society? How does the Chinese majority live? If you think my characters are 'marginal,' then the majority of the Chinese could also be labeled 'marginal.'"[5]

This refocusing can be seen not only through the types of characters Jia features but also through the environment in which he positions them. For decades, the vast majority of Chinese-language films—and films about China produced in the West, for that matter—were set in one of two locales, the countryside or the city. Over time, a visual shorthand came to be projected on these locations as they took on often overly simplistic symbolic meanings—the city as stand-in for modernity, alienation, and westernization while the countryside represented tradition, community, and cultural roots. But in a bold move, Jia drew his viewers' attention to the often-neglected provincial towns and smaller-scale cities off the beaten path of development. Jia began with his hometown of Fenyang in Shanxi Province, the setting for *Xiao Wu*, *Platform*, and later *Mountains Will Depart*. This attention to liminal spaces can be seen not only in the macro-locations of his films (Fenyang, Datong, Fengjie, etc.), but also on a micro-level in the actual spaces where he shoots, with locations such as street-side noodle stalls, bus station waiting rooms, and illegal gambling houses also highlighting a sense of "in between." Liminality is further displayed, enhanced even, not only through the locations but through their very disappearance, which plays out in the camera's repeated interest in documenting destruction, demolition, and construction.

Throughout Jia's films one can find backdrops of buildings being torn down, sweeping expanses of rubble and waste. These images further isolate the already marginalized characters, destabilizing them and alienating them from their surroundings. These powerful images of desolation and destruction can even be seen as refracted allegorical portraits of Jia's protagonists, who themselves navigate the same treacherous transformation as their environment. Along the way, careful viewers can see the signposts of the abandoned socialist utopia—faded political slogans hiding in the backdrop in *Platform*, ruins of old Soviet-style apartment buildings in *Unknown Pleasures*, or the factory that takes center stage to make room for a modern real estate enterprise in *24 City*. Eventually, Jia's cinematic portrayal of Fenyang would take on a looming presence in his body of work, like Joyce's Dublin, Faulkner's Yoknapatawpha County, or Mo Yan's Northeast Gaomi County. The liminal space of Fenyang would later be expanded to other locales—such as Datong in *Unknown Pleasures*, Chengdu in *24 City*, or Dongguan in *Touch of Sin*. But nowhere provided a more ideal canvas for Jia's meditation on transformation than the drowning city of Fengjie in *Still Life*, *Dong*, and *Ash Is Purest White*. Cecilia Mello has observed that Jia is conscious "of how a disappearing space implies the loss of memory. From this, he derives an urgency to film these spaces and these memories, felt to be always on the cusp of disappearance. At the same time, he cultivates a seemingly contradictory slowness in observation, almost as an act of resistance in the face of the speed of transformations, which he regards as a 'form of violence,' imbued with a 'destructive nature.'"[6]

Equally remarkable as the characters and places he depicts in his body of work is the cinematic form he appropriates; content to settle into the uncomfortable space *between*, allowing his camera to linger on the unsettling space of transition itself. This in-between space speaks to a longing nostalgia toward the socialist world being abandoned while projecting an uneasiness about the uncertain future rapidly rising up to take its place. While Chen Kaige, the director of *Yellow Earth*, the very film that first inspired Jia's cinematic epiphany, has long eschewed the experimental filmmaking of his early days in favor of more mainstream commercial fare, Jia Zhangke has continued to take up the mantle of Chinese art cinema. Going against the current of the mainstream, Jia continues to make films that ask difficult questions and push the boundaries of cinematic form: one can see subtle intertextual bleeds between his own films, which function like a nuanced cinematic conversation: hints of the martial arts film genre in *Touch of Sin*, echoes of science fiction in *Still Life*, shadows of the 1980s Hong Kong gangster film in *Ash Is Purest White*, and a probing interrogation between the boundaries of narrative film and documentary. He experiments with different mediums—16mm, 35mm, digital—and different genres, and over time has created a cinematic vocabulary that is all his own.

In dissecting the philosophical underpinnings of the director's formal approach to filmmaking, film scholar Qi Wang has offered the following insight:

> Jia Zhangke exercises what I call "subjective metanarrative vision" and creates conscious subject positions for the spectator to encounter cinematic representations of past and present. The encounter is an epistemological experience of the "superficial" nature of time and space: traces left on the surface of a wall as an embodiment of the past and debris as a spatial index of the memory of space, for instance. In the face of the richly suggestive surface of the present pregnant with the past, Jia's camera remains non-intruding yet attentive, anonymous yet conscious, placing the spectator in a sensitive position, from where cinematic interventions and the real historical world informing them are seen and experienced simultaneously as a whole.[7]

Wang's description allows us to appreciate a key facet of Jia Zhangke's film style, which is at once seemingly detached and observational yet somehow "conscious." And it is through this visual consciousness that viewers are invited to experience the subjects as being thoroughly rooted in time, even as Jia repeatedly reminds us of how history, and time itself for that matter, is continually being broken down and stripped away. While many of the other early Sixth Generation filmmakers became known for their "on-the-spot realism," Jia went further than anyone else in rooting his camera's documentary-like captures of the here and now inside a larger meditation on the passage of time.

Another facet that sets Jia apart from his contemporaries is the way he has self-consciously positioned himself as one of contemporary China's leading public intellectuals. Jia's documentary films have garnered almost as much critical acclaim as his feature films. He is a popular public speaker who appears frequently on Chinese talk shows and lecture tours. In addition, he is a prolific essay writer and has published more than half a dozen companion books related to his films, such as a collection of interviews with workers released in conjunction with *24 City*, various screenplays, and the highly acclaimed two-volume collection *Jia Xiang* (the first volume is available in English under the title *Jia Zhangke Speaks Out*). Jia has run his own production company, Xstream Pictures, since 2006 and serves as a prolific producer, fostering the work of several other up-and-coming directors like Han Jie, Diao Yinan, and the poet Han Dong. Jia appears in Hitchcock-esque cameos in nearly all of his feature films and has also appeared in cameo roles in films by Han Han and other directors.

However, since 2012, Jia's film activities have taken on a markedly entrepreneurial flavor. In 2012, he became the second-largest investor in Turn East Media (Yihui chuanmei), a company involved in developing television, film, and variety shows. In 2015, Jia formed Fabula Entertainment (Shanghai nuanliu wenhua chuanmei) with Cao Guoxiong, Wang Hong, and Wu Xiaobo, a company aimed at "film-related lifestyle building." And in 2016 Jia registered three new companies in his hometown of Fenyang: Fenyang Jia Zhangke Arts Center, Fenyang Zhongzi Film Exhibition, and Shanxi Mountains May Department Food and Beverage. The following year, he founded the Pingyao Crouching Tiger Hidden Dragon International Film Festival, which in just a few short years has developed into one of the most dynamic and influential independent film festivals in China. Two decades after Fenyang first appeared on-screen in *Xiao Wu*, Jia Zhangke seemed determined to reinvent his hometown as a major hub for cinema and the arts via theater construction, cafés, an arts center, and his own film festival. Perhaps one of the most notable shifts in Jia's public persona came in 2018 when the onetime underground director was elected a deputy of the National People's Congress, the highest organ of state power in China. All of this points to Jia's enormous impact on the contemporary Chinese cultural scene and his transformation into a cultural critic, a producer, a film mogul, and ultimately even a politician. However, it seems uncanny that a director whose films once championed the underdog and leveled unflinching criticism at the mechanisms of power that create alienation and oppression now finds himself situated at the very center of those corporate and state centers of power. At the same time, within Jia's body of work we witness a telling synthesis of the three phases of Chinese film history mentioned at the beginning of this introduction: socialist cinema, art house film, and commercial cinema. Throughout Jia's body of work, we have seen a keen engagement with the fate of socialist China's legacy, and experimental or New Wave cinema has always been the primary language through which Jia has expressed his attachments, concern, and often suspicions about China's socialist legacy in the Reform Era. However, his more recent commercial and entrepreneurial activities are telling indicators that even someone once described as a "migrant director" and as "A Director for the People from China's Lower Class" cannot escape the uncompromising commercial nature of Chinese film culture today. It also begs the question as to whether Jia's commercial activities are used to fund his art house films or that instead his cultural activities are used to leverage bigger business moves. However, as Dai Jinhua reminds us in her afterword to this book, a big part of Jia Zhangke's contribution has been breaking down binaries, and not falling into them.

All the while, Jia Zhangke's voyage from Fenyang to the world needs to be considered not only within the context of contemporary Chinese film history but also through the director's engagements with global art cinema. As scholars like Jason McGrath and Li Yang have observed, Jia's style of aesthetic realism can be seen as a marriage between the dual influences of postsocialist realism in Chinese fiction and documentary films from the 1990s and the tradition of international art house cinema.[8] Stressing the "synergy" between these two forces, Li Yang argues that "it was Jia's ingenious blending of gritty realism and formalism to address contemporary social issues in unmistakable aestheticism, that ultimately produced his success and the lasting power of the new realist style."[9] But Jia Zhangke's interface with the international art house film movement went far beyond its influence on him as a young director. Perhaps more than any other contemporary Chinese filmmaker, Jia Zhangke not only has been embraced by the global network of elite film festivals, from Venice to Cannes and from New York to Tokyo, but has become a central figure in that world. Jia has been awarded prestigious prizes such as the Golden Lion at Venice for *Still Life*, and five of his films have been screened in competition at Cannes. Whereas *Yellow Earth* may have been the film that ignited his early interest in cinema, he would go on to study the works of Ozu, Hou, Antonioni, and Bresson. More commercially minded directors like Martin Scorsese and John Woo would also leave their mark on Jia's aesthetic. Jia came to perfect a style and cinematic diction that firmly positioned him alongside the auteur masters of the global art house tradition. In fact, Jia further enmeshed himself in this world through active collaborations with figures like Eric Gautier (cinematographer for filmmakers like Agnes Varda, Olivier Assayas, and Hirokazu Koreeda); Matthieu Laclau (French film editor who has worked with Jia since 2013); Lim Qiong (Taiwanese composer and frequent collaborator with Hou Hsiao-hisen); and Shozo Ichiyama (Japanese producer who has also worked extensively with Hou). Jia has even had the global art house camera turned on him when he became the subject of a documentary by Walter Salles, the Brazilian director of films such as *The Motorcycle Diaries* (2004), *Dark Water* (2005), and *On the Road* (2012). The resulting film, *Jia Zhang-ke, A Guy from Fenyang* (2016), was screened at Berlin and helped to further establish Jia as part of the canon of global art house cinema.

To understand Jia's political positioning, body of work, and aesthetic signature, it is essential to position him within the dual environments of the local Chinese film industry and international art house cinema. Between these two poles, Jia's body of work takes on conflicting meanings and alternative arcs of reception and dissemination. The tensions between these two worlds can be seen through his first three films—*Xiao Wu*, *Platform*, and *Unknown Pleasures*—which were embraced by the international art house community while being commercially restricted in China. They can also be seen through the complex lines Jia walks when he accepts Chinese projects like the documentary *I Wish I Knew* (2010), which was commissioned by the Shanghai World Expo, or corporate projects like directing a 2019 iPhone X commercial or opening the 2020 Prada Mode show in Shanghai. Perhaps the example that best crystallizes these tensions is *A Touch of Sin* (2013), which was recognized by Cannes and even selected by the *New York Times* as one of the best twenty-five films of the twenty-first century even though, as of 2021, the film had yet to be commercially distributed in China. Another example of these tensions was revealed in October 2020 when Jia suddenly announced that he and his team were stepping away from the Pingyao Crouching Tiger Hidden Dragon International Film Festival, which had just completed its fourth run. While no clear explanation was given for why he felt the festival needed to be "unburdened from the shadow of Jia Zhangke,"[10] lurking behind the announcement were certainly deeper tensions between state-sponsored film festival models in China and a politically unfettered vision of what a true *independent* film festival can be. This results in two Jia Zhangkes or, at the very least, two different bodies of work and artistic personas between China and the West. While a film like *A Touch of Sin* may be absent from Chinese theaters, Jia's shorts and numerous producing activities have left a powerful mark on the industry in China, all of which is largely invisible to Western viewers. At the same time, Jia's previously discussed persona as a public intellectual, cultural entrepreneur, and political player is also largely left out of his presence in the West, where he is still received primarily as an auteur of pure cinema. But one of the reasons Jia Zhangke has managed to flourish as a filmmaker, even under the crushing tide of commercial cinema in mainland China over the past two decades, is because he has been able to so successfully navigate these two poles, from the Chinese film market to the global art house, standing up for an uncompromising artistic vision while traversing the complexities of censorship and shareholders, from Fenyang to the world.

WHILE THIS BOOK PROJECT came together fairly quickly, with the majority of conversations recorded over the span of one week in 2019, in some sense it took much longer because the book includes interview content recorded as early as 2002 and as recently as 2021. Jia Zhangke began making films just a few years after my first trip to China, and his work has been a core part of my academic life for the past twenty years. I started taking note of Jia's films in the late 1990s, when I was a PhD student at Columbia University. I first watched *Xiao Wu* and *Platform* on poor-quality VCDs and later in their proper format at the Film Society of Lincoln Center. Those films had a tremendous impact on me during those years, partly for their sophisticated use of film language, their powerful images, and the humanistic portrayal of characters but also because the world they portrayed was so close to my personal memories from my time as a foreign student in China during the early and mid-1990s. While I had seen dozens of Chinese films from that period, none of them captured the sights and sounds, spaces and faces of 1990s China like *Xiao Wu* and *Platform*.

I had the opportunity to finally meet Jia Zhangke in 2002 when he traveled to New York with his producer Chow Keung for the New York Film Festival, where *Unknown Pleasures* was screening. I served as Jia's interpreter, handling all of the postscreening Q&As, various press interviews, and even an unforgettable private meeting with Martin Scorsese. I also managed to squeeze in my own two-and-a-half-hour interview with Jia, which was published in *Film Comment* and later reprinted in my first book, *Speaking in Images: Interviews with Contemporary Chinese Filmmakers*. Gradually, Jia's films became an increasingly important part of my teaching and research; I would use his films in my classes and even taught a graduate seminar on his entire body of work. In 2009, I published the first English-language monograph on Jia: *Jia Zhangke's Hometown Trilogy: Xiao Wu, Platform, Unknown Pleasures*, which was included in the British Film Institute's Contemporary Classics series. Five years later, Jia wrote a preface to my full-length interview book with Hou Hsiao-hsien, *Boiling the Sea: Hou Hsiao-hsien's Memories of Shadows and Light*. Thus, much of my work has somehow been linked to Jia Zhangke.

In 2017, my colleagues Susan Jain from the UCLA Confucius Institute, Paul Malcom from the UCLA Film and Television Archive, and curator Cheng-Sim Lim were beginning to plan for the 2018 China Onscreen Biennial. I suggested inviting Jia Zhangke, but the idea was not to simply screen his new film *Ash Is Purest White*, but to create an artist-in-residence program around which we could program a series of screenings, dialogues, and a master class with UCLA film students. The other motivation behind this program was this book—to produce a record of discussions with Jia on cinema that would take place during his visit.

During the Jia Zhangke retrospective at UCLA, we screened eight of Jia's films over the course of five nights: *Xiao Shan Going Home, Xiao Wu, Platform, The World, Still Life*, the short film *Revive, A Touch of Sin*, and *Ash Is Purest White*. Besides the first night, each of the subsequent four screenings was followed by a 90-to-120-minute dialogue. Jia also participated in a two-hour master class, which was conducted as part of our running conversation but was more focused on issues of professionalization and film technique. In February 2019, on the eve of the official US commercial release of *Ash Is Purest White*, Jia and I were able to record two additional conversations at the UC Berkeley Art Museum and Pacific Film Archive (BAMPFA) on February 10 and at the Asia Society Southern California on February 12. Then on June 3, 2021, Jia Zhangke and I engaged in an online dialogue to discuss his documentary film *Swimming Out Till the Sea Turns Blue* (2020). These more than thirteen hours of conversations, combined with some material from our 2002 interview, form the basis of this book.

Jia Zhangke on Jia Zhangke is divided into six chapters, which in large part chronologically follow the director's body of work. Chapter 1, "A Portrait of an Artist as a Young Man," focuses on Jia's formative years, his comments on film music, his student films, and reflections on some of his primary collaborators, such as cinematographer Yu Lik-Wai. The second chapter, "The Hometown Trilogy," centers on Jia's first three feature films: *Xiao Wu*, *Platform*, and *Unknown Pleasures*. The third chapter, "Documenting Destruction and Building Worlds," is devoted to *The World* and *Still Life*, two films that are generally regarded as important works in the transition of Jia's style and engagement with the Chinese market. Chapter 4, "Film as Social Justice," explores *24 City* and the controversial *A Touch of Sin*. Chapter 5, "Return to Jianghu," primarily engages with *Ash Is Purest While*, with some discussion of *Mountains May Depart*. Chapter 6, "Toward an Accented Cinema," is drawn largely from Jia Zhangke's master class with UCLA film students. This chapter begins with Jia's reflections on his time as a film student at the Beijing Film Academy and a detailed account of his own student film *Xiao Shan Going Home* before moving on to discuss the aesthetic principles of designing an opening shot (by way of *Still Life* as an example) and concludes with his advice to young filmmakers. The book concludes with a coda, "To the Sea," which uses Jia's documentary film *Swimming Out Till the Sea Turns Blue* to reflect on the relationship between literature and film in modern China, Jia's approach to documentary filmmaking, and film structure.

The fact that most of the dialogue included here originally took place in a public forum inevitably had an impact on the content of this book. In a private interview setting, one has more freedom to explore highly specialized topics, pursue points that would otherwise be brushed aside, and gradually ease into sensitive topics. In public dialogues, the presence of the audience immediately alters the nature of the conversation; the audience brings a certain energy to the forum, while at the same time, one becomes more sensitive to the constraints of time, audience engagement, and technical matters of interpretation. I also realized that the public forum tended to bring out Jia Zhangke's witty side, whereas he was much more serious and reflective during our private interviews. Most of the dialogue was tied to film screenings, which also had a direct impact on the content: for instance, films not screened at UCLA during Jia's visit—such as *Unknown Pleasures* and *Mountains May Depart*—are discussed in far less detail than films in the series. And while we did discuss his views on documentary filmmaking via

Swimming Out Till the Sea Turns Blue, there is relatively limited extended analysis or discussion of his main documentary films, *Dong, Useless*, and *I Wish I Knew*. Instead, most of the dialogue is focused on his feature films, with special emphasis on his major works. Over the course of this extended dialogue, certain themes are revisited and expanded on with new details and nuances: the art of working with actors, intertextuality between his films, the shifting meaning of music in film, and the importance of various sites—like his hometown of Fenyang—in his work. Limitations aside, this book contains the single most extensive collection of interviews with Jia on his life, major works, and views on cinematic art.

CHILDHOOD IN FENYANG
POPULAR MUSIC
STUDENT FILMS
FILM COLLABORATORS

1 A Portrait of an Artist as a Young Man

1.1 Jia Zhangke shooting one of his student films

Naturally there are some directors who neglect reality in their work, but my aesthetic taste and goals don't allow me to do that—I can never escape reality.

Your first three films are often referred to as the "Hometown Trilogy," and your own hometown of Fenyang in Shanxi Province is also the primary setting of *Xiao Wu* and *Platform*. In your later films, such as *Mountains May Depart*, Fenyang also repeatedly reappears. Why don't we begin with the concept of *guxiang*, or "hometown"? Could you describe your childhood experience growing up in Fenyang? And what has the concept of "hometown" meant for you over the course of your career?

My hometown of Fenyang in Shanxi is a provincial town and it has indeed been very important to me. The thing about these provincial towns is that they are quite unique in terms of how they have been viewed from an administrative perspective; they are essentially a bridge between the countryside and the cities. If we take the example of Shanxi Province, the largest city is Taiyuan, which is also the provincial capital. As the provincial capital, there are naturally a large number of cinemas, theaters, dance halls, television stations, and film studios; there are an incredible number of cultural organizations that are concentrated in that single city. In the countryside there is basically just land—the only thing they have there is agriculture. But in these provincial towns you could find all kinds of cultural elements as well as an abundance of material goods like television sets and washing machines, which all make their way to the countryside via these provincial towns. At the same time, it is also through these same provincial towns that agricultural products make their way into the cities. So growing up in a provincial town provided me with a unique perspective through which I was exposed to all of the information that came from the big cities, while also having a deep understanding of the countryside.

Take me, for example. My father's family has always lived in one of these provincial towns, so all my dad's relatives live in Taiyuan. My mother, on the other hand, grew up in the countryside, and all of my aunts and uncles on my mother's side still live in the country, where they are basically peasants. So whenever I had summer vacation as a child, I would spend half my summer in Taiyuan with my aunt's family, where we would play tennis and go to the movies, and the other half of my summer in the countryside with an aunt on my mom's side of family, where I'd spend all my time herding sheep with my cousins. So growing up in a provincial town like Fenyang gave me a really unique perspective from which I could understand both rural and urban culture; I have always deeply treasured that perspective.

My hometown, Fenyang, has a long and rich history. Fenyang's place in history during the late Qing and early Republican era is especially interesting because during that time some of the earliest educational and medical institutions in Shanxi Province were established there. Fenyang Middle School was built in 1905, and the local hospital was built in 1907. Although Fenyang was a leader in these areas, it was actually a very small town. On bicycle, you can traverse the entire town in just ten minutes, and once you reach the city limits, you are basically surrounded by fields and the countryside.

Back when I was growing up, people were quite poor, and nobody ever went on trips out of town. Of course, part of the reason was that during the Cultural Revolution and its immediate aftermath, people still did not have the freedom to travel where they wanted. I remember my father going on a trip to Shanghai around that time; his work unit had sent him to purchase a set of musical instruments for their performance troupe. At the time, you needed an official introduction letter to go to Shanghai, otherwise you wouldn't even be allowed to purchase a train ticket or book a hotel. That meant that from a very young age I always had the impression that Fenyang was a particularly isolated place.

When I think back about that time period now, it almost feels like I spent my childhood in ancient China! That is because all of the houses and buildings there dated back to the Ming and Qing dynasties. People rarely left Fenyang during their lives. This sense of isolation and a closed-off feeling impacted me in many ways during my childhood. It led me to entertain all kinds of fantasies about the outside world. In *Platform* there are some scenes where the characters are listening to the radio and hear about a cold front coming in from Ulan Bator; that is actually drawn from my own childhood memories. When I was a kid, there was really nowhere for us to go. If I had to imagine the most distant place in the entire world, it was Ulan Bator! And that was because whenever the northwestern winds picked up, we would get a cold front in from Ulan Bator! [*laughs*] After I shot *Xiao Wu*, I actually had plans to visit Mongolia and see Ulan Bator for myself, but I had to cancel the trip due to a visa issue. But somehow, in my imagination, Ulan Bator has also stood for a very distant place.[1]

Growing up in such an isolated place meant that when the Reform Era kicked in during the early 1980s and all kinds of new things began to enter into our lives, the utter shock we felt was even more powerful. Whenever I talk about my hometown, I always feel the need to link it up with this period of extreme change. When it comes to this era of radical transformation, I need to start with the changes taking place on a material level, but besides those external changes, there were also radical changes taking place on a spiritual level. The Reform Era began back when I was seven or eight years old and had just started elementary school. Things were just on the verge of changing, but when I think back to that time, what left the deepest impression on me was the sensation of feeling hungry all the time. I definitely lived with the sensation of hunger during that time. That was because food staples were still being distributed centrally according to how many people were in your family. We were a family of four, so the two adults would be allocated a certain amount of rice and flour, and my sister and I would be allocated a smaller amount—everything was distributed according to these quota allowances. One of the primary staples at that time was cornmeal, which we would prepare as steamed buns referred to as *wotou*. We would eat wotou for breakfast, but by noon I would already feel hungry. That's because wotou has very poor caloric value; it gets quickly absorbed into the body and you are left hungry. This feeling of lingering hunger stayed with me throughout my entire childhood. So one of the first things I remember about the Reform Era during the early 1980s was how quickly that sensation of hunger disappeared.

Shortly after that all of those material objects that had always seemed like distant fantasies—things like television sets and washing machines—suddenly began to appear in our lives. This shift in the material nature of our lives was extremely exciting. How can I describe this sense of excitement? I remember the shock when I first learned what a washing machine was. Back when I was in school—that must have been around 1983 or 1984—my school showed us a documentary called *New Face of the Nation* (*Zuguo xinmao*), which introduced new products and architecture from that era. That episode was about a factory in Shanghai that had just begun to produce washing machines. At the time, what I saw on-screen all felt so distant, but a year or

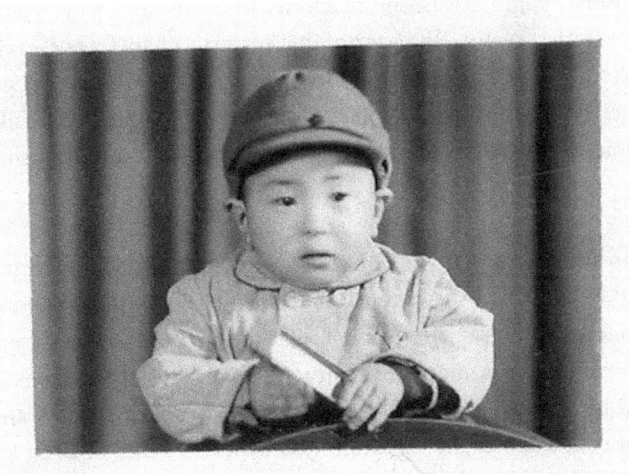

1.2 Jia Zhangke as an infant

1.3 Jia Zhangke as a young boy

two later my family bought a washing machine! In an instant, what I saw on-screen had become a reality. The pace of that material change and development was extremely rapid. This form of transformation was so powerful. Besides that, society began to remake itself in leaps and bounds; suddenly there were all kinds of new pop music from Hong Kong and Taiwan that came in as well.

Speaking of pop music, virtually all of your films highlight the place of music in everyday peoples' lives, often representing a variety of themes. Sometimes music can portray the passage of time or becomes a means of unspoken communication between characters, while at other times it serves as a kind of cultural signifier. Whether it be karaoke, opera, Cantopop, rock and roll, a subtle melody hummed by a character, or even an electronic melody played by a cigarette lighter, music seems to be ever present in your body of work, and although your employment is often quite subtle, it brings an enormous power to your film narratives.

I have always loved music. Even when I was in college I once wrote a thesis essay on the relationship between film narrative and music. I feel that there are all kinds of structural aspects to music that can be incorporated into a narrative. So even then I was already playing around with these rather abstract thoughts about the relationship between music and film. In the years preceding the shooting of *Xiao Wu*, karaoke became extremely popular in China. I went with a bunch of friends to a karaoke club in my hometown where we saw a guy all alone who kept singing the same songs over and over again. His voice was really terrible; at first I found him annoying, but as time went by I suddenly found myself quite moved by his singing. That experience really made me look at popular culture in a new light. In such a cold and difficult environment [popular culture] provides a place to come home to, it serves as a means of providing self-comfort. So it was really that experience that led to all of those karaoke scenes in *Xiao Wu*.

Another factor stems from the fact that I was born in 1970, so I was in my formative years in the early eighties when popular music began to take root in China. I grew up with pop music. Popular music really played an enormous role in the lives of people of my generation as we matured and came of age. At first it was all popular music from Hong Kong and Taiwan, and only later did Western music start coming into China. One of the reasons [popular music] was so important was because, previous to this, China really didn't have any popular culture to speak of. The closest thing we had were revolutionary model operas and things made in that mold. I still remember so clearly the first time I heard the music of Teresa Teng.² The experience was exactly as it was portrayed in *Platform*, where the characters listened to illegal shortwave radio broadcasts from Taiwan. At the time, I was quite young and couldn't really say what it was about her voice, but it was so moving—I was utterly hypnotized. There was a special time every day when they would play her songs, and I would always tune in.

Later, when I went to college and reflected back on this time, I realized that her music represented a massive change in our cultural landscape. When I search my earliest memories from childhood, I realize that back then China really didn't have such a thing as so-called pop culture, nor did we have pop music. All our radios ever broadcast were revolutionary songs. If I recite the names of some of those songs, you will understand just how unique that period was. When I was a child we used to always sing "We Are the Successors of Communism" ("Women shi gongchanzhuyi de jiebanren"), or in the eighties we sang "We Are the New Generation of the Eighties" ("Women shi bashi niandai de xin yidai") and "We the Workers Have the Power" ("Zamen gongren you Liliang"), all of which highlighted "we"—the collective. But it was around 1978 or 1979 that cassette tapes from abroad began to get smuggled into China, and suddenly artists like Teresa Teng and Chang Ti came into our field of vision.³ When Teresa Teng's music first made its way to our provincial town, the first song we heard wasn't "My Sweetie" ("Tian mimi") or "The Moon Represents My Heart" ("Yueliang daibiao wo de xin"), but "Wine with Coffee" ("Meijiu jia kafei"), which featured a line that went "Wine with coffee, I want a glass!" [*laughs*] When you think about it, wine and coffee are both capitalist luxuries, and then you add in the "I" and it becomes a song completely about individualism! When you put songs like that side by side against "We Are the Successors of Communism," you get such a radical juxtaposition. But it was precisely this type of new music that attracted the younger generation.

All those kids a little older than me would walk down the street carrying a tape recorder that would be blasting these pop songs. I remember those older kids walking around with their boom boxes being the epitome of cool during that time; they were so fashionable. You can even see a few scenes that portray that in *Platform*. But Teresa Teng's songs were always about "me"—the individual. Songs like "I Love You" ("Wo ai ni") and "The Moon Represents My Heart" were something completely new. So people of my generation were suddenly infected with this very personal individual world. Before that everything was collective, we lived in a collective dormitory, our parents worked as part of a collective, and our schools were structured in the same manner. In our educational system, the individual belonged to the nation, and we were all part of the collective. But in the 1980s everything changed, and it all started with popular music.

This is especially evident in *Platform*, where I tried to consciously inject all the music that moved me over the years into the film. So there is a historicity immediately built into the narrative through the music. There are also several specific songs that really represent what the Chinese people were going through during a given historical frame, For instance, in 1980 with the beginning of the Open Door Policy, when the government was trying to let people know how optimistic the future awaiting them was, there appeared an incredibly popular song entitled "Young Friends Come Together" ("Nianqing de pengyou lai xianghui"). The key line in the song is "In twenty years we will realize the Four Modernizations. We will come together then and the world will be a beautiful place." This song represented a kind of promise from the country to its people that the future will be brighter and tomorrow will be a better day. During the early days of the Open Door Policy, practically every young person in China was singing that song. They were filled with excitement and hope. By 1988 or so we start getting songs like "Go with Your Feelings" ("Gen zhe ganjue zou"), which came during the initial thawing-out period [after the Cultural Revolution], when we saw the beginning of free thought and expression.[4] And then later came Cui Jian's anthem, "I Have Nothing to My Name" ("Yiwu suoyou").[5] Each of these songs really represents a snapshot of the social reality of the time. So for a director of my generation, I really cannot escape the influence of popular music; it is everywhere. There is a historical reason why these songs move us.

Besides music, popular culture in general seems to have an incredible power in your films, but it is a power that is alternately both liberating and oppressive.

It is only natural for there to be a kind of oppressive component at work. When there is all of a sudden a voice that is telling people to start paying attention to their personal desires, there is bound to be this kind of phenomenon. Take loneliness, for example. I have no doubt that in the sixties and seventies the Chinese people were often very lonely, but at the time they didn't know what loneliness meant. People then also had feelings of loneliness and desperation, but they would never feel that those were natural human emotions. Only once our minds were liberated and we started paying attention to ourselves as individuals and began to read Freud, Nietzsche, Schopenhauer, and other forms of Western thought and philosophy did we begin to understand ourselves, and with that came a kind of loneliness and desperation. But this is all actually a very natural phenomenon.

What other forms of popular culture had a major impact on you in the 1980s during the early days of the Reform Era?

The most important aspect of the 1980s was the awakening of a new form of self-consciousness. If you look at *Platform,* when the film begins, the young people in the song-and-dance troupe are performing a bunch of propaganda programs, but they have no personal attachment to any of that music. Gradually, however, they begin to perform more pop music and rock and roll. They begin as part of a collective, but over time this breaks down and they end up as a touring song-and-dance group. The 1980s brought with it an awakening—a renaissance, if you will—of individual consciousness. At the same time, families started to purchase television sets, and with that came TV dramas from America, Japan, Hong Kong, and Taiwan. At the time, there were two American television miniseries that were particularly popular, *Garrison's Gorillas* and *Man from Atlantis.*[6] Another popular one was the Hong Kong series *Huo Yuanjia.*

Besides these examples of mass culture, this was also the period of time when books by authors like Nietzsche, Sartre, and even Freud began

1.4 Jia Zhangke (*right*) with childhood friends on the set of *Xiao Wu*

to appear in bookstores. Who would believe it, but even in a provincial town like Fenyang, reading works by these masters of Western philosophy became all the rage! My friends and I would get together and discuss things like the subconscious! [*laughs*] At the time, my favorite was Freud; that's because you could read his work as a kind of pornography! [*laughs*] It wasn't long before video rooms came to town—they were small, privately run places where you could watch all kinds of films and videos—I spent virtually of my time from middle school through high school hanging out in these video rooms. Most of the video rooms were just equipped with a single television and a single VHS player, and we would mostly watch films from Taiwan and Hong Kong. It was during that time that I first became exposed to the films of King Hu, Chang Cheh, and John Woo, along with an assortment of *wuxia* martial arts films, action films, gangster films, and other genre films. At the time, the most popular type of films among the young people who frequented those video rooms were sex education documentaries. And just like in *Platform*, we would often end up getting ripped off; sometimes we would buy a ticket only to discover they were showing a cartoon! [*laughs*]

It was a few years later, in 1987, that an American film entitled *Breakin'* made it to China, and virtually everyone my age fell in love with that film.[7] I personally watched it over and over again! Why did I watch it so many times? Because I was into break dancing! I wanted to learn all the moves in the film. But after I had seen it seven times, it stopped playing in Fenyang, so my friends and I had to rely on our memory to copy all those dance moves. Since I was one of the better dancers in my hometown, [*laughs*] I received an invitation one summer to tour with a dance troupe that was one person short. I had a lot of homework that summer, but I really wanted to go—I wanted to get out of Fenyang and see the world. So I told my parents that I was going to go with a classmate of mine on a two-week study trip to improve my English! [*laughs*] When they heard that, my parents encouraged me to go. So I went with that song-and-dance troupe from Fenyang across the Yellow River and stayed with them all the way up until they almost reached Inner Mongolia. That was my first time away from home, the first time I had left Fenyang, and the first time I had made money on my own—I earned money through dancing! [*laughs*]

That was an age when I would secretly read Freud and discuss sex. I could write a dozen love poems in a single afternoon, I would practice my break dancing, and I would read novels. That was an age when our thoughts and bodies were all liberated. Every day there were new philosophical and literary books to read. And there were so many things we could discuss—it wasn't just intellectuals that were discussing these things—even peasants were discussing these sophisticated topics. Take, for instance, the novella *Life* (*Rensheng*).[8] Another example was a film that starred Zhang Yimou, *Old Well* (*Lao jing*, 1987).[9] These were being discussed by everyone. But then it all stopped in 1989, and suddenly that era was over.

It was as if we were on a train that had suddenly stopped moving. One of the very first Chinese rock songs of that era that I heard was called "Platform" ("Zhantai"). The song made me think of the first time I ever saw my sister perform in public; she played violin in a performance of "Train to Shaoshan" ("Huoche xiang zhe Shaoshan kai"). The performance began with a violin solo, and without realizing it, I somehow unconsciously ended up linking those two pieces of music together. I felt like I should write a screenplay.

You have discussed your childhood as a form of *jianghu*, hanging out with gangster types and hoodlums, listening to rock and roll, break dancing, et cetera. How much impact do you think those formative experiences had on your later films? I ask this because many of your films, from *Xiao Wu* to *Touch of Sin*, all the way up to *Ash Is Purest White*, all emphasize a certain jianghu sensibility.

If you want to talk about jianghu, I spent my entire childhood in a kind of jianghu. By the time I started to mature a bit, the Cultural Revolution was over, and there were a lot of young people who ended up disenfranchised—they were unemployed, some had graduated and ended up back home, others had returned after having spent years in the countryside during the Cultural Revolution. Somehow my group of friends and I—we were all around seven or eight years old—ended up hanging around with that group of teenagers and young adults. We constituted our own kind of jianghu. Our most frequent activity was fighting. [*laughs*] There was no real reason for these fights, and one wrong stare could set off a war between two people. It didn't take much for a simple fight between two people to develop into an all-out battle between two factions from different sides of the street. All of these kids were just filled with raw energy and seemed to be looking for any opportunity to release their frustrations.

At the time, there were a lot of kids who didn't get past third grade of elementary school. That is because by the time they got to third grade, they had covered basic math, and their parents thought that was enough for them; for them, being able to count money was good enough to get a job. That meant there were a lot of kids who just dropped out, but they were still too young to get a real job, so they just ended up as part of this jianghu. Back then I had quite a few friends who were part of this jianghu. Elementary school was five years, and a lot of people thought that was enough to learn basic literacy skills, so they just dropped out. By the time I got to middle school, there would always be a dozen or so kids hanging out around the school gate—they were all my buddies, but none of them went to school. That was a kind of jianghu. In the first segment of *A Touch of Sin*, Dahai picks up a hunting rifle and sets out to exact revenge. Back when I was in elementary school, the mom of one of my classmates came after me with a hunting rifle! At the time, she scared me half to death! [*laughs*] But I had a lot of experiences like that as a child. That is the kind of environment that I grew up in, and it had a rather powerful impact on my later work as a filmmaker. I always felt as if I was a part of that group. But growing up in that environment I always craved independence, I longed for the day when I would no longer be reliant on my parents, and I felt the need for adventure. The entire process is a long story, but to put it simply, I felt that independence, adventure, understanding Chinese society, and understanding people were what constituted my individual jianghu.

As a kid I was already a master negotiator. Whenever anybody got into a fight, I was always the one to smooth things over. I've always been good at helping to make peace because I have a knack for clearly communicating who's right and who's wrong and how to resolve conflicts. I somehow always ended up being the peacemaker. In some way, I feel that cinema has helped people like me who grew up in this jianghu. My love for film and literature seemed to bring out my good side. Whenever I would write a poem or later when I started making movies, it was as if art helped me discover this other kindhearted side of my personality.

You became heavily interested in the arts as a youth, spending a lot of time painting, drawing, writing poetry, and reading. How important was that early artistic stage on your later work in film?

Being born in 1970, much of my formative years were spent during the 1980s. While I still have some very early memories from the Cultural Revolution period, the majority of my childhood memories really begin only after the Reform Era of the late 1970s. Before that time, there wasn't a lot going on in terms of Chinese culture; there was really no entertainment to speak of, nor were there many books available for us to read. Actually, we had some books at home, but they were all the same old stuff—*The Selected Works of Mao Ze-*

dong, *The Complete Works of Marx and Engels*, and political books like that. As for nonpolitical books, we had at the most two books, *The Water Margin* and *Dream of the Red Chamber*, but that was it! [*laughs*] We didn't even have a collection of Tang poetry because all of those types of books had been destroyed during the "Destroy the Four Olds" campaign. But in the late 1970s and early 1980s, copies of books by Nietzsche, Freud, and all kinds of other Western literary and philosophical works started to appear in our small-town bookstore. For me it all started with reading. Actually, it is kind of hard to express just what the act of reading meant to a kid like me during that era; all I knew was that I loved reading. At the time, a friend of mine gave me a copy of one of Freud's books and told me: "This book is all about sex!" [*laughs*] So I read it like it was some kind of pornographic literature! [*laughs*] Of course, there was no real erotic content in the book; it was instead a book that was primarily about the subconscious and our internal world, which immediately led me to a new place of self-discovery and self-understanding.

But I spent even more time reading contemporary Chinese literary works, and there was one book that had a particularly powerful impact on me—Lu Yao's novella *Life*. The book was about a talented young man from the countryside who moved to a provincial city, where he became a reporter. However, he didn't have the required *hukou*, or residence permit, to work in the city, and after someone reported on him, he ended up getting sent back to the countryside. Before this time, I had never really given much thought to China's *hukou* system. Although I was living in a provincial city, I somehow qualified as a city resident, but for most citizens in China at that time, the only way to become a city resident was through the high school entrance examination system. It was only after I read Lu Yao's *Life* that I was suddenly struck by just how unfair the whole system was. Why is someone's lot in life predetermined simply by the fact that they were born in the countryside? And why is everyone else somehow not a peasant, just because of where they were born? So, reading started me on an early path toward self-discovery and reflection about the society I live in.

It was in that context that I began to fall in love with literature and try my own hand at writing. In the beginning I wrote poetry, which was inspired by all the Misty Poets I read at the time.[10] Those types of poems were fairly easy for me to imitate; all you had to do was jot down some strange, enigmatic phrases and you had a poem! [*laughs*] Speaking of the Misty Poets, there was one poem in particular that really had a tremendous impact on me; that was the poem "The Answer" ("Huida") by Bei Dao.[11] The poem had a line, "I don't believe . . . ," which kept repeating. That was the coolest poem in the world for me at the time! I absolutely loved that line "I don't believe" because our educational system at the time kept emphasizing "You have to believe everything!" But Bei Dao's poem represented the spirit of questioning; it taught us to challenge. At the very least, the words "I don't believe" filled me with a kind of excitement! I ended up trying my luck at poetry, and later I wrote fiction.

On the one side, there was literature, but on the other side there was life experience. I lived in a small provincial city, so I could get my hands on things like Misty Poetry and other literary works—all of those literary journals made their way to Fenyang—but on the other hand, I also got firsthand experience about what life in rural China was like. I saw the impact those dramatic changes had on the lives and fates of everyday people. Our house was in a mining area where life was hard, and I often had the opportunity to witness firsthand just how fragile life really is. After seeing that, I felt an even greater desire to find an outlet to express myself; I needed to find a way to write about my experience and feelings. But I never thought about making films—that was a dream that felt too distant, but literature was always something much closer to our everyday lives.

When did you first become interested in film?

I first became interested in film in 1991. I was already twenty-one years old at the time. After high school I failed to get into college because I was never much of a good student. My parents, however, didn't give up on their hope that I could still someday pursue a college education. So they proposed the

1.5 Jia Zhangke during his Beijing Film Academy days

CHAPTER ONE

option of attending an art institute because most art colleges have relatively lax requirements when it comes to subjects like math and physics. In my hometown of Fenyang there are a lot of people who studied art as a way of improving their social situation. So I went to the provincial seat of Taiyuan and took a preparatory art class at Shanxi University. One day during that year at Shanxi University I went to a movie theater next to our art studio where we did our painting. The theater was called the Highway Movie Theater (Gonglu dianyingyuan), because it was run by the Department of Roads and Highways—it was actually their social club. They used to screen a lot of old films, and the tickets were dirt cheap, just a few cents to get in.

Were these Chinese or foreign films?

They were all domestic films. On that afternoon in question I went in and they happened to be showing *Yellow Earth*.[12] *Yellow Earth* was actually made in the mid-1980s, but I had never seen it. So I bought a ticket and went in—I didn't have the slightest notion who Chen Kaige was or what *Yellow Earth* was about. But that film changed my life. It was at that moment, after watching *Yellow Earth*, that I decided I wanted to become a director and my passion for film was born.

Actually, before I became taken with film, I had long been interested in art and literature. I have actually written several works of poetry and fiction.

Did you publish any of your early literary work?

Yes, in some Shanxi-based literary magazines. But going back to my interest in film, it all started with that afternoon in Taiyuan when I saw *Yellow Earth*. Before I saw *Yellow Earth*, virtually all of the other Chinese films I had seen were basically state-sponsored works laden with propaganda, all made in a very conservative mold. So my cinematic imagination was always very limited; I never realized there were other possibilities for film. But all of that changed after watching *Yellow Earth*. Suddenly I was struck with a new paradigm for cinematic expression.

And soon after you applied to the Beijing Film Academy?

Not right away, I didn't get into the Beijing Film Academy until 1993 and majored in "film literature" (*dianying wenxue*), which was basically a film theory major.

The Beijing Film Academy has an almost legendary place in the history of Chinese cinema and has produced many of China's top filmmakers. What were those four years like, and how did what you learned there shape your later directorial vision?

As it happened, my time at the Beijing Film Academy coincided with what was the single most prosperous time in the careers of many Fifth Generation directors. Just before I was accepted, Zhang Yimou had completed work on *The Story of Qiuju* (*Qiuhu da guansi*, 1992) and was close to finishing up his production on *To Live* (*Huozhe*, 1994). In addition, 1993 was the year that Chen Kaige's *Farewell My Concubine* (*Bawang bieji*, 1993) met with great international success.[13] This brought a breath of fresh air into the film academy and gave the students a burst of real confidence.

But as for what the academy actually provided for us . . . well, most of the professors there are still extremely conservative. For me the most important thing I got out of the academy was that for the first time I was actually able to watch true films—and a lot of them. There has always been a lot of censorship and control regarding films in China. For instance, even as late as 1993 let's say you wanted to watch some popular American films like *The Godfather* (1972) or Coppola's *Apocalypse Now* (1979). Unless you were a film director or a film student, you had absolutely no access to those types of films. So the greatest thing about film school for me was being able to finally see actual prints of all those films that up until that point I had only read about in books. At the film academy we had two movie nights a week. Every Tuesday was Chinese movie night, and every Wednesday was foreign movie night. So during those four years I really felt as if I had entered into a world of cinema.

I am also very thankful that the Beijing Film Academy maintains a library of film books from Hong Kong and Taiwan. Film theory in the PRC is primarily based on all the classic Western theorists like Bazin and Eisenstein; then there are more contemporary theories like feminism, new historicism, and semiotics that we learn later. But there are very few available books that contain biographical writings on film directors or even primary sources featuring interviews with filmmakers. So when I went to the Hong Kong–Taiwan Film Library I was finally able to read books like *Scorsese on Scorsese*, Andrei Tarkovsky's *Sculpting in Time: Reflections on the Cinema*, and volumes of collected interviews with Hou Hsiao-hsien and other directors. At the time, none of these works had been published in China, and that library was the only place you could get your hands on them.

My interest was in directing; the only reason I majored in film theory was because there were a lot fewer applicants to that department. I figured that I would get my foot in the door first and worry about the rest once I was in. At the time the Beijing Film Academy was extremely hot, and entry was very competitive. But what really opened my eyes at the academy were those film screenings and books.

The academy, however, was also supportive when it came to helping students branch out in other directions. Gradually I started to gravitate toward directing, and around 1995 my classmates and I established an experimental film group. As part of this project I managed to raise some money on my own to shoot a short. It was a ten-minute documentary entitled *One Day in Beijing*. We shot it in Tiananmen Square, and it was a work of documentary portraiture. After that we shot two subsequent dramatic shorts, *Xiao Shan Going Home* and *Du Du*. *Xiao Shan Going Home* won an award at the Hong Kong Independent Film Festival, and it was during that trip to Hong Kong that I met producers Chow Keung and Li Kit-ming and cinematographer Yu Lik-Wai, who would later become the core of my creative team. Together, we decided to make films.

For the past decade, you have been a great supporter of young Chinese filmmakers, even serving as a producer for filmmakers like Han Jie. Back when you were just starting out in the industry, what teachers or filmmakers provided you with support and encouragement?

I thought I was still a young filmmaker! [*laughs*] When I entered the Beijing Film Academy in 1993, there were not a lot of resources for film students in China. If I hadn't been admitted to the Beijing Film Academy, there is no way I would have been able to see all of those classic films. But once admitted, I was immediately exposed to the classic films of directors like Akira Kurosawa, Yasujiro Ozu, and Jean Renoir. We had access to all of those important masterpieces of world cinema. The education model used at Beijing Film Academy was very close to the Soviet model; it was basically the same system employed by the former Soviet Union. But when I enrolled, things had started to change, and many of the younger teachers had experience studying in the United States, France, and Japan, and this introduced some new teaching methods. Take, for instance, our screenwriting classes, where some of the teachers employed the Soviet style while others preferred the Hollywood style. Each style had its benefits, but my generation was unique in that we could have the freedom to select which style we preferred. The Soviet method required all screenplays to achieve a very high level in terms of their inherent literary quality. You needed to produce a literary screenplay of publishable quality—it should be able to be read as a literary work independent of any film. When it came to details like word choice and descriptive passages, it needed to be a true work of art. But all of our teachers who had studied in the United States would say: "Film scripts are meant to be shot! Just focus on the dialogue and make sure the setting is expressed clearly and you'll be fine!" The script is just a working tool. These represent two very different methods of thinking about and approaching filmmaking. But I always had a preference for the Soviet method, partly because I didn't have confidence that any of my screenplays would ever be made into movies, so at the least I wanted something that was highly readable.

And what was the most influential part of being in school for you?

The most influential elements of that atmosphere were those new ideas that my teachers shared with us. They all directly translated those ideas and explained them to us because at the time there still no real teaching materials available, but they still did their best to introduce us to theories like postmodernism, structuralism, neo-historicism, and all the other "isms" that were in vogue at the time! [*laughs*] Most of the time we thought that these ideas had a real freshness to them, even though those methods of thought and understanding the world had not yet been widely disseminated in Chinese research communities. But for a filmmaker, the most important thing remains the method through which you see the world, and those theories provided a whole palette of ways in which to grasp and understand different methods of viewing the world. This leads to a certain openness and tolerance, and for many filmmakers it brought a new modern perspective to their way of thinking.

On one occasion, I had a teacher who gave me a homework assignment. He said: "Jia Zhangke, next week I want you to give us a mini-lecture on structuralism. I haven't had time to prep my lecture, so I want you to prepare something and teach structuralism to the class!" [*laughs*] I ended up spending an entire week in the library trying to figure out what the hell structuralism was! [*laughs*] I'm sure that what I ended up talking about was just what I imagined structuralism to be after a week of torturing myself over this! [*laughs*] As I reflect on all of this, I find that those years as a film major were very important to my development, but even more important is being able to have an open mind when it comes to different methods of understanding the world.

One person who had a particularly strong impact on me was my Chinese film history professor Zhong Dafeng. He had spent time in the United States and was a specialist in the theatrical tradition in Chinese film history. He felt that Chinese cinema had been deeply influenced by drama and various theatrical traditions, going all the way back to the very first Chinese film *Dingjun Shan*, which was adapted from a Peking opera.[14] Over time, this tradition had gradually contributed to the formation of a unique perspective of film in China. Even today when we shoot film, we usually say in Chinese "pai xi," or "shooting a drama"; when audiences go to the movies, they say they are going to "kan xi," or "see a play." When they watch documentary films, they never look at them as cinema; it is as if only fiction, drama, and work with more dramatic qualities can qualify as cinema. Professor Zhong's research was really eye-opening to me. It made me realize that sometimes Chinese culture can lead audiences to form certain fixed ideas when it comes to cinematic form. What is cinema? For most mainstream audiences, the preference is clearly highly dramatic fictional films. When facing this type of an audience, what should our approach be? What is cinema? I too have been heavily influenced by this tradition, so early on my screenplays were also filled with great spectacles and fantasies, just like all those other mainstream films you see in the multiplexes! [*laughs*]

Those first three efforts, *One Day in Beijing* (1994), *Xiao Shan Going Home* (1995), and *Du Du* (1996), are largely unavailable. Could you talk a bit about these early student works and what they meant to your early trajectory as an aspiring filmmaker?

One Day in Beijing was my first effort as a director, and I also served as cinematographer on the shoot. It was shot on Betacam, and it was really the first time that I looked at the world through a lens. The excitement I felt during that shoot is so difficult to express in words. The shoot lasted for only a day and a half, but that first experience of describing the world through the perspective of the camera was simply riveting. There is really not much to say about the work itself as it is a relatively naive film. But even though it is a short and immature work, standing there in the street during the shoot got me to start asking myself about the people I was filming and how to approach these subjects. The film is basically a short documentary portrait of tourists in Tiananmen Square, but what left me with the deepest impression were those people from the countryside who I seemed to naturally gravitate to during the shooting. Naturally, there are all kinds of people in the square, maintenance people who work there, Beijing locals taking their kids out for a stroll, people flying kites, but for some reason I was naturally attracted to those people from the countryside. On an emotional level, there was just something that drew me to them.

After *One Day in Beijing*, I wanted to make a film built around the story of some of these provincial workers who come to Beijing for work. So I wrote a screenplay entitled *Xiao Shan Going Home*. Xiao Shan is the name of a provincial worker from Henan, and the story takes place just before the Spring Festival when the protagonist wants to go home to visit his family for the New Year, which is a custom in China. But Xiao Shan doesn't want to go alone so he starts looking around Beijing for someone from his hometown to accompany him on his trip. Among these people from his hometown are construction workers, scalpers, prostitutes, and university students—but no one is willing to go with him. Finally, he puts up an announcement on the street, and the film ends with him at a street-side barber stall having his long hair cut off.

It is a fifty-eight-minute work that is quite linear; the basic narrative motive follows his search for people from his hometown as a means of expressing some of the fundamental issues faced by many of the provincial workers who find their way into the big cities in China. These issues include illegal workers, the harsh realities faced by construction workers, and prostitutes who live between the lines of morality and self-respect. This was without question my most important work prior to the making of my full-length features. It established my direction. For instance, the kind of characters that I care about in my work and my stylistic approach are both already becoming clear in *Xiao Shan Going Home*. Naturally, it is also an immature and unpolished film, but it nevertheless remains very important to me and truly marks the beginning of my work as a filmmaker.

From a production perspective, I also learned so much with *Xiao Shan Going Home*. I learned how to get funding, how to put together a camera crew, how to edit and mix, and how to publicize and promote the finished work. After *Xiao Shan* was finished, we took the film to several universities around Beijing, including Beijing University, the Central Drama Academy, People's University, and the Central Academy of Arts, to screen the film and interact with student audiences. Looking back on *Xiao Shan* after having completed *Xiao Wu* and *Platform*, I realized that with *Xiao Shan* I had already gone through the entire filmmaking process. Although it is crude work, with it I completed a full education in how to produce a film, from shooting to editing to promotion. In the end, we sent the film out for competition in the Hong Kong Independent Film Festival, and it took home an award, which was a huge encouragement for a student filmmaker like myself and proved to be a big confidence booster. That trip to Hong Kong also led me to my core creative team.

So today when young aspiring filmmakers ask for advice, I always tell them that no matter what, they must persevere and get through their student film and see it through to the end. Even if halfway through the shoot they are already convinced that it is garbage, they still need to finish it, edit it, and show it to people. Filmmaking is a field that relies heavily on experience. And the only way to acquire a complete experience as a filmmaker is to go through the entire process yourself. So although my first major work, *Xiao Wu*, was not made until 1997 and didn't start getting international notice until the following year when it was distributed in France and gradually several other European countries, I had already been through the entire process before—just on a smaller scale. Later, when I began to attend international film festivals and see all kinds of films, I could approach everything with a very composed attitude because through my shorts I had already established my own direction as a filmmaker. One problem facing Chinese artists is that after living in a relatively closed society, once they leave China and are exposed to the diversity of the artistic scene abroad, they end up losing their cultural self-confidence or sacrificing their artistic values. But I feel that through my early shorts I had already established an inner artistic world—something that is essential for any artist.

After *Xiao Shan*, I made a third short entitled *Du Du* about a college student who, on the verge of graduation, is faced with an array of potentially life-changing choices. These decisions involve her career, her family, and pressure to get married. This film represented a new kind of cinematic experiment for me because we worked without a script and with only one actress. It was very spontaneous, and we would only work out the plan for each day of shooting the night before. It was an incredibly spontaneous film, which helped develop my skills on set. I am not terribly proud of *Du Du* and rarely show it to anyone, but from the perspective of my growth as a filmmaker, it really did the most to hone my directorial instincts while shooting. I would suddenly realize what kind of actor I needed or what kind of angle I needed for a particular shot. The whole thing was completed with us figuring out what we needed as we went, including the narrative continuity and even the very structure of the film.

The shooting schedule for *Du Du* was very strange. We only shot two days a week.

That was because you were still in school and had to rely on the Beijing Film Academy's equipment?

Right, we didn't have money to rent our own equipment, and the school camera could only be taken out on the weekends. We'd borrow the camera on Friday night, shooting on Saturday and Sunday so we could get it back before Monday. It took six shooting days spread out over four weekends to finally complete the film.

Let's talk about some of your collaborators. Some filmmakers put together a new crew for each project, yet you have been working with a stable group of collaborators for many years; this group includes editor Kong Jinlei, sound designer Zhang Yang, and cinematographer Yu Lik-Wai. What is it that having a stable core group of collaborators brings to your artistic process? How important are they to your method of filmmaking? And what does each one bring to the table?

Generally speaking, it comes down to the fact that we all share the same goals and values. We have very similar sensibilities when it comes to our views on filmmaking. Although I am a graduate of the Beijing Film Academy and have a lot of classmates I went to school with there, our perspectives on and understanding of film are not necessarily compatible. One thing that is quite unique about my approach is the drive to capture people in their natural state when shooting, and I have always had a distaste for overly dramatized shooting styles and overly theatrical methods. Whenever I'm shooting, I am always trying to capture a natural sense of time, a natural sense of space, and the way things are in their natural state. But this is a perspective that not all filmmakers can subscribe to. Back when *Xiao Wu* and *Platform* were released, there was even a film critic who came out and accused my films of not even qualifying as film! He felt that film wasn't supposed to look like *that*! [*laughs*] So it is important that I find collaborators who share the same view of cinema as I do.

Yu Lik-Wai, Zhang Yang, and Kong Jinlei each admire these types of films, and our overall views on cinema are quite similar. I was struck by how similar my views on sound mixing were with Zhang Yang when I first started working with him. Part of the reason he was able to appreciate my views on sound had to do with the fact that Zhang Yang is also a rock musician, so he appreciates noise and discordant sounds like me. If I were to work with a different sound designer, he wouldn't necessarily be able to accept my vision of what film sound should be. Zhang Yang recorded the sound for *Xiao Wu*, and we had a wonderful working relationship back then. I kept wanting to add more and more street noise and pop music into the mix because that would reveal a more accurate and realistic soundscape of what small towns in northern China are really like. Those towns are so noisy. They are filled with all kinds of sounds: people talking, cars, motorcycles, and all kinds of other noise elements from the environment. So when working on sound design, Zhang Yang and I both like to add more sounds to the mix. Our views on sound also impact the quality of the sounds we record and the use of pop music. When we utilize pop music, we never run the music clean through our computer, nor do we use any special effects to alter it. Instead, we insist on using actual radios and cassette players that are historically accurate to the environment and period; then we play the music through those players and record it on site. So any music you hear in the film is being played through a tape player or CD player that is on set during the shoot. This is an extremely unusual vision of film sound that not a lot of people use. For instance, many of Zhang Yang's classmates would be utterly disgusted by our approach to sound recording. According to them, our approach to sound is "too dirty." A lot of sound designers insist on a clean soundtrack; they want to preserve the quality and clarity of every sound, which should be clear and distinctive. But both Zhang Yang and I are looking for something very different when it comes to sound design, and it is precisely because we share similar aesthetic tastes that our collaboration has lasted all these years.

Another core member of your creative team is Yu Lik-Wai.[15] **A brilliant cinematographer and a director in his own right, Yu has a unique style that juxtaposes jarring handheld work reminiscent of Christopher Doyle with steady long takes in the spirit of Hou Hsiao-hsien's works. Could you talk about your working relationship with Yu?**

My working relationship with Yu Lik-Wai began in Hong Kong at the Hong King Independent Film Festival when I saw a documentary he directed entitled *Neon Goddesses* (*Meili de hunpo*, 1996). I really admired his cinematic approach and felt that it was extremely close to what I was going for in my own work. I really fell in love with his cinematography. Since we didn't really know each other, we didn't have much to say at first, but as soon as we discovered that we were both fans of Robert Bresson, we started to hit it off.[16] I never imagined that Bresson was also one of Yu's favorite filmmakers, so immediately there was this instant connection. We got on so well that we started collaborating almost immediately. One critic in China described our collaborative relationship as perfect partners in crime. [*laughs*] One of the main qualities that sets our collaborative relationship apart is that we're not just business partners but very close friends. We see each other almost every day, and usually before my next screenplay is even written he already knows exactly what it is about because I'm constantly sharing my ideas with him. So on set there isn't much need for communication because he already knows what I'm after.

So in some way Yu Lik-Wai is your most important collaborator.

Without question. A good director really needs a very strong cinematographer by his side to support him. His vocabulary of visuals is what supports my aesthetic vision. I have seen a lot of films made by my fellow filmmakers, and I always feel it is such a shame to see films by directors with vision who lack the visual support they need. Naturally, there is a lot of room for aesthetic critique of the Fifth Generation directors, but one reason for their overall success is that they all have an incredibly strong visual support team; people like Gu Changwei and Zhang Yimou have such a strong aesthetic sense. In my graduating class at the Beijing Film Academy, we had a lot of cinematography majors, but there really wasn't anyone that I felt was speaking the same aesthetic language as me. But as soon as I saw Yu Lik-Wai's *Neon Goddesses*, I instantly realized that he was someone I should collaborate with. What's funny is that after seeing my film, he also wanted to work with me. So it was very interesting the way everything came about, as if it was all meant to be.

What is it about your collaboration with Yu Lik-Wai that has allowed you to attain such a deep chemistry?

I think that the fundamental foundation lies with the fact that our views on cinema are quite close to one another; moreover, even more important, we have the same taste in film. We are both tuned in to the same channel. It is absolutely essential for a director to work with a cinematographer who is on the same page. After all, everyone has a different understanding when it comes to the aesthetics of visuality. To give you an example, there are a lot of

1.6 Yu Lik-Wai (*right*) with Jia Zhangke (*center*)

people who love photos and images of the beach during sunset; they think they are so beautiful. But I have always despised those images! They are so difficult for me to look at! I could never work with a cinematographer who shot those kinds of aestheticized images! Instead, I need to find a cinematographer who despises shots of sunset beaches as much as I do! [*laughs*] So in Yu Lik-Wai I finally found a cinematographer who hated beautiful sunsets as much as me. [*laughs*]

Mutual understanding is also essential for us. When we were shooting *Platform*, I told Yu Lik-Wai that I wanted to add a green tint. Yu Lik-Wai asked me, why green? Why not blue or yellow? At the time, I didn't have an answer for him, I just felt that it should be green. Then one day when we were setting up one of the shooting locations, I told the art designer to paint one of the walls green because when I was a kid all the walls like that were green. Yu Lik-Wai overheard me and suddenly understood why I wanted green. Back then I was a little kid and was not very tall, so when I looked up all I saw were these green walls! [*laughs*] Taking that information, Yu Lik-Wai was able to create the gorgeous green tints that you see in *Platform*. [*laughs*]

From the perspective of collaboration, my relationship with Yu Lik-Wai is indeed quite unique. I don't have any special preproduction routine; the main thing I do during that period is location scouting. I usually go together with Yu Lik-Wai to scout the locations and decide on angles, colors, and lighting. We usually settle on these things during location scouting so by the time we are actually shooting there isn't too much we need to discuss.

Sometimes when on set there are times when I suddenly find myself at a complete loss as to what to shoot. That is because I don't storyboard. I just bring my literary-style script to the location, but then we sometimes need to take an hour or two to set up all the camera angles. Usually the other crew members have no idea what we are doing when this happens. But later I discovered that Yu Lik-Wai has a method to deal with this—he just starts tinkering with the various props on set. That way the rest of the crew members will think we are doing something important! [*laughs*] In actuality, he is the only person on set who understands that I still haven't decided how to shoot that particular scene!

For instance, when we were shooting *A Touch of Sin*, we spent most of our time together discussing how to link the film style up with the tradition of wuxia films. At the time, we decided on using wide-screen because all of the old Shaw Brothers wuxia films were shot in wide-screen. So that is what we did. The way we arranged items in the foreground was also indebted to the style of those early Shaw Brothers films.

I have a short film entitled *Revive* (*Fengchun*), in which we added some special effects to the overall look during postproduction, and that was entirely Yu Lik-Wai's idea. When the film begins, audiences often think they are watching a classical Chinese costume drama, and it is only later that they discover they are actually watching a contemporary story. Yu Lik-Wai asked me, "Do you want to make the characters appear even more like they were from a classical drama?" So he experimented with the images to make the characters' faces appear longer, just like those palace girls in old Chinese court paintings. What he did was really amazing, and their faces indeed were stretched, but in a subtle way that most audiences wouldn't even notice. But it indeed helped to enhance the classical effect of the film.

One time I went to a dance performance with Zhao Tao; the performance featured a woman dancing on the shoulders of her male dance partner. The show was a big hit in China, and everyone loved this part of the show. But when Zhao Tao saw it, she said it was terrible! She explained that dance was not a contest to show off difficult tricks; after all, how are you supposed to express emotion when you are doing fancy tricks? This performance was more like an acrobatic performance—everyone in the audience was on the edge of their seats, afraid that the woman might fall off her partner's shoulders. How can you call that a good dance performance? I'm telling you this story because it serves as a metaphor for cinematography. A good cinematographer should express his emotions through his images; it shouldn't be about accomplishing some sort of technical feat. When it comes down to it, what we want to see most in any film is how people live their lives; we want to explore their inner emotional lives, and technique should always be in the service of revealing those core truths.

After working with Yu Lik-Wai for so many years, his style seems to constantly transform as you explore different visual strategies for each of your films.

My relationship with Yu Lik-Wai is indeed quite special. One of the most unusual things about our relationship is that from *Xiao Wu* all the way up until *Ash Is Purest White*, Yu Lik-Wai participated in the preproduction process of all these films. *Ash* was actually shot by Eric Gautier, but that was only because Yu Lik-Wai's schedule was busy, but he was there from the inception of the film. So he is in many ways my most important collaborator. I never discuss my stories with Kong Jinlei or Zhang Yang; they are always so busy, and I don't want to bother them. Naturally, Yu Lik-Wai is also very busy, but we have already settled into a habit of collaboration. Even before I have a screenplay, I always share my stories with him as they are evolving. While I am writing I call him almost every day to update him on what I wrote that day. Sometimes when I get tired of writing and need a break, we meet up for dinner and we talk about the screenplay and where the story is going. When we talk we never get into the details of cinematography, but he serves as a sounding board for me. He is always willing to share his thoughts on my projects. On a spiritual level, Yu Lik-Wai is my most important interlocutor. So on some level he has participated in the production of almost all my films, he is like a producer. That is not to say that he carries out the traditional role of a film producer by locking up funding or booking shooting locations, but he provides me with all kinds of input. For instance, for *Ash Is Purest White*, it was actually Yu Lik-Wai who recommended I use Eric Gautier.[17] Because *Ash* required a broad palette of different shooting styles and equipment, he felt that Eric's style would be better suited to this film.

XIAO WU (1997)
WORKING WITH ACTORS
PLATFORM (2000)
UNKNOWN PLEASURES (2002)

2 The Hometown Trilogy

2.1 Jia Zhangke on the set of *Platform*

I increasingly feel that the single most difficult thing in film is to create a new image of what a protagonist should be. That is where the absolute heart of cinematic innovation lies. You need to create a new type of person, and capture that new character on film.

Let's talk about your first full-length feature film, *Xiao Wu*. What made you decide to focus on a pickpocket? Did you know people like Xiao Wu when you were growing up in Fenyang?

Before getting to work on *Xiao Wu*, I had originally wanted to do a short about a man and a woman and their first night together. I wanted to make a short film that featured one location (a bedroom), one time (a single night), and just two characters. We were getting ready to shoot, and my cinematographer Yu Lik-Wai came in from Hong Kong. Spring Festival was just around the corner, and it had been a full year since I had been home, so I went back to Fenyang. When I arrived, I was suddenly struck by how dramatically the city had changed in just one year. The rate of Fenyang's modernization and economic growth, not to mention the impact the forces of commodification had on people there, were all unbelievable. Shanxi is already a relatively backwater province in China, and Fenyang, being on the bank of the Yellow River and close to Shaanxi, makes it a rather remote place even in Shanxi, so the fact that these changes were reaching even Fenyang and in such a visible way had an incredible impact on me. The changes stunned me, especially when I discovered that so many old friends of mine were no longer even speaking to one another. I also had several friends who after getting married were starting to have problems with their parents and barely spoke to them.

Then there were friends who had just gotten married and were now already divorced. I just felt that people were changing so quickly, everything was a blur. All in the course of a year, it seemed as if all of those interpersonal relationships and friendships I had were completely transformed.

Then there was the sudden appearance of countless karaoke clubs and karaoke girls, who were basically prostitutes; all of this became so commonplace. There was an ancient road near the neighborhood where I grew up, and that entire road was to be ripped up, just like the scene portrayed in *Xiao Wu*. All of this radical change playing out right there before my eyes left me with a pressing urge to shoot it and capture it before it was gone. China's hinterland was in a state of massive transformation—not on the eve of great change or just after a great change—it was all happening right there before my eyes. I knew it might not last long, perhaps one year, maybe two, but it was a time of immense pain. So amid this excitement I decided to make a movie about an ordinary Chinese man living in this environment of upheaval and massive social change.

Another reason for why I decided to make *Xiao Wu* is that in 1997 I was getting ready to graduate from the Beijing Film Academy, and after four years of watching Chinese films, I still hadn't seen a single Chinese film that had anything to do with the Chinese reality that I knew. After the Fifth Generation's initial success, their artistic works started to undergo a lot of changes. One of these big changes came with Chen Kaige, who once said, "I increasingly feel that film should be used as a vehicle to convey legendary stories." I, however, could not disagree more. Sure film can describe legend, but where is it written that film can't depict other things as well? Unfortunately, most of the Fifth Generation directors all followed this trajectory. Moreover, it became increasingly common to see Fifth Generation directors imitating each other. For instance, Huang Jianxin, who I am very fond of, made a film called *The Wooden Man's Bride* (*Wukui*, 1994); He Ping also did a film in this style called *Red Firecracker, Green Firecracker* (*Pao da shuang deng*, 1994). These kinds of imaginary representations of traditional Chinese society became increasingly common [after the success of similar period pieces by directors like Chen Kaige and Zhang Yimou]. But there was a very clear disconnect between these films and the current Chinese reality that we are living in. There is something about this phenomenon that left me feeling very unsatisfied, and it was partially out of this frustration that I decided to make films. I told my collaborators at the time that I wanted to express "the here and the now" (*dangxia xing*) in my films, and that has been the aim of our films ever since. Although *Xiao Wu* was made in 1997, today China still faces many of the same problems and exists in a state of agony, brought on by its current state of massive change and transformation. For an artist this can be a double-edged sword because, on the one hand, living in this environment of constant change can generate a lot of creative inspiration, especially with the camera; however, the other side of the coin is the multitude of problems brought on by this change and all the hardships the people must go through in this process.

On the surface, *Xiao Wu* adopts a realist documentary style, yet the film actually had a very complete structure. So on the one hand there is a natural shooting style, yet hidden beneath that is a tight three-act structure centering on the protagonist's relationships with his friend, lover, and family. How did you develop the structure of this film, and how did the screenplay take shape?

When it comes to the structure of *Xiao Wu*, what really drove me to make this film was seeing just how profoundly the changes playing out in society had impacted people's interpersonal relationships. But just what do these "relationships" entail? There are relationships with friends, family, and romantic relationships. Coincidentally, just as I was getting ready to start working on the screenplay for *Xiao Wu*, I read an old article from the time of the Cultural Revolution. The article's structure was something like "Ding Ling's friend, Chen Huangmei's nephew, so-and-so's uncle." It was basically a personal attack on an individual, but the article began by laying out the network of personal relationships surrounding him. [*laughs*] This is very much in line with Chinese people's worldview. Since I wanted to tell a story about changing times, I decided to use interpersonal relationships as my entry point. So the structure begins with practical, real-world relationships and develops from there.

The original title for *Xiao Wu* was actually *Hu Meimei's Sugardaddy, Jin Xiaoyong's Buddy, Liang Changyou's Son: Xiao Wu*. [*laughs*] I really loved that title. But after we shot the film, my producer forced me to drop everything that came before *Xiao Wu*! *laughs*] Otherwise, it may have been one of the longest titles in film history! So in the end we just went with *Xiao Wu*. Even up until today, I still like to settle on a Chinese title early on in the screenwriting process; without that it is hard for me to really capture the spirit and emotion of what I want to convey through the film. I normally don't settle on an English title until after the film is complete, but I always have a Chinese title early on.

2.2 Wang Hongwei (*left*), Zuo Baitao (*center*), and Jia Zhangke (*right*) on the set of *Xiao Wu*

There is one funny anecdote regarding *Xiao Wu*'s Hong Kong distribution: The local distributor there wanted to change the name to *The Thief and the Beauty* (*Shentou qiaojiaren*) [*laughs*], but I wouldn't agree. In my mind that was an oversimplification—after all, if all you have is a thief and a beauty, what about Xiao Wu's parents? [*laughs*] And what about his good buddy? So we just stuck with *Xiao Wu*. [*laughs*]

Although you grew up in Fenyang, and shooting there must have been a homecoming of sorts, was there also a kind of alienation after having been away during this time of rapid change?

Right, the transformation of Fenyang is really incredible. So whenever I go back, part of me feels like a stranger. For instance, the means by which young people today communicate with each other and get along is really completely different from what it had been. This really showed me how to capture the transformation of my surroundings with a kind of sensitivity, which should always be the responsibility of a director. Naturally, there are some directors who neglect reality in their work, but my aesthetic taste and goals don't allow me to do that—I can never escape reality. So in *Unknown Pleasures*, I made a film about a younger generation with different values and characteristics than my generation. Growing up, I always played with at least three or four other kids, often all the kids on the block played together—the power of the collective was extremely strong, and culturally speaking, we always had a lot of confidence. But the younger generation are faced with a new kind of cultural oppression. This is in part due to the lifestyles they hear and learn about through the media—especially the internet and cable television—which exists on a completely different plane from their everyday reality. It is this radical contrast between the reality of their environment and the picture of the world they get through the media that creates an enormous pressure in their lives.

We completed *Xiao Wu* in just twenty-one shooting days, and a big part of my goal was to capture transforming relationships. Chinese people live in a world where they are dependent on interpersonal relationships. Whether they be family relationships, friendships, or husband-wife relations, we are always living in the context and confines of a relationship. And describing the structure of these relationships was really what I wanted to express through *Xiao Wu*. So the first section of the film is about the relationship between two friends. Amid this relationship there is a fundamental change brought on by broken promises and the loss of trust that the friendship was once based on. The second section of the film is about love and Xiao Wu's relationship with Mei Mei. In the past, the Chinese view of love was always an eternal one, from now until forever; the relationship between Xiao Wu and Mei Mei, however, is only about the moment, the now. Fate is destined to tear them apart. The final section is about family and the relationship with one's parents, another source of many problems. Of all the radical changes confronting the Chinese people in recent years, I feel the most fundamental and devastating change is in the realm of interpersonal relationships.

In one sense, it is as if all the characters are wearing a mask, pretending to be someone they are not. Xiao Yong, once a thief, is now a model entrepreneur, Mei Mei calls herself a karaoke girl while she works as a prostitute and her parents think she is studying acting in Beijing . . .

2.3 Wang Hongwei (*left*) and Zuo Baitao (*right*) on the set of *Xiao Wu*

Right, that's something I wanted to express. In China there are two kinds of people, those who can adapt to the changes around them, like Xiao Yong, Xiao Wu's childhood friend. In the film he takes part in all kinds of illegal activities, like importing contraband cigarettes, but he describes himself as "working in the trade industry." He uses wordplay to completely alleviate any moral burden or responsibility. Or, for example, when he opens up a dance hall, which is actually a place for prostitution, he says, "I'm in the entertainment industry." He has the power to cover up his behavior with language. He knows how to adapt to his environment, unlike Xiao Wu, who is helpless in this regard. Take, for example, his profession; for Xiao Wu a thief is a thief. There is nothing he can say or do to change his inferior moral

2.4 *Xiao Wu* French film poster

position. This is further augmented by his idealized view of friendship and interpersonal relationships.

Platform has been considered by numerous critics to be a key work of independent Chinese cinema. Could you talk about how the film came into being? You began work on the screenplay even before you conceived of *Xiao Wu*?

That's right, *Platform* was the first full-length screenplay that I wrote. It was already completed long before I began shooting *Xiao Wu*. Back when I was still shooting short films, I kept thinking about what kind of film I should make as my first full-length feature film if I were to ever get the opportunity. The first thing that came into my mind was *Platform*—a film about the 1980s and pop culture. For most Chinese—myself included—the 1980s was

THE HOMETOWN TRILOGY

an unforgettable decade. Just from the perspective of material culture, the transformation was utterly soul-stirring. I remember back when I was seven or eight years old, my older brother told me: "If I could buy a motorcycle, I'd be the happiest person in the world!" At the time, only police officers and mailmen had motorcycles, but for everyone else, owning a motorcycle was a luxury no one could even dream of. For my brother the very thought of one day having his own motorcycle was the pinnacle of happiness. But just three or four years after making his wish, the streets of China were utterly filled with motorcycles! By the same token, when we were kids you could only find television sets in large public facilities like the conference room at the police station or the local union's meeting room, and there would always be several hundred people crammed into those places to watch the television. But just a year or two later practically everyone was buying their own televisions sets!

The other big transformation taking place during this time was on a spiritual level. Previous to the Reform Era, there were very few books we could get our hands on, there were no avenues through which we could access outside cultural influences. But as the cultural thaw began, we suddenly had access to foreign literature, and by 1983 or 1984 the rate of that thaw seemed to increase. Even in a remote place like my hometown of Fenyang, you could buy books by Freud and Nietzsche at the local book vendor on the street. And even though none of us really understood what we were reading, we still devoured those books with great relish! [laughs] The change was so rapid, and throughout the entire decade of the 1980s, China was in a phase marked by idealism and excitement. Deep down we were all filled with hope and optimism for the future. We started to win all kinds of freedoms that we never had before, but then in 1989 came the setback. . . .

It was only after 1989 that people began to attain true independence in terms of their lifestyles. If I look at myself as an example, I was not part of a so-called work unit, and didn't have a traditional job. Suddenly a lot of independent intellectuals and artists began to appear, and, gradually, more aspects of the economy started to privatize. Many of us were determined to seek out an independent life for ourselves and break away from the system of state-controlled work units. This is also the period when independent or underground cinema began to arise: in 1989, Zhang Yuan started making films. These are all some of the things that the 1980s culture gave us. Whenever I look back and reflect on the 1980s, I always get particularly excited, and that is where the idea to make a movie about the 1980s first emerged. But there was always the question of how to find the right angle to approach that decade. It was only later that I realized I could use a song-and-dance troupe to reflect on the changes taking place during that era. These *wengongtuan*, or song-and-dance troupes, were the lowest on the rung of so-called cultural workers, and I thought that through their transformation we could gain a perspective on the changes taking place throughout the country at that time.

Were you a member of a song-and-dance troupe?

Not an actual member, but I participated in a lot of performances. In high school we saw an American movie called *Breakin'*. I must have watched that movie ten, twenty times, and learned all the moves from that movie. I became a break-dancer. It was right about this time that song-and-dance troupes were cut off from state financing and had to tour poor provincial areas to sustain themselves economically. Since I could break-dance, they often took me on tour during my summer vacations, adding a break-dance showcase to the performance. In addition to my experience, my older sister was also a violinist with a song-and-dance troupe in the early eighties. It was a combination of these two experiences that inspired the film.

Once the script was written, I started negotiations with my Hong Kong producers about a full-length feature film. At the time, however, the available funding was extremely limited, and I felt that *Platform* would require a larger investment to accurately re-create the historical background and cover the expenses of all the travel (since the film is about a touring troupe). All they initially offered us was just over 200,000 RMB, and there was no way to shoot *Platform* on that small amount, so we went ahead and shot *Xiao Wu* first. After the success of *Xiao Wu*, funding came easier; suddenly there were many international producers interested in working with us. In the end, we decided to collaborate with Shozo Ichiyama from Japan. A main factor in my decision to work with Shozo was the fact that he had produced Hou Hsiao-hsien's *Goodbye South, Goodbye* (*Nanguo zaijian, nanguo*, 1996) and *Flowers of Shanghai* (*Haishanghua*, 1998). Hou Hsiao-hsien is a director I have greatly admired for many years, so I felt that based on Shozo's relationship with Hou, we should be able to understand each other artistically. He came on to produce *Platform*, and he indeed turned out to be a wonderful producer.

Is it a fair assessment to say that *Platform* is the most personal of your works? Or even autobiographical?

I would agree with that. Naturally, there are a lot of differences between the characters depicted and myself; they are actually about ten years older than me. But several scenes in *Platform* are derived from things I saw growing up, and the latter half of the film was influenced heavily by my own experiences.

How did you discover your lead actor, Wang Hongwei? What is it about his performance and acting style that attracted you initially to him and led you to continually recast him?

Wang Hongwei was a classmate of mine in college. We were both film theory majors. When I made *Xiao Shan Going Home*, he played the role of Xiao Shan. I really admire his work. One thing that initially attracted me to him was the plainness of his appearance; his face looks just like countless other Chinese people.

And *Xiao Shan Going Home* was his first film as an actor?

Yes, that was his first film.[1] What really attracted me to him as an actor is his sensitivity and self-respect.

Wang was the lead actor in *Xiao Shan Going Home*, *Xiao Wu*, and *Platform*; he also appears in cameo roles in several of your later films, including *Unknown Pleasures*, *The World*, *Still Life*, and *A Touch of Sin*. Since he is not a professional actor, can you talk about just what it is that draws you to his performance style and makes you keep going back to collaborate with him?

Actually, back when I first cast Wang Hongwei, I was at a stage where I was quite rebellious and was consciously trying to resist the images I was seeing on-screen, which I had a great distaste for. Back then, all of the lead roles in film were portrayed by handsome young men and beautiful young women, but I wanted to try to present a more moving and realistic image for my lead characters. That's not to say I have a distaste for handsome and beautiful actors! [*laughs*] The real issue is that these professional actors have all been trained; when they speak, there is a certain standard inflection to the way they deliver their lines. You could line up ten actors for a role, and they will all read their lines exactly the same—speaking beautiful, pitch-perfect Mandarin Chinese and delivering their lines with the same air of artificial theatricality. When your average person speaks, their manner of speech is

2.5 Wang Hongwei in *Xiao Wu*

usually quite natural, but as soon as those actors open their mouths, there is a theatrical tone; it just immediately reads as fake. I don't want those types of people in my films. So those actors may have training and be very good-looking, but they are completely removed from those people I see around me in my everyday life. I started to ask myself, why can't the characters in my films resemble those people in my everyday life? I wanted to create a new image, an image built on authenticity, which up until that point I had never seen on the big screen. So I started to search for those individuals that drew me in, and they were precisely the kind of people that you rarely see in film. They are instead people imbued with real life. And that is what led me to Wang Hongwei.

Xiao Shan Going Home was the first time I worked with Wang Hongwei; at the time, we were both enrolled in acting class at the Beijing Film Academy. Our instructor thought that Wang Hongwei and I were such abysmal actors that when we did our acting workshop exercise we were both assigned to portray corpses! [*laughs*] But when I would see Wang Hongwei hanging out around the dormitory, I was also mesmerized by his expressive body language. Sometimes he would shake his sleeves and just that action was enough for me to know exactly what he was thinking. At other times he might be angry, anxious, or looking down on someone, but he was always able to express those emotions with a really creative and rich set of physical gestures. There was so much depth in his movements that I felt like he could have the potential to be an amazing actor.

In short, that was an era in which the image of the rebel was extremely popular on the silver screen. But after twenty years of filmmaking experience, I increasingly feel that the single most difficult thing in film is to create a new image of what a protagonist should be. That is where the absolute heart of cinematic innovation lies. You need to create a new type of person and capture that new character on film.

Another important facet of my working relationship with Wang Hongwei is that he has an innate ability to understand what I am trying to achieve—much more than any other actor. He always *gets* what I'm trying to do in my films.

What is interesting is that although your first films end with the shockingly powerful credit "This film was made with nonprofessional actors," by the time we get to Unknown Pleasures, **Wang Hongwei in the role of Xiao Wu is a kind of cultural icon, which you playfully reference.**

Right, he has changed and on one level is already a cultural symbol of sorts, which we see toward the end when he tries to purchase bootleg copies of *Xiao Wu* and *Platform*.

All of your films employ large numbers of nonprofessional actors. What are some of the pros and cons of using nonprofessional actors?

During the early phase of my career, I used exclusively nonprofessional actors in my films, starting with my early shorts. This really has to do with my aesthetic taste and my desire to make films about people in a very natural and realistic state. Professional actors have all undergone extended speech training and long periods of study on how to act with their bodies. So it is very difficult to adapt their methods of movement and speech into the kind of documentary-esque type of narrative film I am making. An actor trained in body movement is bound to stick out when walking down the streets of a place like Fenyang; it is extremely difficult to get them to fit in with their

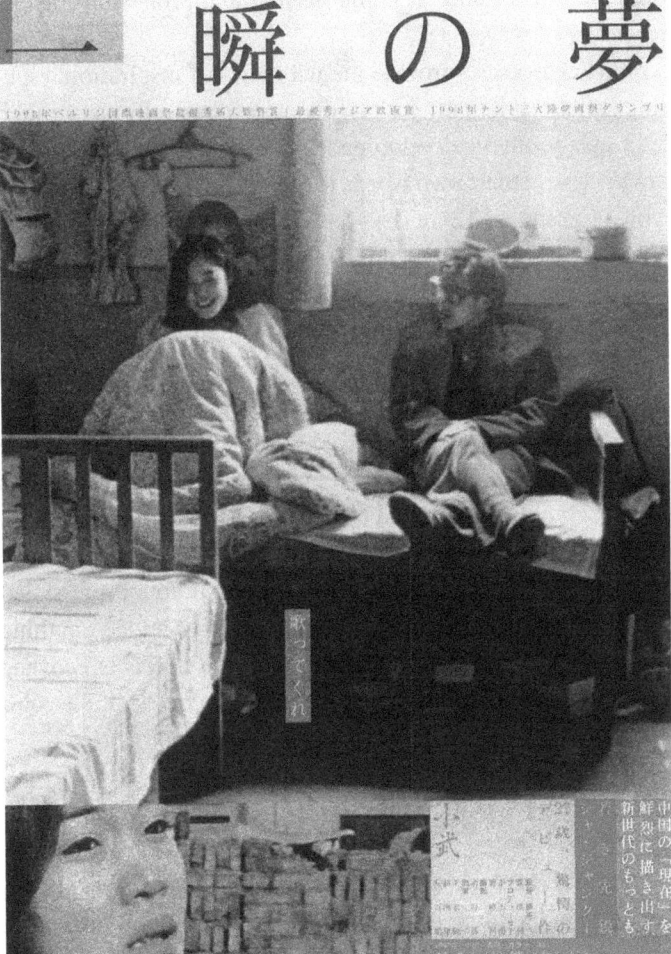

2.6 *Xiao Wu* Japanese film poster

surrounding environment. So the benefit of using nonprofessional actors is that their speech and movements are extremely natural.

The other reason is that nonprofessional actors can really understand what I am trying to express with the script. Since they grew up in a very similar atmosphere, they can believe in the script; they believe in the characters and their universe. For instance, the actors we used in *Xiao Wu* and *Platform* grew up in that very environment. We would shoot scenes on streets that they had been walking back and forth on for twenty or thirty years, so they all had a natural confidence and "at home" feeling that professional actors can't compare with.

Nonprofessional actors also provide me with a lot of inspiration, especially in the linguistic realm. In my scripts, dialogue is basically just a rough blueprint with ample room for development. I always leave it up to the individual actors to choose their own words to interpret what is on the page. Let me give you an example. There is a scene in *Platform* where Zhao Tao is doing a scene with Zhong Ping where they are both smoking. So before we began to shoot, I explained the scene to her and told her, "You just came in from the street to tell her that Zhang Jun has gone to Guangzhou." So she walked in and said, "Hey, they're parading some criminals down the street!" As soon as I heard this, I was so moved. Back in the early eighties it used to be quite common to see sentenced criminals paraded down the streets of Fenyang for public exhibition. Her creativity in throwing in this line was something completely inspired by her experience of growing up in the streets of Fenyang. These moments of spontaneous creativity added so much to the film, really making it come alive. If I had used a professional actor, on the other hand, they probably would never have added anything like that because they have no idea what went on in the streets of Fenyang during that era. It is details like this that really added so much subtle color to *Platform*.

And the challenges?

Well, at the same time there are also a lot of complications involved with nonprofessional actors due to their unfamiliarity with the art. It takes a lot of work to help them build up confidence in the characters they are playing. For example, if I ask a nonprofessional actress to play a woman going for an abortion, she will often have an internal resistance to playing such a role. Or if I want her to perform a certain dance, she will ask why. All of this requires extra effort on the part of the director. The link between the director and nonprofessional actors is very vulnerable and demands a lot of time and attention. Unlike professional actors who basically have a professional working relationship with the director, nonprofessionals require you to build up friendship and trust. If the actor loses their trust in the director, there is basically no hope of inducing a genuine performance. The whole process takes a lot of time. Another factor that comes into play here is the spontaneous style with which I make films, which tends to influence the rhythm of the work. Often an actor will deliver lines spontaneously during shooting, and although the words are incredible, it sometimes gets too long, making the scene go over and influencing the rhythm of the film. Gradually, however, I am figuring out ways to deal with these types of problems. After all, that's what film is about—it's all based on experience.

But the biggest challenge is simply the amount of time you have to invest in nonprofessional actors; after all, there are several factors you have to take into consideration when working with them. The first issue has to do with the type of language I employ when writing screenplays. When I write I almost always use my local dialect for the dialogue—this is true even for my most recent film, *Ash Is Purest White*. That is because it is impossible for me to imagine my characters without knowing where they are from. So whenever I write, I need to first settle on where exactly my characters are from to establish their background. China is, after all, a massive country: So where in China are they from? In what city do they live? Where did they grow up? Since I am from Fenyang in Shanxi Province, the characters in my head are almost always from Fenyang and they speak Shanxi dialect. Once you start using Shanxi dialect, the language itself has its own unique methods of expression and emotional texture. Every region is unique when it comes to this. If you compare people from Shanxi, Shanghai, Beijing, or Guangzhou, you will quickly discover that everyone has their own unique qualities. And since their dialects are different, the vocabulary they use is different, as are their ways of expressing and understanding emotion. So when I begin to imagine a new character and how he expresses himself, I need to know where he is from. That means that I almost always create characters from Shanxi, which also means that when I cast actors for these roles I try to find actors who can speak this dialect. So if an actor from Shanxi is performing in one of my films, they are speaking their native tongue—this is the language they have been speaking since childhood, which makes the performance more natural. That's why I used nonprofessional actors almost exclusively for my first few films. After all, there aren't many professionally trained actors from Fenyang—there aren't even that many from Shanxi! [*laughs*] It can be really hard to cast these films. Take Zhao Tao, for example. She is from Shanxi but isn't actually a native of Fenyang; she is from the provincial capital of Taiyuan. But the dialect there is quite similar to Fenyang dialect, so it isn't too hard to adapt.

Given your extensive experience working with nonprofessionals, what are some of the tactics you use to get them to feel comfortable in front of the camera?

The single most important quality to have when working with nonprofessional actors is patience because shooting a film is a totally new experience for them. You need to take time to allow the actors to familiarize themselves with the set and the general shooting environment. And another challenge is teaching them to put their guard down and let themselves go. Not everyone is able to feel comfortable and relaxed in front of the camera and truly let their vulnerable side be seen. Professional actors are trained in how to do this, but nonprofessionals rely on the director to help them adapt to this new environment.

Early on, my crew was usually quite small. At the early phase of my career, I needed only around thirty people to shoot a film, since I had a fairly nimble crew. One method I often would use was to have the nonprofessional actors spend all their time with us starting about three weeks before shooting. We would go to karaoke together, play mah-jongg, sing songs, go out to eat, and basically spend all our waking hours together. This isn't just so the actors become familiar with me; it is also so they can get comfortable with the cameramen, the soundman, and everyone else in the crew. I want them all to be like old friends who really understand each other by the time we start shooting; that way, the actors feel like they are part of the crew.

Besides that, another factor is the importance of rehearsal for nonprofessional actors. I don't rehearse every scene because I still really love the freshness and spontaneity when actors are performing. There is a direct and spontaneous emotional release that occurs when acting a scene that hasn't been overrehearsed. But for nonprofessionals, there are always certain scenes that require a run-through. That's because even rehearsal is something quite foreign for a nonprofessional actor. However, through the process of rehearsal, nonprofessional actors can become acquainted and comfortable with this thing called acting. If you don't rehearse with them and just throw them in front of a camera, they find themselves suddenly faced with two forms of pressure: the stress of performance and the stress of the camera. However, if you rehearse with them and allow them time to get comfortable with the cameramen and the rest of the crew, you can significantly reduce these two stress factors. I usually like to select a few of the more difficult scenes for them to rehearse. For instance, the scene in *Xiao Wu* where Wang Hongwei visits Jin Xiaoyong to ask why he wasn't invited to his wedding and ends with Wang Hongwei stealing Jin's lighter. That is probably the single most important scene for those two characters, so I began with that scene and we spent a lot of time rehearsing. As we ran through the scene, I would explain the screenplay and discuss the actors' understanding of their respective characters; this of course touches on their overall understanding of plot that I discussed earlier. These are some of the basic methods I use when trying to resolve the challenges faced when working with nonprofessional actors.

Another issue when working with nonprofessional actors is the need to really understand them: their conception of self-respect, their personality, the level of sensitivity. Sometimes all it takes is a deeper understanding of an actor in order for me to create a method through which he or she can really break through and assume the role.

While your first few films all employed a cast of nonprofessional actors, you later began to branch out and work with more and more professional actors: in *24 City* **you worked with Joan Chen, Lü Liping, and Chen Jianbin; then you went on to work with more Chinese celebrity actors in** *Touch of Sin***, such as Wang Baoqiang and Jiang Wu. These collaborations represent a very different approach than what you were used to early in your career, but what new challenges did working with celebrity actors present? And in what ways was the collaborative process more comfortable?**

The most comfortable thing was not having to do all of that prep work on the front end. Instead, the real work came down to acclimating to these different actors. I needed to find a way to let these different actors understand what I was trying to do through my films and allow them to get used to my approach to filmmaking.

For my three most recent films—*Touch of Sin, Mountains May Depart,* and *Ash Is Purest White*—I employed quite a few professional actors. *Touch of Sin* featured Jiang Wu and Wang Baoqiang; *Mountains May Depart* featured Dong Zijian and Sylvia Chang; *Ash Is Purest White* costarred Liao Fan; and of course all of these films featured my wife! [*laughs*] This shift is partially due to the fact that, ever since *Touch of Sin*, my views about cinema began to undergo some changes and I started to play with genre cinema in a much more overt manner. From the portrayal of characters at the screenplay stage to the final character designs, *Touch of Sin* was heavily influenced by the *wuxia* genre, especially the classic novel *The Water Margin*. All of the characters in the film are like the protagonists from that classic novel, and you can even detect traces of Wu Song, Lin Chong, and Lu Zhishen in the story.

When you appropriate a set genre, you end up needing to increase the dramatic elements in the film. This is an area where the specialized training of professional actors comes in handy, allowing them to capture these more challenging characters with greater ease. Another factor for working with more professional actors has to do with a change that began to take place among actors in the industry. In the 1990s, when I first began making movies, there were not a lot of films shot in the realist mode. Since most films were more dramatic, actors held on to a view of performance that made it difficult for them to accept a director who asked them to go for a more realist tone that was closer to everyday life. Since there were so few films being made in that realist manner, most actors faced real challenges when it came to nailing a performance that was both naturalistic and realistic in tone. Their perspective on what performance entails was simply too far off. This required me to waste a lot of time explaining things to actors and carrying out all kinds of experiments before we could begin shooting. Nonprofessional actors, on the other hand, didn't have any of that baggage and could deliver performances that I wanted much easier. But after twenty years, there is now a crop of actors who can take on dramatic roles while also being able to deliver very natural, true-to-life performances. This new breed of professional actors are fully able to appreciate films that accentuate a style that shuns any hint of an actor's "performing." There has indeed been a shift in performance styles. So now when I work with celebrity actors like Liao Fan and request they go for a more natural acting style, they are only all too happy to accommodate. They now also have a deep understanding of what kind of performance style I am looking for as a director. In some sense, this is just like how we handle technical aspects of film like lighting. Of course, we need to have lighting for our films, but I always stress a lighting style that falls on the side of natural lighting. Since these films are genre films, there are naturally some essential dramatic elements, but for the performance approach I always stress a more natural style.

Could you describe the screenwriting process for *Platform*? How was the story first designed, and how did you figure out the structure for the film?

Platform is actually the first full-length screenplay I ever wrote; I wrote it during my sophomore year at the Beijing Film Academy right after I had completed shooting *Xiao Shan Going Home*. However, when I was eventually able to raise close to 300,000 RMB in funding to shoot a feature film, I was concerned it wouldn't be enough for *Platform*. Since the screenplay was so long, the story spanned such a long time period—from the 1970s to the late 1980s—and because the troupe tours around different provinces, it required

2.7 Jia Zhangke (*left*), Wang Hongwei (*center*), and Zhao Tao (*right*) on the set of *Platform*

shooting at numerous locations: these were the factors that led me to shoot *Xiao Wu* first. But *Platform* will always be my first screenplay.

So, what led me to write this screenplay? I left my hometown in Shanxi to study at the Beijing Film Academy in 1995, and it was actually only after arriving in Beijing that I started to gradually begin to understand my hometown. Before that time, I had basically spent my entire life in Shanxi. It is like the old saying, "It is only when you leave your hometown behind that you can truly know that place called home." That's because it is only after you have this spatial distance—only after I arrived in Beijing—that I began to have all kinds of memories about home that came back to me. Once I was in Beijing, I began to experience a new set of emotions regarding my hometown.

Another reason I wanted to make *Platform* has to do with that era—the entire film is basically an ode to the eighties decade—the entirety of Chinese society was experiencing the single most explosive era of social change and individual liberation of the modern era. That was the age when people were all longing to get out and see the outside world, and when that era came to an end in 1989, all kinds of things ended with that. I have always felt that the period during which I wrote the screenplay was at a particular moment when the Chinese reform period was at its most stagnant; it had basically come to a complete halt. The social atmosphere at the time grew very heavy and grim, and even people like me who were only twenty-five or twenty-six years old keenly felt that the 1980s were gone and this was truly the end of an era. This led me to also have a different understanding of my hometown and also created a deep nostalgia for that lost atmosphere of the 1980s. This is the backdrop against which I began writing the screenplay for *Platform*.

When it came down to shooting the screenplay for *Platform*, there was actually an intense process of subversion where I had to turn a lot of elements upside down. At first the screenplay was extremely long, with so many characters undergoing all kinds of changes in their lives that I wanted to portray. I decided to shoot the film in a way that traced their movements, starting from an extremely isolated environment and eventually moving from the collective to the individual, and then from the individual back to a family structure. In the end, my protagonist gets married, settles down, and returns to a highly structured life within the confines of a social system. That's the story I wanted to tell, and that was the basic narrative structure.

Once it came to the production phase, in what ways did you have to adjust the original screenplay?

In the original screenplay, every detail in the characters' lives was clearly delineated: you could easily trace out all of the causes and effects in their lives. For instance, the reason that Zhao Tao's character made all of those various decisions in the film were all spelled out in black and white: the reason she didn't go on the road with the song-and-dance troupe was because she got a better job with the local tax bureau. The original screenplay even had a segment where her family tried introducing her to all kinds of prospective suitors after she left the troupe, but she didn't like any of them. By the time Cui Mingliang returned to Fenyang from his years of touring, Zhao Tao was beginning to get a bit old to be a single woman, which is why she married him. In the early version of the screenplay these were all details that were clearly spelled out. But after one week of shooting I decided to throw out that version of the screenplay because I realized it had some problems.

So what led me to halt shooting after only one week? The main reason was that I realized how much I hated that omniscient perspective where the camera seems to know everything. In our real everyday lives we often understand people through scattered fragments. Take the example of my neighbor. They have a daughter who usually goes to school every morning at a set time, but then I started to occasionally see her during the day shopping with her mother—immediately I knew that she wasn't in school anymore. She only made it halfway through high school before deciding to drop out. I don't know why—I don't think any of the other neighbors knew why either. Sometime later I discovered that she must have gotten a job at the post office because I would see her wearing a postal uniform. Before long I started to see her with a young man in the morning who would walk her to work—I knew that she must have a boyfriend. Then one day I heard the sound of firecrackers and knew that she must have gotten married. Normally, these are the kinds of fragmented details that everyday life gives us. So how come when we make films we suddenly have an omniscient perspective? At the very least, I knew that at least for this film I did not want to have an all-seeing eye that would capture everything my characters were doing. I instead wanted to bring the narrative perspective back to what my understanding of these characters would be in real life, but in order to achieve that, I needed to severely limit my perspective. I consciously wanted to shoot a film without that omniscient point of view. So as we shot *Platform* I kept revising the screenplay to adjust it to this new perspective and ended up making some very dramatic changes.

You have a quite a few shots where the camera gradually pans across an environment, and as the camera moves, so too the characters reposition themselves, creating a radically different mise-en-scène within a single shot. In other cases, you have a fixed camera but the characters are constantly moving, also changing the mise-en-scène in interesting ways. One such example of the latter approach occurred in *Platform* when Wang Hongwei's and Zhao Tao's characters are atop the city wall discussing their relationship. How much of shots like that is planned out in advance, and how much is improvised on set?

In order to answer this question, let me begin by explaining a bit about my working method: I always start with a literary screenplay. That's because when I was studying at the Beijing Film Academy our curriculum was heavily influenced by Soviet film training methods, and Soviet screenplays are quite literary—they require screenplays that can stand on their own as pieces of literature. So my screenplays have a lot of rich descriptive language. Even today I still prefer to write screenplays in this style because it provides a method by which I can clearly convey the type of story and overall tone I am trying to achieve to all of my collaborators. This is also the screenplay I use on set during shooting—I usually don't prepare a separate shooting script with all of the shot breakdowns. So when it comes to the actual shot breakdown and camera setup, we usually work all of that out when we actually start shooting.

Let's talk about the scene you mentioned in *Platform* where Zhao Tao and Cui Mingliang are atop the city wall, but as they move about, the wall periodically obscures them in the shot. As I was rehearsing that scene on set, I discovered that this perspective would be a perfect complement to the subtle and awkward nature of their relationship—he was constantly walking in and out of her life, close one minute and distant the next. So that led me to utilize that approach for the scene. Just a few subtle movements on the part of the actors, and they would suddenly be out of the shot and then back in. And it matched the story perfectly because at that point in the narrative the nature of their romantic relationship was quite ambiguous; it was precisely the point where things were teetering on a brink.

The scene also marks the only time in the film that Wang Hongwei asks Zhao Tao about the nature of their relationship. We decided to shoot the scene on top of the city wall, and I kept feeling that using words alone to express their feelings wouldn't carry the weightiness that I was going for. So I started thinking about the possibility of playing with the angle to visually accent the characters' feelings. Suddenly I discovered that corner with that hidden angle. Basically, Wang's pacing in and out of frame represents his inability to completely enter her world and the fact that they seem destined to keep going back and forth, unable to really be together. We actually shot that scene in several ways, but none of them seemed to click. Finally, I had everyone take a break while I tried to work out a way to handle the scene, and that's when I thought of using that cornered angle, and it seemed to really bring the scene together.

When it comes to true-to-life documentary-style shooting methods, there is often a sense of dislocation between the subject and the camera. What do I mean by this dislocation? If you are in a real-life location and trying to record the surroundings—and not just re-create a realistic environment—whenever your attention moves from one spot to another, the characters never wait for the camera to follow them. They never cooperate with you. They always end up walking away or eventually start doing something else. But I have always felt that this is precisely one of the most beautiful things about the truth of documentary-style films. This is the beauty of truth, the beauty of reality. In traditional narrative films, the camera always follows the actors and they have a close relationship. In narrative films, your camera might pan away from an actor, but when it returns, the actor has actually been waiting all along for the camera to return so he can resume his performance. But in my method of making narrative films, I really hope to occasionally employ methods and angles that are more common in documentary films and convey a deeper sense of reality. My camera may pan away from an actor, but when it eventually returns, there is no one waiting for the camera. They may have already walked out of frame, or gone on to do something else. This is one of the subtle things that I have taken away from documentary filmmaking and attempted to apply to my feature narrative films. Of course, it is not something I can employ all the time, but when you occasionally sneak this technique in, it can bring a subtle change in texture to certain scenes.

People often talk about the fact that my feature films have a documentary-esque sensibility, but as far as I'm concerned, what they are more concerned with is the notion of reality in and of itself, because what is "true" will always be relative. So for me the most important thing about film is its sense of truth, its sense of authenticity. Deep down I have always felt that since the invention of this medium we call film, the most beautiful aspect of this art form is the way in which it can present the world with a sense of authenticity: the way we eat, the way we walk, the sky, nature, our cities. The most powerful medium when it comes to reproducing the authenticity of the real world is film. And this is what I take to be the most enticing aspect of cinema. Given these feelings, when I make films I am always striving to create this sense of reality. I would never dare to say that my films are "real"—after all, that is a different category, it is also a different concept—but "realism" is an aesthetic concept, and I always strive for a kind of beauty in my films and that is the beauty of realism.

Back in 2013, when I was shooting *A Touch of Sin*, there was a scene featuring Wang Baoqiang buying a train ticket at a crowded train station during the Spring Festival holiday. The station was packed with people buying tickets, and when we were shooting we needed to control the location. The greatest challenge was how to ensure that the thousand extras we had there for the shoot revealed an order that was natural and true to life. We needed a kind of natural logic to arrange such a large-scale location; it is not enough to just take this crowd of people and stick them into that location. We needed to boil it down to the everyday real-life world and have a logical reason for why each person was there; what are they doing there at the station? So you have to figure out who is buying tickets, who is just standing around, who is shopping at some of the stores in the station. All of this needs to be designed. Over the course of the past few years my films have moved closer to genre cinema: *A Touch of Sin* was designed according to the structure of martial arts films; *Ash Is Purest White* borrows elements from gangster films. But even as I move closer to genre films, I still strive to make films in which the characters, natural environment, and the overall tone and mood are all true to life and realistic. This is extremely important for me.

2.8 **Yu Lik-Wai** (*left*) and Jia Zhangke (*right*) on the set of *Platform*

Earlier we talked about some of the subtle changes in your shots, such as camera movement, but in *Platform* you are also documenting a much bolder form of historical change. The film explores the transformation of an entire era, social movement, and the passage of time. Given the limited budget you had to work with, what techniques did you use to convey the passage of time? Can you talk about how you used subtle changes in costume, props, hairstyle, art design, and character design to convey the passage of time?

Platform spans an entire decade from the late 1970s to the late 1980s, and conveying that radical change was indeed challenging—a decade is simply too long! When you are dealing with such a long time span, there are a lot of elements that end up getting mixed together: some things change, others remain the same, and then there are some elements that superficially look the same but are actually completely different. Given this situation, one of the first things you have to do is deal with the issue of making a judgment call on how to deal with these issues. Let's start with the issue of costume design. The first proposal my costume designer gave me planned to use exclusively Mao-style tunic jackets for the late 1970s and then switch to light jackets in the early 1980s, then gradually we would switch those out for Western-style suit jackets. By the time we got to the late 1980s, the plan was to transition to cream-color windbreakers, which were very popular then. The benefit of that costume design plan was that each time period was very clearly delineated. Just one look and you knew exactly what year you were in. However, when I scrutinized the overall proposal, there was something that didn't sit right with me. There were certainly clear fashion trends in China during that time; people did indeed suddenly start wearing different types of clothing that came into fashion, but that wasn't exactly how things played out in real life during that time. For instance, in the early 1980s there were a lot of people who started wearing Western-style jackets, but it was just one segment of the population—definitely not everyone. What was really going on was that while some people were wearing Western jackets, others were wearing suit jackets, and then there were still a lot of people wearing their old Mao-style tunic jackets. I felt mixing it up like that would be a much more convincing approach. After all, what we were going for was historical accuracy, but not some kind of historical time stamp. If you just want to produce something that will immediately read as the product of a certain era, well, that is easy to do. What we were attempting to do with this more hybrid approach was much more difficult. Later my costume designer and I figured out a method to achieve what we were going for: we went back to my old school and looked up the old class graduation photos from the 1980s. Once we looked at that decade of class photos side by side, we quickly realized that the fashions were indeed quite uneven and mixed. Once we saw that, we began to utilize this hybrid approach for the costume designs in *Platform*.

Then there were some very minor details that I was also insistent upon paying attention to. For instance, there is one scene in *Platform* that takes place in the late 1970s where a group of girls are rehearsing for a performance, and at one point, they kick their legs up, exposing their socks. They were wearing synthetic fiber socks. When I saw that, I immediately knew that those types of socks didn't come into fashion until the 1980s. In the 1970s everyone was still wearing coarse wool socks—there is no way that anyone would be wearing those synthetic fiber socks in the 1970s! If we wanted to switch out the socks for fifty or sixty actors, it would have been a major project—we simply didn't have the appropriate socks on hand and were not prepared. But in the end, I decided we had to make the switch. So we shut down production and went on to shoot some other sequences before coming back to reshoot that dance rehearsal scene. I felt that since *I* noticed the socks were inaccurate and felt they didn't look right, I knew we had to change it. My cinematographer argued that it was the kind of detail that no one would ever even notice on-screen! Who would even be able to tell the difference between synthetic fiber socks and wool socks!? [*laughs*] But, as a director, I felt that once I noticed something was wrong, how could I still include that in my film? How could I knowingly include something that is historically inaccurate? If I had cut corners like that, I probably would never be able to look at that film again! So it is a good thing I insisted on changing the socks because now I can at least watch the film without feeling too embarrassed! [*laughs*] So a lot of what I do is tied to the accumulation of these types of fine details.

If you were to ask me about how we were able to shoot *Platform* on such a tight budget, I think the best example I can give you has to do with costumes. When we were looking for costumes for Zhao Tao's character, we tried out all kinds of outfits, but none of them were quite right. Later I found some of my older sister's old clothes from that era, and when Zhao Tao put them on they really felt just right. My sister is six years older than me, and the characters in the film are all basically from her generation. The opening of *Platform* takes place around the time I was seven or eight years old, which was in 1978 or 1979; so the film is really the story of my older sister's generation. So we dug all of my sister's old clothes out of the closet and had them washed and disinfected, and that is what Zhao Tao wore in the film. In the closing credits we even list the two "clothes washers," who were really amazing! They collected all of these old clothes, washed them, and prepared them for the actors so they would all feel comfortable. So this was one way in which we truly captured the pulse of the era in an accurate way but also saved a lot of money!

Another reason we needed to save money was because the vast majority of our budget was devoted to production costs. When we were shooting *Platform*, we had fourteen-hour workdays. A lot of people commented on our low production costs; actually the production costs for my films are extremely high because we invested our youth in those films! By the time we

2.9 Zhao Tao (*left*) and Yang Lina (*right*) on the set of *Platform*

got to the last week of shooting, we had burned through our entire budget and were almost broke. We had no choice but to quickly wrap up the shoot. By the end, my producer was buying me cans of Red Bull just to get through each day. They kept my body going forward, but my mind started to slow down! [*laughs*] But I indeed invested my youth in that film.

Critics of traditional Chinese literature sometimes use the dynamic between *jing* (stillness) and *dong* (movement) to describe a certain literary technique in classical Chinese poetry. On some level, I feel that *Platform* also engages with a similar dialogue between stillness and movement. In *Platform* "stillness" is epitomized by Fenyang, the city wall, tradition, and daily life; "movement" can be seen through those external elements that present the world outside such as Guangzhou, Wenzhou, the Reform Era,

THE HOMETOWN TRILOGY

and the troupe's life on the road. What are your thoughts on the film's relationship with stillness and movement?

Well, the film is a story about movement. After the first third of the film, the protagonists are basically on the road as touring performers. So it is the story of them leaving behind an isolated place and traveling from one place to another. But in the end, Cui Mingliang returns home to the order of everyday life. Toward the end of the 1980s there was a period of time when everything seemed to stop and there was a genuine feeling of stillness. Then by 1995 or 1996, society started to come back to life again. After 1989 there was a dark period where things were quite oppressive, but then by the mid-1990s there was the so-called Second Wave of the Reform Era. This second-wave of reforms were directed primarily at the economic realm, while culture and intellectual trends just continued along the same lines as in the 1980s. But the economic changes were quite dramatic. All of *Platform* is revealing the transition from a closed society to when things started to move and eventually leap forward, but in the end, everything goes back to everyday family life where it began—that's the cycle of change I wanted to express. According to the Chinese perspective, the concept of family represents a kind of stillness. So in the end, Cui Mingliang returns to the structure of a family system. For me it is this system that is most important: when the film begins he is part of an official song-and-dance troupe, which is also a type of system or organization. He and the other protagonists are all part of that system. After all of his travels and touring around the country, he returns home, gets married, becomes a father, and is now part of the family system. I wanted to use this as a foil to set against all those years of restless travel. As far as I am concerned, this journey that they are on is a journey in search of freedom.

Each installment of your Hometown Trilogy is quite different stylistically, but they are also very different in terms of the technical approach you took on each film. *Xiao Wu* was shot on 16mm, *Platform* was shot on 35mm, and *Unknown Pleasures* was shot on digital. How does shooting in different formats and using different technology impact the style and content of your work?

The transition from 16mm to 35mm was due to clear technical considerations. For *Xiao Wu* I was hoping to really capture that "on-the-scene" aesthetic and record what was happening in the "here and now." At the time, I really wanted to use handheld cameras, and 16mm handheld cameras were lighter, smaller, and more convenient to shoot with. This allowed me to get closer to my protagonists and navigate around the real-life environments of my characters. So when we shot *Xiao Wu* we didn't use any dolly tracks or any other special equipment. Instead, we just put the camera on our shoulders or on a tripod, and 16mm was enough for us to capture that documentary aesthetic.

For *Platform* we decided to use 35mm because we were facing an era that had passed us by, and I wanted to create a greater sense of distance between the camera and the characters. Moreover, I wanted to keep the number of shots down and instead focus on fixed camera angles, long takes, and long shots as the overriding look of the film. With that aesthetic in mind, I knew that 16mm wouldn't deliver the kind of quality image that 35mm could. And that is why I switched to 35mm for *Platform*.

By the time I got to *Unknown Pleasures*, I decided to switch to digital. From an aesthetic perspective, I didn't give this switch too much consideration at first. I just thought it was a new film medium to explore and it was quite convenient. It was just as convenient as 16mm, and it had fairly low requirements in terms of lighting. That meant that we could shoot in low lighting situations without many special light sources. It was that simple, and that's how I came to first experiment with digital film. But as I was shooting I quickly realized that the format had a big impact on my methods and approaches.

Did the amount of footage you shot greatly increase when you started shooting in digital?

It increased quite a bit. I also did a lot more experiments with different characters and locations. To give you an example, back when I shot on location in *Xiao Wu*, I had two basic approaches: either prepare the scene with actors in advance or just go in quickly and do one or two takes before packing up and moving on. However, after the transition to digital, I could shoot in the same location for several days, allowing the environment to gradually grow accustomed to our presence. In the past I needed to rely on a style of guerrilla filmmaking where I would try to get some footage in the can before people even had a chance to register what we were doing. With digital I could set up in a train station or pool hall and just stay there a few days. In the beginning the presence of our camera would create a disturbance in the environment, but after two or three days, you become part of the environment and people stop paying any special attention to you. So after shooting in digital I started to utilize this method.

At the time, the deepest impression that digital left on me was that when shooting in public spaces it somehow allowed me to get a kind of abstract feeling. Why do I say that? Once everyone is completely comfortable with your presence, the environment around you begins to reveal its natural texture and sensibilities to you. But somehow through that process you are left with an abstract feeling. In films like *Xiao Wu* we would barge in, shoot shoot shoot, and everyone on camera was touched with a kind of excitement and energy. The camera would change the feeling of the space and alter the mood in the room.

Unknown Pleasures also featured a richer color palette than my earlier films because adjusting color in postproduction is much more convenient when working with digital. Back then we would still have to transfer the digital back to celluloid after we had adjusted the color. Then, once transferred to celluloid, we would have one last shot at adjusting the color a final time before locking the picture. So for *Unknown Pleasures* we adjusted the colors in digital; then, after transferring to film, we did some further manipulation to the colors during the development process. For this second color adjustment, we used a special technique called "portrait method" (*liuying fa*), which allowed us to add a coldness to the colors we were adding. This is something that you can only do with digital, and we really tried to accentuate that. For the entire postproduction period, we were continually searching for the right texture and color. We wanted to find a visual style that was unique to digital film and not use digital to re-create the style of celluloid film. They are, after all, two completely different mediums that really can't be compared. From that point on, my cinematographer Yu Lik-Wai would spend most of his time experimenting with different possibilities for digital cinema.

In 2002, when you first shot *Unknown Pleasures*, digital cinema was still in its infancy. A lot of directors were just beginning to experiment with digital as a less expensive alternative to celluloid. But, at the time, there were still a lot of questions about the feasibility of a true digital revolution due to the technical and aesthetic limitations of the medium as well as the complications associated with transferring work shot in digital to traditional film stock. At the time of its release, however, critics called *Unknown Pleasures* the most successful film ever shot with DV technology.

Actually, I feel that there are a lot of problems with *Unknown Pleasures*. One issue was that in the process of resolving some of the problems associated with shooting in digital, we sacrificed a lot. For instance, we cut back heavily on exterior shots due to the poor quality of filming in the sunlight. Another problem was with the different camera lengths, some of which were too long for me to utilize—so there are some restrictions when working with digital. But working in digital was really a new experience; I found that there was much less pressure on the shoot. It was a very relaxed atmosphere. We had the freedom to experiment with many different things.

For instance, the second-to-last scene in *Unknown Pleasures* when the character Xiao Ji is riding his motorcycle down the highway—that whole scene is purely the result of digital. In the scene Xiao Ji's bike starts to stall, and suddenly it begins to thunder and rain—the whole scene came together beautifully; it was as if the environment was complementing his internal feelings. Actually that scene had already been finished, and we were packing up for the day when the sky suddenly grew dark and it looked like it was going to pour. Now, if I had been making a traditional film, I would have just told everyone to pack it up and go home for the day; after all, we already had a good take. But since we were shooting in digital, there was no pressure, we were completely free, so I suggested one more take. That final take [with the rain] was the one we used in the film.

Digital film also seems to bring a certain degree of abstractness when shooting in public spaces. This required some readjustment on my side because when I was first experimenting with digital video, my impression was that the medium would bring a new life to public spaces, but in actuality the result was an abstract quality. Every space has a kind of abstract order. Traditional film works to break up this order, making people appear active and excited, but digital interacts with its subjects in a very quiet way, enabling me to capture a cold, distant, almost abstract quality. This is something I realized a few days after shooting and adjusted to fit the story. Actually, it worked quite well for a film about lost youth like this.

Let's talk a moment about the place of destruction and ruins in your Hometown Trilogy. Toward the end of *Xiao Wu* an entire block is being torn down, but by the time we get to *Unknown Pleasures*, it appears an entire city is in a state of utter ruin. Can you talk a bit about the politics of destruction in your work, from the destruction of youth or the destruction of locales?

2.10 *Unknown Pleasures* French film poster

There are definitely some connections between *Xiao Wu* and *Unknown Pleasures*; not only is there the cameo reappearance of the character Xiao Wu, but there is also the echoing of the motif of destruction. The entire city exists in a state of desolation. All of those old industrial factories have stopped production, leaving a cold, abandoned feeling that permeates the city. Datong left me with all kinds of feelings of desperation and devastation. In one sense, it is truly a city in ruins, and the people who inhabit it very much live in a spiritual world that reflects their environment.

One very interesting difference between Fifth Generation filmmakers and the younger generation of filmmakers like yourself lies in the realm of adaptation and source material. Virtually all the major cinematic works of Fifth Generation and older-generation filmmakers are adapted from literary sources, while the Sixth Generation, or Urban Generation, as they are sometimes called, have often opted for a more spontaneous approach and have preferred original screenplays over adaptations.

This is indeed a major change. One reason for this change is that Fifth Generation directors seem to need to extract their material from historical and literary texts in order to carry out their cinematic creativity. Younger-generation filmmakers seem to pay more respect to their own life experience. They are willing to directly express their lives through film. Naturally, Fifth Generation filmmakers express their life experience through their work as well, but it is not as direct. They create a space between themselves and the cinematic text, and this space often comes through the intervention of adaptation. My big turning point in this respect came when I saw Hou Hsiao-hsien's *Boys from Fengkui* (*Fenggui laide ren*, 1983), which really taught me to trust my own experience. At the same time, I'm not at all against adapting a novel or literary work for film. I plan to write my own screenplays for my next two features or so, but in the future I would really love to adapt a novel. Actually, [right after making *Unknown Pleasures*] I was considering adapting a French novel called *La condition humaine* (*The Human Condition*) by French author André Malraux.[2] It is a story about Shanghai in the 1920s, and if we ever do it, we would probably shoot in Southeast Asia.

One of the themes in your work is the repetition of actions. Examples of this include the continuous opening and closing of the switchblade in *Platform*, the repeated slapping of Xiao Ji, and the pushing game between Qiao San and Qiao Qiao in *Unknown Pleasures*. What is the function of these repetitive games in the narrative fabric of your films?

They represent a kind of mechanistic lifestyle. For instance, the pushing game between Qiao San and Qiao Qiao—actually their relationship is nothing but a cycle of mutual provocation. They are blind in their relationship, neither knows what love is—all that they have left is this rote and mechanical method of antagonizing one another as a futile attempt to change their situation. Or in the karaoke bar where they are beating Xiao Ji and continually repeating that same line, in that scene the two of them are using their stubborn stances to express the pain they have inside. At least, that's what was going through my mind while shooting those scenes.

I was wondering if you would mind playing a little game. I would like to describe a handful of key scenes from each of your three features and have you tell me what was going through your mind from a filmmaker's perspective as you were filming each respective scene.

Starting with the opening scene of *Xiao Wu*, our first visual introduction to the protagonist, the first thing we see is a close-up of Xiao Wu's hands lighting a cigarette before he boards the bus. The scene culminates with the climactic juxtaposition of Xiao Wu picking the pocket of the passenger next to him and the mini-portrait of Chairman Mao hanging from the rearview mirror of the bus.

Well, the second half of that scene is a standard montage. Basically, I wanted to describe a new phenomenon playing itself out under the gaze of [a symbol of] traditional hegemony. I decided to open the film with a shot of his hands because he is a pickpocket; as a thief, his hands are the tools of his trade. The package of matches in his hand actually has Shanxi written on it. I decided to add this prop to provide a spatial reference point to the viewers, which is very important. The whole issue of locale was extremely close to me when I made the film, and I wanted to highlight the fact that this was a story about Shanxi. It was really a rarity for a camera crew to come to a place like Shanxi and face the reality there, so I wanted to make this clear from the beginning—so the hands for the thief and the matches for Shanxi.

There is a scene in *Xiao Wu* where the protagonist's childhood friend Xiaoyong touches a brick wall. Just a few scenes later, Xiao Wu caresses the same wall. What is the symbolism here?

You might not notice it, but there are height marks carved and scraped into the wall. Those scrapes are actually markers that come from a popular custom in northern China where children the same age who are good friends measure their height by marking a wall. So those marks are a record of their childhood, a record of them growing up. The wall, in this sense, is a symbol of their friendship and their past.

Another moving scene in *Xiao Wu* is when he visits Mei Mei when she is sick. Mei Mei sings a popular song by Faye Wang (Wang Fei/Wang Jingwen), but when she asks Xiao Wu to sing a number, all he can do is flick open his singing cigarette lighter, which plays a mechanical version of "Für Elise."

In my mind Xiao Wu is the kind of character who is not good at expressing his thoughts and feelings. But in that situation he needs to find some way to express his feelings for this girl. I kept trying to figure out a way for him to express his feelings when I suddenly thought of the cigarette lighter. So he responds to her with music as a means of expressing his feelings for her.

What about the conclusion of *Xiao Wu* where we see Xiao Wu squatting like a dog, handcuffed to a pole on the street, surrounded by a crowd of onlookers? It is a scene of incredible power, and I was curious, what led you to end your film with such a sudden, and in some sense brutal, conclusion?

In the original script the ending was supposed to be of the old police officer leading Xiao Wu through the street, eventually disappearing into a crowd. But as I was shooting, I was never really completely satisfied with this original ending. It is a safe ending, but also a rather mediocre one. During the twenty days of the shoot, I was constantly trying to come up with a better ending. Suddenly, one day when we were shooting a crowd started to gather around to watch us filming, and I was struck with a kind of inspiration. I decided to shoot a crowd scene of people staring at him. I felt that in some way, this crowd could serve as a kind of bridge with the audience. Like the audience, the crowd are also spectators, but there is a shift in perspective. As soon as I thought of it, I felt a kind of excitement. Naturally, I also thought of Lu Xun's conception of the crowd.[3]

In *Platform* there is a short but endearing scene where three people pile on to a single bicycle and one of the passengers extends his arms as if he can fly.

Fleeting happiness.

There is a very charming scene in *Xiao Wu* where a beeper is being passed around to the different members of the protagonist's family, eliciting radically different expressions from each person.

Right, for them, the beeper is a strange, unknown device. And when these new things enter people's lives for the first time, they are beside themselves as to how to deal with them. During that era, the Chinese people had to continually deal with the introduction of new things, and we really had no idea what they were. It is a kind of cultural blindness.

2.11 *Platform* film still

It is difficult to find a scene of such understated melancholy and cinematic power as the climactic scene in *Platform* where Wang Hongwei dozes off in a chair on a lazy afternoon as his wife takes care of their baby. It is a scene that has been described by Kent Jones of the Film Society of Lincoln Center as "one of the finest moments in modern movies."[4] Can you talk about that scene?

I wanted to arrange an ending where they return to a state very close to that of most other Chinese. They were once rebellious, they once pursued their ideals and dreams, but in the end they return to the pace of everyday life—which is where most young people eventually end up. They return to the trappings of the everyday.

The challenge came with how to go about expressing the state of the everyday. And then I suddenly thought of an afternoon nap. I can't speak for life in southern China, but in my hometown after starting their careers and getting married, most people end up living a very repetitive life where they do the same things every day and the possibilities for variations are extremely limited. A lot of men living this type of life spend all their time at their work unit and come home for afternoon naps. And I decided to use this to conclude the film.

The scene conveys such a lonely existence, and does so with such incredible power.

It is a lonely existence. No longer is there any possibility for miracles to happen. There is no hope for change. And then there is that late afternoon sun, shining down as he naps, which also adds another layer to the scene.

2.12 Zhao Tao (*left*) and Wu Qiong (*right*) in *Unknown Pleasures*

Let's talk about Xiao Ji's motorcycle in *Unknown Pleasures*. Did you intend for the cycle's continual breakdowns to serve as a metaphor for the youth in the film who are young and full of energy but are always "breaking down" and apparently going nowhere?

In the original screenplay there is nothing wrong with the motorcycle, so that scene was something that came out spontaneously during shooting. Suddenly the motorcycle wouldn't go up the hill and began to stall. I should have yelled cut right there, but I discovered that the actor's expression at that moment was so close to what the character was going through. He looked so anxious, he wanted to make it up the hill, he wanted to get through his youth, and to get the scene right. He kept trying, and I kept shooting. Only after this scene did I get the idea of revisiting the stalled-out motorcycle again at the end of the film. So in the penultimate scene we decided that we would have him run out of gas, but then it rained and the scene was brought to a whole other level.

You discussed your preference for literary screenplays over more technical screenplays. But during the screenwriting process are you already conceiving shots and imagining the look of the film? Or do you design the visual tone of your films later?

I often have some ideas about the imagery I want to use. When I was in college there was a really interesting situation where half of the teachers were graduates of the Moscow Film Academy. That is because the entire film education system in China was imported from the Soviet Union during the 1950s and 1960s, so many of our professors came out of that tradition. But by the time I went to the Beijing Film Academy there was a new generation of professors who had studied in America, Japan, and France, so when it came to screenwriting there were two distinct approaches we were exposed to: the Soviet style and the American style. The two methods were completely different. The Soviet approach required a very literary style similar to a novel but did not have any practical requirements when it came to actually shooting. [*laughs*] Instead, the main goal was to write something of publishable quality that was highly readable. That was my earliest training, and even today I still write screenplays according to this method. Part of that is tied to the fact that I have always been drawn to the process of description. I love the process of describing colors, environments, smells—the latter of which you can of course never depict on film! But for me, that process is extremely important because it helps me understand the kind of mood I want to create for the film. The more detailed my descriptions, the clearer I am about what I want to shoot. By the time I am done with the screenplay and start to direct the film, I have a very good understanding of what kind of atmosphere I want to create for the picture. So as I am writing I am already very clear about what kind of image I want to capture. Another essential part of this is that the screenplay provides a blueprint for the crew to understand the style and mood of the film. So I have always stood by this practice of writing detailed literary screenplays for all my films, and it is a process I really enjoy.

When it comes to shooting, I am very much reliant on the process of location scouting. When I do location scouting, I usually visit each location three times. The first time I go alone; usually I have two to three options to select from for each location. For instance, if I want to shoot a scene in a karaoke bar, I will select a few locations and get a clear understanding of each one. As I'm visiting these locations I am usually simultaneously going back to the screenplay and making all kinds of adjustments and revisions to account for the logistics of the locations. That is my first round of location scouting. For the second round, I bring along my cinematographer Yu Lik-Wai and we look at all the locations together. That is when we start

2.13 Jia Zhangke on location

to have deeper conversations about shot breakdowns and camera angles; that is when we play with different options for the overall visual design. The third visit includes the core creative team: sound designer, producer, production manager, and even the lead actors. We go together and go through everything as a team. I never draw storyboards or write shot-by-shot breakdowns, but over the course of this third trip to visit the locations I always have a complete shot-by-shot breakdown in my head. And by then the shot-by-shot breakdown is not something abstract, it is grounded in specific locations: I know exactly which house and which street each shot will take place in.

How big is the difference between your first draft screenplay and your final film? Do you usually add new scenes during shooting?

More often than not, I cut scenes. There are never any major changes when it comes to the overall structure of my films. In the case of *Platform* I ended up shooting less and less as we went along; for *Still Life* I shot more and more! Every film presents a set of unique circumstances to navigate.

In your entire body of work, which film diverged most greatly from the original screenplay?

That would have to be *Platform*.

•

THE WORLD (2004)
STILL LIFE (2006)

3 Documenting Destruction and Building Worlds

3.1 Jia Zhangke on location shooting *The World*

But there is one element that is of particular importance when you are writing a story, and that thing is emotion. Once you are moved by something, your imagination becomes extraordinarily rich, and all kinds of details start to come to you. Every one of us has the power of observation, every one of us has an extraordinary capacity to remember details, but often when we can't remember those details, it is simply because there is nothing about them that moved us—there is no emotional connection.

When you first came on the scene all the films in your Hometown Trilogy were considered "underground films." Your 2004 film *The World* was your first film to be commercially distributed in China. What were the considerations that led you to transition from a so-called underground filmmaker to someone who could operate above ground? What were your concerns? Was there a fear that through this process you would lose some of your freedom and autonomy?

I began shooting my first film, *Xiao Wu*, on April 10, 1997—at the time I hadn't even graduated yet and was still a student at the Beijing Film Academy. At the time, I just thought I was shooting another student film and didn't give the process that much thought. Jumping ahead to February 1998, *Xiao Wu* was selected for competition at the Berlin Film Festival, and before I even realized what was going on, the film started to get picked up for distribution in several countries, including France and Korea, and it started to make an impact. Things continued like that for a while until one day some people from the Film Bureau came to have a chat with me. It was only when they told me, "You have violated the rules," that I realized I had indeed not followed proper protocol when submitting the film! [*laughs*] Somehow, without even realizing how it really happened, from that point forward I was labeled a so-called underground director! [*laughs*]

Later, when I was preparing to shoot *Platform*, I really hoped the film would be able to be commercially distributed in China. It was really important for my film to be seen by Chinese audiences, so I was very careful to go through all the proper channels to apply for shooting approval. However, because of my previous record with *Xiao Wu*, they did not approve the film. I decided to go ahead with the film anyway, and later I also made *Unknown Pleasures*.

During that period the film censors and I didn't have a great desire to reach out to each other. [*laughs*] I actually didn't even know how to get in touch with them; there were no open channels. Fast-forward to 2003, I had just completed the screenplay for *The World* when the dean from the Beijing Film Academy called to inform me that the Film Bureau was planning a symposium with underground film directors. He asked me to attend, so I went. When I arrived, I discovered fifty directors sitting there! I had no idea China had so many underground film directors! [*laughs*]

That meeting turned out to be quite famous, and a lot of books on independent Chinese cinema make reference to that symposium. The gist of the meeting was that the Film Bureau expressed its hope that, moving forward, underground directors would all go through the proper channels to apply for the required permits and permissions when making films. They also said that the nature of Chinese cinema was changing, and they expressed their hope that everyone's film could be commercially exhibited in China. Since I had just completed my screenplay for *The World*, I submitted it to a state-run film studio, Shanghai Film Group. The head of the studio (Ren Zhonglun) was a former film critic who used to be the editor of the *Wenhui Film Times*. He really liked my screenplay, but before we moved the project forward I asked him, "Can I expect any interference from you?" He responded by saying, "I will never interfere in your work. I hope that the Shanghai Film Group can make a Jia Zhangke film—what I don't want is Jia Zhangke to make a Shanghai Film Group film!" I was quite happy with that arrangement and went on to collaborate with them on *The World*.

There was something else that was very important about that symposium in that it represented a major shift in China's film environment—from that point on, film was regarded as an industry in China. Before that time, film was still considered a tool for propaganda. But from that moment the government shifted its perspective from regarding film as propaganda to film as an industry. This was an extremely important change. It wasn't just me; from that point on there were quite a few directors in China whose films were suddenly allowed to be officially exhibited. Another thing that came out of that meeting was the decision that underground films shot previously would not be granted any distribution access; they would just remain in limbo. A lot of directors were very much against that decision, but I took a somewhat indifferent attitude to it. After all, so much of the film market at that time was dominated by bootleg DVDs so it didn't really matter; if people wanted to see my films, they could still see them. [*laughs*]

Besides bearing the "Dragon Seal" of the Chinese Film Bureau, another important thing about *The World* was the shift in your overall film style. One rather dramatic change was the incorporation of Flash-style animation sequences in the film. I remember how shocked I was the first time I saw those sequences because their tone was so radically different from the rest of the film, as well as your previous work. Later, however, I realized that in some way those sequences fit perfectly because they represented the inner desires of the characters, a kind of artificial world, and the digital escapist world of the cell phone. Could you talk about those animated sequences?

Actually, China has been in a state of constant transformation, so although this story is inspired by people's lives playing out in the here and now, the film captures some of that change in the atmosphere of the now. The period of time from the initial conception of *The World* up until the time shooting began corresponded to the outbreak of SARS in China. Before the outbreak, China's economy was developing at breakneck speed, and the economy was expanding rapidly. Another thing that was happening was that the internet was becoming a regular part of young people's lives in China. The internet at that time was mostly centered on sending email and looking up news stories, but by 2002 or 2003 a lot of internet forums started to appear, and young people began to invest huge amounts of time on online virtual games. Suddenly young people found themselves living amid two worlds—the virtual

3.2 Zhao Tao in *The World*

world and the real world. This period represented the very beginning of that dichotomy between the virtual world and the real world. Before that time there was really no such thing as a so-called virtual world for most people; we were all living the real-life, everyday world. But the rise of the internet added a virtual or artificial world to our lives, and this was a shocking change for me. Then you factor in the fact that this film takes place at World Park, which is already a kind of artificial fantasy space. Within World Park you have miniatures of all the world's famous tourist destinations: the Eiffel Tower, the Arc de Triomphe, the White House, all open for visitors. The park's slogan is "See the world without ever leaving Beijing." It is truly an entirely artificial world. So when I was writing the screenplay I decided to combine the actual atmosphere of World Park's artificial world with the artificial world of the internet and intertwine them. I felt that this combination did indeed capture the new situation that many young people found themselves in, living amid two different worlds.

3.3 Zhao Tao in *The World*

And how did the screenplay come about?

The story behind *The World* was inspired by my future wife, Zhao Tao. Zhao Tao is a dancer, and before she went to Beijing Dance Institute she had been enrolled in a dance school back in Shanxi, Shanxi Provincial Arts College. I once asked her why she came to Beijing to study at the Beijing Dance Institute, and she told me that after she graduated she had been assigned to work at Window of the World in Shenzhen, which was another version of World Park. At first she was extremely happy there. Shenzhen is a very liberal and open place, and at the park you can basically see the world without ever needing a passport—you can go from Niagara Falls to the Arc de Triomphe in a matter of minutes. But after just two or three months she started to feel extremely frustrated and closed off. She would have to perform at different sites every hour or two, and for an entire year they just mechanically performed the exact same dance routines. So the place that at first gave her the impression of being an extremely open, global, and international fantasyland turned out to be an extremely closed-off and isolated corner. So, on the one hand, the park is dazzling and beautiful, filled with all kinds of sights and sounds and imbued with the feelings of freedom and openness, but for those people who actually work there, it is still like some backward corner cut off from the world. This relationship between "the world" and a "small corner" really enticed me and put me on the path to write the screenplay.

I do have one anecdote about the screenplay: *The World* was the first screenplay that I wrote on a computer. I had just bought a laptop and learned how to write on a computer. Just as I was finishing the first draft, I had to take a trip to Belgium. Although I had learned some of the basics about the computer, I still hadn't learned the importance of backing up my files or emailing files to myself. In the end, I ended up losing my laptop in Belgium! I was so depressed that I spent the whole day in bed at my hotel! [*laughs*] I was so upset! I had no idea how to go about rewriting this entire screenplay. It was only after taking a break for a few months that I finally rewrote it! [*laughs*] I guess this is one lesson I learned from the virtual world! [*laughs*]

You mentioned the setting of the film, Beijing World Park, which is a site imbued with all kinds of allegorical meaning. The film itself also seems to engage with some of the major keywords present in Chinese society during the early 2000s—"globalization," "migrant workers," "consumerism," "*shanzhai*" (copycats), et cetera. How important were these keywords as you were conceiving the screenplay and making this film?

I live in Beijing, and after the successful application to host the 2008 Olympics in 2001, the entire city became an overnight construction site, and there was a huge influx of migrant workers from outside the city. That was the moment when many of us living in northern China began to really sense this tide of human movement as all these new migrants were flowing into the city. At the time one of the most common expressions was "migrant worker." Owing to the lack of a local labor force in Beijing, large numbers of people from rural areas began funneling into the city. *The World* really began with the phenomena of populations of people from remote regions who began to move into the cities. Of course, this human flow can be seen much earlier—it is even there in *Xiao Shan Going Home*. Back when I shot *Xiao Shan Going Home*, you couldn't call it a "tide," but by the time we get to *The World*, urban populations began to rapidly expand, traffic worsened, and everything began to change.

3.4 *The World* Chinese film poster

SARS was also an important factor when I wrote the script because, amid the SARS crisis, Beijing basically turned into what felt like an abandoned city. The first, second, and third rings were basically empty—at the time I lived along the third ring, and because there were no cars on the road, I would walk in the middle of the street on those major traffic arteries and not see a single car! One day when I was out for a walk during the SARS period, I suddenly started paying attention to all of those advertisements that you drive by every day but don't really take notice of. I was especially shocked by those real estate advertisements: they were all advertising new developments with names like "Roman Gardens," or "Vancouver Forest"! There was even one called "Venetian Waterside Village" [*laughs*], but the actual place probably only had a little stream running through it! Without exception, all of these real estate advertisements that were selling homes and condos were named after various international locations. Just like World Park, this was another reflection that the age of consumerism had arrived and with it had come an extremely complicated psychological state through which you could see the decline of our own cultural self-confidence. All of this pointed to a longing for the outside world, but on the other side of that, there was also something very negative being reflected. Take, for instance, that place called "Roman Gardens," which wasn't far from where I lived: the place was constructed right in the middle of a traditional neighborhood filled with courtyard-style houses. My feelings about the whole thing were quite complex. I remember at one point writing down the following question: "Is globalism actually Americanization?" In the age of globalization, I became keenly aware of this crisis regarding cultural self-confidence. Somehow this had become intertwined with the concept of consumerism. At the time, McDonald's and

3.5 Jia Zhangke (*left*) and Yu Lik-Wai (*right*) on location

DOCUMENTING DESTRUCTION

Kentucky Fried Chicken restaurants were popping up everywhere, and then one day I discovered that my niece's CD shelf didn't have a single album by a Chinese artist—all of her CDs were in English.

The World and *Still Life* reveal two completely different worlds. In *The World* we have an artificial theme-park version of globalism, but in *Still Life* you peel away this gaudy facade, and what is left is an empty, haunted world literally in ruins and on the verge of being submerged. Looking at these two films side by side creates an incredibly powerful juxtaposition. How do you reflect on this rather absurdist juxtaposition, from the construction of a completely artificial "plastic global city" to the submersion of an ancient Chinese historical city? At the time of making *Still Life*, were you in some way intentionally trying to display the underbelly of *The World*?

At the time I was shooting *Still Life* I never really considered its relationship with *The World*, but after hearing your comparison, it is indeed quite interesting. [laughs] Because I am a native of Shanxi who has lived in Beijing for many years, southwest China and the area around the Yangtze River have always been quite unfamiliar territory for me. When they were building the Three Gorges Dam, there was a lot of attention focused on that, and many of my fellow filmmakers went out there to shoot documentaries and feature films. Initially I didn't intend to shoot anything related to the Three Gorges Dam, even though I knew what was happening there was very important. What drew me there was the painter Liu Xiaodong.[1] Liu Xiaodong was planning on going to that region to paint a series of paintings. For a long time, I had been wanting to shoot a documentary film about Liu Xiaodong, so I followed him there as part of that documentary (*Dong*). Once I arrived there and saw the ruins, I was utterly shocked. The city I went to was called Fengjie; it is an ancient city with more than three thousand years of history. The famous Tang poet Li Bai has a well-known line of poetry, "The cries of the monkeys from both sides of the shore never cease, as my small boat traverses ten thousand layers of mountains"—he wrote that line while in Baidi Fortress, which is in Fengjie. When you visit such a famous place so filled with history and to see it completely reduced to rubble, it is really an indescribable feeling—I was utterly stunned. The whole city was in ruins. By the time I arrived, the demolition was already nearing its tail end. It was only taking the demolition teams a week to bring down massive buildings, and they did everything by hand; there was no heavy machinery—just men with sledgehammers. You might wonder why they didn't just use heavy machinery or explosives. That's because they wanted to recycle all of the bricks, steel, and other materials. When I stood on the bank of the Yangtze River and saw the remnants of what was left amid a landscape of ruin, my first impression was that it looked like the aftermath of an alien invasion! [*laughs*] It was completely surreal. As I spent more time there I began to feel increasingly drawn in by those workers laboring amid these ruins. They were filled with such an incredible drive and energy. I arrived there in summer, and the workers' skin was all sweaty and blackened from the relentless sun and the soot. It was the juxtaposition of these dead ruins and the life force of those workers laboring amid the remains of the city that drew me in and made me want to make a film about the Three Gorges. As I wrote the screenplay, the story was completely related to my direct observations and emotional response—immediately I knew I wanted to make this film.

Once the government made the Three Gorges Dam project a priority and decided to make Fengjie the site, individuals had no recourse or means of resisting. One decision ended up bringing about massive change. More than a million people would be relocated, and a city with more than three thousand years of history would be erased, buried beneath the river. *Still Life* reveals the helplessness of the individual when confronted with rapid change; instead the individual simply gets pushed aside and swept away. It was within that kind of environment that I stood amid the ruins reflecting on what a person can do when faced with such monumental changes. What can any single individual do? Perhaps we need to start by resolving our own issues as individuals and make some difficult decisions. You may not have any power over whether or not this city will be flooded, but perhaps you can exert control over who you love. While this made me somewhat depressed, it helped me understand just what it meant for someone to truly have a passion for life—it is not that they are able to resist the raging tide of their times, but rather are able to grab hold of themselves as the floodwaters crash down. From there, two characters gradually emerged: one of them wants to get divorced and the other is trying to save a failed marriage. Han Sanming is a coal worker who was once illegally married, which eventually ended in divorce. They are reunited after many years, and although they love one another, they don't have the power or ability to be together again. The other character is a nurse played by Zhao Tao who wanted to terminate a marriage that had long been devoid of any love. The question of whether or not she is able to resolve this problem and get out of her marriage hints at the basic question of whether or not we are able to take control over our own fate. In

China there is a lot of jargon about being "the masters of society" or "the masters of our nation," but often people aren't even able to be the "masters of their own *lives*." For me the definition of modernism is the individual being able to be his or her own master. That is how these two characters emerged out of the backdrop of the massive transformation surrounding the Three Gorges Dam project.

The greatest challenge I had to face when making this film was the fact that time was running out—the entire city was being ripped apart and about to be submerged. If I had followed my normal timeline for making a film, which would be to write a screenplay, lock up funding, and cast the film, I would have been looking at eight months to a year, perhaps even longer. But by then the entire city would be underwater! So the screenplay was written under a very special set of circumstances. I wrote the screenplay in five or six days. During the day I was shooting the documentary film *Dong*, and at night I would go back to my hotel with the assistant director and producer from my documentary; each of them had a laptop, and I would act out scenes and they would record everything. There was something audacious about what we were doing—it was as if we were taking on the gods! [*laughs*] From that very first sequence on the boat I just acted the whole thing out. After a few days of that we had a screenplay, which we then ran through. I took that early version of the screenplay, did some hasty revisions, and then called up Han Sanming and Zhao Tao and asked them to come down to Fengjie and we started shooting. It was literally that quick.

Since you were essentially shooting amid the ruins of a city being dismantled, what kinds of technical challenges did that present to you in terms of equipment, lighting, power sources, et cetera?

Since we were in Fengjie to shoot a documentary film, we only had one digital camera, a Sony DSR-PD150, which is a rather small model. That was it! Now that we were going to shoot a feature-length narrative film, we had no choice but to just use that same camera since we didn't have time to get funding or have other equipment shipped in. If we had been shooting on celluloid or in high definition, we would have required special lighting, an external power source, and the whole thing would have gotten quite complicated. But given the circumstances, we had to let all of that go and just get what we could get on camera and worry about other details later. The good thing was that the DV technology provided us with a lot of freedom. We could shoot around the ruins with very low lighting and in other places like the workers' dormitory and get really close to the subjects we were shooting, so our pared-down equipment actually gave us a lot of flexibility. I really feel that given the specifics of this story and the shooting situation, this is the kind of film that could only have been shot in digital.

At one point while I was shooting the documentary *Dong*, I suddenly noticed that one of the electrical wires had a short circuit and a light was flashing. I really regretted not getting a shot of that, and when we were shooting *Still Life* I asked my cinematographer, "In this scene, can we make the light bulb flash like there is a short circuit in the wire?" He replied by saying: "I'm not sure if we are able to do that." So he handed the task off to our art designer to find a way to create that effect. [*laughs*] My art designer came back to me and explained: "We don't have any of the safety measures in place to do that. I'm afraid that if we try someone might get electrocuted!" Finally, my cinematographer just said: "C'mon, we're shooting in digital! Let's just fix it postproduction!" [*laughs*] In the end, we were able to create the exact same effect using digital effects in post, and it was quite affordable. That's the benefit of shooting in digital!" [*laughs*]

As we were shooting *Still Life* I really felt that Fengjie was a surreal place. As I mentioned earlier, my first impression when I got there was that this place had been invaded by an alien race—and they did not have good intentions! I would often have these kinds of thoughts as we were shooting. For instance, there is a building in the film called Commemorative Tower of the Immigrants—I always felt like that whole building was ready to launch off into the sky. It just didn't belong there. So later in the film I decided to let it fly off—those effects also cost almost nothing to produce! [*laughs*]

The film is filled with all kinds of embellishments from the world of my imagination, such as the tightrope walker and the flying saucer. As shooting continued I gradually started to feel like I not only wanted to capture the surrealistic aspects of the Three Gorges region, I also wanted to capture those surrealistic reflections coming out of my imagination about that place. My rationale for placing these surreal elements into a film that was otherwise rooted in realism was because the dramatic pace of China's development during that time often felt as if it was somehow not real—it all felt surreal. Actually, what I most wanted to capture at the time was this surreal feeling that people living in that environment must have been experiencing. A big part of *Still Life* is about allowing myself to be free enough to follow my instincts, and just because we were telling a story about the real world in contemporary China doesn't mean we can't employ surrealistic methods. As long as you are free, you can employ whatever techniques you like. And even when you do utilize these methods, lurking behind them there is still a clear realist intention.

Earlier we talked about your collaborative relationship with Wang Hongwei in your first three films. But for the past twenty years your most consistent collaborator has been your wife Zhao Tao. You first worked together on *Platform*, and starting with *The World*, she seemed to take on a more central role in your films. How did you first cast her, and how has your collaborative relationship changed over time?

This is quite the story. [*laughs*] We started worked together on *Platform*. At the time, the screenplay for *Platform* called for a girl who had experience with a performance troupe, knew how to dance, could speak Fenyang dialect, and was around twenty years old. We started to search for actors in Fenyang but couldn't find anyone suitable. We then expanded the search by opening it up to anyone who could speak Shanxi dialect, but we still came up empty. Later we broadened the search again with a call that stated any actors who could speak Shanxi, Shaanxi, Henan, or Mongolian would be considered. [*laughs*] But even after that we still couldn't find anyone!

3.6 Zhao Tao in *Still Life*

Just as I was getting to the point of despair, a friend told me that there was a university in Shanxi that had just established a dance department, so I went there to check out the students. I had been focused on the students, but suddenly Zhao Tao appeared—she was actually their instructor and was just starting class. She was criticizing one of the girls in class and told her: "If you want to dance you need to imagine yourself to be mute—whatever feelings or emotions you have must be conveyed through your body language in dance. You have to dance with emotion." That was the moment I noticed Zhao Tao. She had just graduated and was actually fairly close in age to the students. I patiently waited for her to finish class and told her that I wanted to collaborate with her on a movie. Starting from that first film together, Zhao Tao gradually began to display a truly singular understanding of what was required for her roles.

Because *Platform* is set in the past, the costume designer had to artificially age all of the clothes so they would look authentic. But the first time Zhao Tao went out to the costume truck to try out her outfit for the film, she immediately told me: "Director, this isn't right!" I asked her: "What isn't right?" She replied: "This isn't what I would call 'making the clothes look old,' it's called 'making the clothes look dirty!' All of the clothes from that era are old, but they should look clean, especially for a girl who is a dancer with a performance troupe. There is no way she would ever wear clothing that dirty! Can't you get the costume designer to make sure the clothes all look clean and proper?" What she said made a lot of sense. At the time, we were quite inexperienced and took a lot of shortcuts—in our eyes, making clothes dirty was the only thing we thought of when we tried to make them look aged. And once they were dirty, we didn't understand how to properly clean them in a manner that would be period accurate. But from a woman's perspective, Zhao Tao immediately knew that there was a big difference between aged clothes and dirty clothes—she knew there was no way her character would wear dirty clothes. Even if a dancer in a performance troupe in the 1970s had only two different outfits, she would still be sure to wash them every day. In the ensuing years over the course of our collaboration, Zhao Tao would often provide this kind of advice that really represented a woman's unique perspective.

Another example is when we were filming *Still Life* and she kept telling the makeup artist to "add more sweat" because we were shooting in an extremely humid environment and she felt that she needed more perspiration on her face to capture that sense of humidity. She has always paid a lot of attention to the physicality of her roles and is one of the few actors I have worked with who has this sensitivity about the physicality of performance. She is able to capture things like the environment and weather through her performance—this is very important for her. She needed the way her body appeared on-screen to convincingly reveal the reality of the environment. These are some of the elements that make Zhao Tao such a unique performer.

There is a scene in *The World* in which Zhao Tao goes down to the basement after getting in a fight with her boyfriend. My cinematographer and I followed her down into the basement, but then we were suddenly dumbfounded. That's because it was a night scene, and you couldn't tell the setting was a basement, it just looked like some room at night. At first I wondered, should we add an establishing shot to make it clear she walked down to the basement? But I knew if I included that shot it wouldn't represent the type of cinematic language that I wanted to employ—my films never intentionally go out of their way to emphasize a particular space. My cinematographer Yu Lik-Wai was discussing what to do with Zhao Tao when she suddenly said: "What if I take out my cell phone to make a call but can't get reception? That way the audience will know I'm in a closed-off space like a basement." I hadn't even thought of such a way to approach this, and so that's how she ended up playing the scene.

The other lead actor in *Still Life* is Han Sanming. He first appeared in your film *Platform*, and you have worked with him repeatedly over the years, including the short film *The Hedonists* in 2010. He has a very different image than most "leading man" film stars like Andy Lau or Chen Daoming. What is it that led you to establish such a close working relationship with Han Sanming?

I actually really like Andy Lau and Chen Daoming [*laughs*], but neither of them very much resembles a coal miner. [*laughs*] There are some roles that even they aren't qualified to portray.

Han Sanming is actually my cousin, and he was a coal miner for many years, so when he plays a character like a coal miner, it is quite convincing. He first appeared in *Platform*, and I later cast him in *The World* and *Still Life*. In all my films he plays characters who rarely speak because in real life he is indeed a man of few words. Although he rarely opens his mouth, he is able to express all kinds of life experience through his body language. As far as I am concerned, he has a true camera face because he is someone with stories to tell. He is also someone with a very rich emotional reservoir to draw from, which allows him to get into character extremely quickly and convey a real

CHAPTER THREE

3.7 **Han Sanming in** *Still Life*

sincerity through his performances. Now he has become a professional actor and has worked in a lot of other films, including comedies! [*laughs*] Another special quality about him is that he is an avid reader. He loves reading screenplays and spends more time reading the screenplay than anyone else in our entire crew—whenever he has a free moment, he is always reading the screenplay.

Speaking of Han Sanming, there have been a lot of questions about the symbolic role he plays in your films. One viewer asked whether or not he represents a kind of "Chinese hero" or "sage figure" in your work. Another viewer felt that he was symbolic of the migrant workers who have been left behind and forgotten amid the wave of social change brought on by the Reform Era.

For me, Han Sanming represents a large category of people. He's not simply a symbol of the migrant worker or honest, hardworking people. I always look at him as someone who stands for those countless people in China who are powerless. When I talk about power, what I am referring to is the power people have to tell their own stories.

DOCUMENTING DESTRUCTION

So many of your films are portraits of those marginalized individuals at the very bottom of the social ladder. What methods do you use to understand their experience and capture the details and nuances of their lives?

This is a difficult question to answer. People often say to me: "Your films are filled with so many details about people's lives. You must have particularly strong powers of observation." Others ask: "Do you carry a notebook around with you to jot down all of these details?" But to be perfectly honest, I never carry a notebook around with me, and I don't believe I have any particularly keen powers of observation. But there is one element that is of particular importance when you are writing a story, and that thing is emotion. Once you are moved by something, your imagination becomes extraordinarily rich, and all kinds of details start to come to you. Every one of us has the power of observation, every one of us has an extraordinary capacity to remember details, but often when we can't remember those details, it is simply because there is nothing about them that moved us—there is no emotional connection. I find that when I am writing a screenplay or am on set shooting, all it takes is that emotional connection to turn on in order for all those details to emerge on paper or in my mind. But as for how to imagine those details, that is indeed a hard question to answer. All I can say is that it is related to your emotional connection with the subject.

From my very early days making films, I have developed the habit of recording various faces I encounter in my life that I think I may be able to use in my later films. These people come from all walks of life. *Ash Is Purest White* has more characters than any film I have ever shot. There are a lot of movie stars, but there are also a lot of people I cast in the film that are simply people I encountered in my everyday life and felt like they had what it takes to act. Often this is simply because they have a look that I find particularly interesting; there is just something that I find enticing about their physical presence. [*laughs*] So I often invite these kinds of people to act in my films, and they are usually amazing. I may not pay particular attention to those everyday details of life, but I do keep my own little collection of character portraits that I draw from. I never know which future film of mine they might appear in, but there is often something about them that tells me they could be a good actor. For instance, that young guy in *Still Life* who imitates Chow Yun-fat is one such example. I randomly ran into him and felt like he would be a really interesting character, so I later used him in *Still Life*.

3.8 *Still Life* Chinese film poster

How does your approach to filmmaking change when you are shooting documentaries as opposed to feature narrative films? Is it the same creative spirit, or are there certain fundamental shifts in your shooting strategies and approach?

There are always some changes in approach because these are indeed very different types of films. When I shoot documentary films, I feel as though I include more formalistic elements. If I think about why that is, I think it has to do with the fact that through the format of documentary film I can capture I lot of things from my imagination. But these things may have never happened—at least not in front of your camera. But at the same time, each and every frame you are shooting needs to be real. In situations like this, it is extremely important for a film director to find a unique cinematic language in order to express those things he knows through visual language. Stories are always fictionalized; fiction is an extremely efficient form that is quite close to reality. So, as a whole, humans have always gravitated toward using fiction as a vehicle for expressing their emotions.

Documentary film—especially during the process of shooting—often impacts one's perspective and attitude in fundamental ways. Documentary film is actually an interruption into daily life. Given these circumstances, I always feel that I should use a more experimental or subjective method when trying to reveal things that did not occur in front of the camera. Let me provide you with an example: My earliest documentary film was *In Public*, and it was shot in all kinds of public spaces; however, over the course of editing I discovered a thread that could tie things together, which was those sequences shot in spaces related to public transportation. Through images of people in motion and those people walking past one another in those public spaces I was able to tie things together. Another important trait of that film was that I edited out all the talking-heads interview footage; I didn't want to have any of that footage of the subjects talking about themselves. Instead, I tried to just capture the image of those people in those spaces together; no one in the film directly addresses the audience, but their being, their state of mind, and the reality of their world are etched on their faces. In other words, I screened out all the language in order to convey the real-life appearance of these subjects: their exhaustion, their excitement, and all the other emotions written on their faces are collected and expressed directly to the audience. Through this method I was able to get at some layer of reality and approach a notion of truth.

Your documentary films often have an innate connection to your narrative films. You just mentioned *In Public*, which has a particularly strong connection with *Unknown Pleasures*. A few years later you shot *Dong*, a documentary about artist Liu Xiaodong, alongside the feature film *Still Life*. In some sense, those two films can be looked at as a couplet, with many interconnecting elements, settings, and characters. Later in your career, the line between documentary and narrative films seemed to get even more hazy. One case in point is the film *24 City*, in which you intentionally play with the interrelation between narrative film and documentary. Could you talk about the connection between narrative and documentary film in your body of work?

This really comes from the fact that I feel there are inherent limitations when it comes to both mediums. When I'm shooting a documentary film, I often feel like it is not able to express the true reality of the subjects' lives as powerfully as a fiction film. Then when I'm shooting a fiction film, I often feel like I'm trying to imitate what I see in documentary films in terms of the overall mood and the natural state of the characters. That's because I always feel like fiction films don't feel natural enough; they never feel like what we see in everyday life. In short, I always feel like there are certain limitations to each medium and each form. So I decided that I wanted to try to break through that dichotomy and combine the two.

When I first started working on *24 City*, the initial idea did not have any components from narrative cinema. It started as a fairly traditional documentary film project: I had interviewed quite a few retired factory workers to hear their stories. But then I ran into a situation after interviewing twenty or thirty Shanghainese workers who had been transferred to Chengdu to work in factories there. The Shanghainese originally didn't want to leave Shanghai, and when they arrived in Chengdu, they ended up forming their own little community—they would all hang out together, eating together, singing together, and they spoke to one another in Shanghainese dialect. I was very much interested in this group, but after shooting twenty or thirty of them, I discovered there wasn't a single one of them who had all the elements to become the main subject of a documentary film. Yet at the same time, the group was really fascinating, and all of them had their own interesting stories. Instead of focusing on one of them, I started to wonder if I could extract some of the more interesting details from several of their lives and create a composite character. I knew that if I could do that, I would be able to create a really interesting character. That is when I finally realized the importance of fiction. What a real-life individual faces in his or her actual life is the everyday, but film is a concentrated art form, and the medium requires you to provide multiple levels of information concentrated in one or two characters. Not everyone's lives are rich enough to provide that, so that is where the process of fictionalization comes in: so I absorbed stories from all of those workers and created a new fictional character. That character can, in turn, represent the entire group. It was also at that moment that I decided I needed to cast some professional actors for those roles. That's because I wanted my audience to be able to clearly differentiate the real-life subjects and the fictionalized characters. So I invited several highly recognizable actors like Joan Chen, Lü Liping, Chen Jianbin, and Zhao Tao so that viewers would immediately know who the actors were. There was a need to differentiate them from the other real-life workers who appear in the film.

You worked for many years with the Japanese production company Office Kitano. How did you establish a working relationship with Takeshi Kitano, and how do they support your work?[2]

I have been working with Office Kitano for years, right up until *Ash Is Purest White*. When *Xiao Wu* was first screened at the Berlin International Film Festival, Takeshi Kitano had just established his production company and was looking to invest in young film directors from Asia. After he saw *Xiao Wu*, he wanted to work with me. I also needed money, so that's where our collaboration began! [*laughs*]

But the producer overseeing day-to-day affairs was Shozo Ichiyama, who had previously produced Hou Hsiao-hsien's *Goodbye South, Goodbye* and *Flowers of Shanghai*.[3] Shozo Ichiyama had previously served as an international producer for Shochiku Company Limited. When Shozu Ichiyama first approached me in Berlin, I didn't know much about him, but I certainly knew who Takeshi Kitano was. I also really admired the films of Hou Hsiao-hsien, which made me feel like this was a company I could trust. So that is how it started.

The first film we worked on together was *Platform*. I remember the contract we signed with Office Kitano stipulated that the running time be no more than two hours, but in the end the screenplay had over one hundred fifty scenes! After Shozu Ichiyama read the script he said: "According to this screenplay, we are looking at film with a run time of at least three hours. There is no way this is going to be a two-hour film." When I heard that I asked him: "So, do I need to write a new draft and cut some scenes out?" He responded by saying something that I will never forget: "If you as the director feel the film needs to be this length to tell your story, then you should tell it that way." After that we ended up working together all the way up until now.

I also remember sending Office Kitano the screenplay for *The World*, and after they read it, they wrote to me explaining, "Our office has already carried out deliberations concerning your project and we feel that this film will result in a profit loss. [*laughs*] However, Takeshi Kitano's new film *Zatoichi* (2003) has been able to perform well at the box office, so we have decided to go ahead and greenlight your film." [*laughs*] I worked with Office Kitano all the way up through *Mountains May Depart*, but when I was getting ready to shoot *Ash Is Purest White*, Mr. Kitano resigned from the company, so Office Kitano did not end up producing *Ash*.

3.9 Jia Zhangke (*left*) and Zhao Tao (*right*) on location filming *Still Life*

Speaking frankly, today in China there are a lot of potential investors that I could get money from; however, I have always felt it is more important to find a producer who shares the same vision and ideals. It is never good to irresponsibly spend other people's money; instead, you need to establish a collaborative relationship built on mutual trust.

You mentioned Hou Hsiao-hsien's collaborative relationship with Office Kitano, but besides working with the same production company, you have a lot of other things in common with Hou. You have both worked with composer Lim Qiong on several of your films, and you even featured Hou in your film *I Wish I Knew*. Could you talk about Hou Hsiao-hsien's impact on your work?

I enrolled in the Beijing Film Academy in 1993, and in the early 1990s Hou had actually donated prints of his films to the academy. So while I was in school I had the opportunity to see most of his films, from *The Sandwich*

Man (*Erzi de da wanou*, 1983) all the way up through *City of Sadness* (*Beiqing chengshi*, 1989). Because I was someone who had just begun to study film, Hou Hsiao-hsien had a very important impact on me. At the time, it wasn't just Hou's films that had an influence on me because alongside them I was also reading Shen Congwen's fiction and Eileen Chang's novels, which had all begun to come back into fashion. Reading those novels alongside Hou's films pointed me in a certain direction, which was a much more personal artistic vision. Younger people might not quite understand what I mean by this, but that is because back when my generation was coming of age, our environment was dominated by revolutionary art and literature. According to the logic of revolutionary art and literature, there is no place for individual artists or authors; they don't exist. Everything was instead about the collective. But a work of art's most important quality is the stamp of the original author, its signature. So for me the films of Hou Hsiao-hsien and the fiction of Shen Congwen and Eileen Chang—artists working in different mediums, different genres, and from different eras, but they all came together, and during the Chinese cultural scene of the early 1990s they represented the return of the artist with an individual style and vision. For me they marked the resurgence of individuality in artistic expression.

Chinese cinema has been dominated by commercial works for the past fifteen years, yet you have remained a champion for independent cinema. You have worked hard to try to help establish art house cinemas, produce up-and-coming directors, and even founded the Pingyao Crouching Tiger Hidden Dragon International Film Festival. What is the situation for independent cinema in China today? And where do you see independent film going in the next few years?

Let me start by talking about the establishment of art house movie chains in China, which we have been deeply engaged in. It started in 2016 when my company (Xstream Pictures) partnered up with several others to establish the Consortium for Arthouse Cinema Exhibition. The main sponsor is the Chinese Film Archive, and other partners include my production company, Edko, and Wanda. As of 2018, we have set up five hundred screens in China devoted to the exhibition of art house cinema. Besides Chinese independent films, we also exhibit international art house films, like the recent *Manchester by the Sea* (2016).

One of the initiatives my own company has been spearheading is the Pingyao Film Palace, which is located in Shanxi Province. Pingyao is an old city with a 2,700-year history; it is also a popular tourist destination. Right now in Pingyao we have a five-screen facility, which is the Pingyao Film Palace, where films are screened every day. In my hometown of Fenyang I also opened a small, three-screen art house cinema, which is currently undergoing renovations. There are also plans to open another small theater in Xi'an next year. If that plan is successful, it will be our first art house cinema in a major city. But the current state of Chinese cinema is hard to predict. [*laughs*] The Chinese film industry has indeed expanded in leaps and bounds: there is a large output of films being produced each year, and we are now the second-largest film market in the world. But while the industry is developing very quickly, there are signs of instability. For instance, these past two months (October and November 2018) there has been a sharp decline at the box office, so we need to wait and see.

Naturally, the large quantity of films being produced is worthy of special attention; however, I personally believe there is room for improvement in terms of the quality. A lot of people are deeply dissatisfied with the state of the Chinese film industry today, and I think that has a lot to do with the fact that there are too many films being produced. When you have a situation like that, the market ends up getting inundated with a lot of poor-quality films. There are actually quite a few really solid films being produced each year, including art films, independent films, and various genre films. The problem is that when you throw them in with eight hundred other films, it is hard for them to carve out a space for themselves, and everyone feels there is a huge gap in terms of the quality of Chinese films.

Good films come in all shapes and sizes, but bad films all have a common feature. [*laughs*] That common feature is that they do not fulfill the basic requirements of what a film should be. This is something that we need to be wary of. One of the unhealthy perspectives floating around right now is that we should all be making commercial films and turning a profit at the box office is the bottom line. Within this context, things like film language and the intrinsic requirements of what a film should be are often overlooked. Though this may be the case, at least there are audiences going to the theaters to see films, and the box office numbers are good. However, the quality of films is very similar to the quality of one's health—you take one look at some of these films, and you can tell that the quality is lacking. Having your film succeed in the market shouldn't be an excuse to cut corners when it comes to the basic quality of film production. On the other hand, no matter what genre you are working in there are certain basic requirements that all films should meet. This has resulted in a strange perspective in China where a lot of people think that commercial films are not art, nor do they require any artistic dimension. But I would argue that commercial film is also an art! How can you say that commercial cinema isn't art? That is such a strange perspective for me to hear. As for where the future of Chinese cinema should go, I feel that no matter what type of genre you are working in, you can never forget that film is an art form and should follow the rules and requirements of art.

In 2017 we held the inaugural Pingyao International Film Festival, and I intentionally included a retrospective of the films of Jean-Pierre Melville.[4] One of the reasons I wanted to highlight his work is because a lot of his films are typical detective thriller genre pictures, but when you watch them you can see his profound interest in the human condition and his incredible creativity. His films are all very deep and probing, yet at the same time they are very enjoyable. Through that retrospective, I wanted to emphasize the fact that there is a huge space for creativity when it comes to genre films. Commercial cinema needs creativity and innovation.

At the 2018 Pingyao International Film Festival the Korean director Lee Chang-dong held a master class. During his master class, he told the audience that he has been pondering the relationship between independent film, auteur cinema, and the audience for these past few years. He feels like there needs to be a realignment of these relationships in order to win back audiences. This is pretty close to my own view regarding independent cinema in China. There is no inherent distance between independent cinema and audiences; nor is there any inherent distance between original and experimental cinema and audiences. Instead, film needs to continually revise its relationship with its audience. A film without an audience is an incomplete film. In short, my thoughts regarding the future of Chinese cinema are that we need to restore what we are currently lacking. If our commercial films are lacking art, then we need to pay more attention to the artistic side of our films; and if our independent films are lacking audiences, then we need to find a way to win them back.

CHAPTER THREE

24 CITY (2008)
A TOUCH OF SIN (2013)

4 Film as Social Justice

4.1 Jia Zhangke on location

Of course you should shoot the kind of film you want to make, but sometimes there is a price to pay for that, especially in China. But, to speak frankly, if you are someone with a strong will, you can bear it, you can make the sacrifice. Because I guarantee you that there are a lot of people out there making much bigger sacrifices for all kinds of things every day. After all, compared to those people that are unemployed, those people facing various forms of injustice, those people who have been falsely arrested, what is this thing called film anyway? We can make that sacrifice; we can pay that price. Once you have seen people who are facing true suffering in this world and those facing injustice, the struggles of making a film aren't even worth mentioning.

Your films *The World*, *Still Life*, *24 City*, and *A Touch of Sin* are all imbued with a strong moral spirit that resists various forms of social injustice. Back in the age of Mao Zedong so much of artistic production was dictated along the ideological lines of Mao's "Yan'an Talks on Art and Literature."

CHAPTER FOUR

From that point on, all film and literature had a clear political responsibility to fulfill in society. That essentially reduced most artistic production under Mao to propaganda. Times have changed a lot since then, but in your view, does film still have a social responsibility?

Let me respond to this question by starting with *A Touch of Sin*. Although *Touch of Sin* has yet to be commercially released in China, a lot of Chinese audiences have already seen the film through bootleg versions. [*laughs*] After everyone had seen the bootleg editions, there was a period of time during which everyone was criticizing the film. Some people said the film was advocating violence during a time when violence in society was already so rampant, while others thought the film was praising criminals. At the time, I responded to these criticisms by explaining that we as humans have developed different structures in society to deal with these issues. Take, for example, the courts of law, where they resolve legal issues, face social problems, and make judgments in accordance with the law; and then there are the churches, which use religion to face these issues. Now why did we later invent cinema? The cinema is a place where we go to understand all the different complexities of human nature; it is there where we can face the dark side of human nature and the dark side of society. The cinema is one such place. If we are unwilling to deal with these darker subjects such as violence in the cinema, then we truly have no hope of ever truly understanding them.

Ever since 1949, Chinese cultural discourse has been dominated by revolutionary art and literature. Revolutionary art and literature have an important requirement, and that is for the arts to function in the service of politics. By the 1980s, when the Reform Era hit, a lot of artists abandoned this politicized view of art. For the younger generation, the independent cinema of the 1990s marked a return to the individual. At that point the individual's relationship with society took on a more normal tone. But amid this transition, some other voices also began to emerge; those voices advocated individualism and avoided political or social engagement in art. Instead, they advocated using art to explore topics like love and romance from an individualistic perspective. But I didn't agree with that line of thought. In China today, each and every individual is impacted by the social, economic, and political changes taking place around us. Each individual's life is constantly being interrupted by various external elements. When we observe people or portray them in films, we should make sure everything we do is built on the foundation of the individual's relationship with society; we need to observe humans within their social environment. What I mean is that we should avoid going from one extreme to the other.

You mentioned the fact that *A Touch of Sin* was never commercially distributed in China. In reality, the story behind this film's release was extremely complex and convoluted, filled with all kinds of setbacks. It was initially approved for release; however, just before its release date, authorities blocked it, which inspired all kinds of heated debate and discussion online. Could you talk a bit about the backstory behind *A Touch of Sin*'s release? As the film's director, how did you deal with this kind of major setback?

A Touch of Sin was completed during the spring of 2013, and we immediately submitted it to be reviewed by the censors. After a period of waiting it was approved, and we received the so-called Dragon Seal from the China Film Administration. As the film's director, I was not present when the censors were reviewing the film, so I have no idea what issues came up during their deliberations; however, I did hear that there were some heated debates about some aspects of the film. In the end, however, several of the censors who supported the film felt that because the four stories told were all based on real-life incidents that had already been widely reported by the media in China, they didn't see any reason why the film could not be shown. So the committee ultimately decided to approve the film, and it met their criteria for exhibition.

The Cannes Film Festival took place just after *A Touch of Sin* had passed the board of censors, so I brought the film to Cannes. It was just after that that we settled on an October release date for the China market. I remember returning from the New York Film Festival to Beijing in October just before the release date when someone from the censorship department contacted me and asked if I could temporarily delay the film's release. When I asked why, he replied by saying that violent events like the ones depicted in the film were still playing out in China, and they were concerned that the film might inspire more people to take to violence. Naturally, I tried to explain my position on the matter, but after a long period of time trying to sway them, I ultimately failed. Later they explained to me that the film had indeed been officially approved for release; it was not banned, they just wanted to temporarily delay the release because now wasn't an appropriate time. [*laughs*] But, as things went on, there was really nothing I could do, and then, as we were still in negotiations about a new release date, bootleg editions of the film began to appear online. [*laughs*] I was really frustrated because these are the types of films that already struggle at the box office when they are theatrically released, but now that bootleg editions were already available online, I knew that it would be even more difficult. It was really a bad situation, but my hands were tied. For me the most important thing was to just move forward and focus on my next film. Even up until now, I still take some time to check in with the censors every three or four months to see if the film can finally be released.

But an even greater crisis for me was the economic side of this. Although the film was not permitted to be screened in China, it was allowed exhibition outside of China, so I was able to earn some money through international

4.2 *24 City* film poster

distribution. But that still wasn't enough because this was a film with a very large budget. We shot in four locations—Shaanxi, Hubei, Chongqing, and Guangdong—and the shoot was quite long; it was actually like shooting four separate films. What we made overseas didn't even get close to allowing us to recoup our losses. That film was primarily financed by a friend of mine. [*laughs*] So after that debacle, I spent an entire year shooting commercials—I shot around two each month for a year—in order to pay my friend back for his investment. [*laughs*] I was so desperate that I not only shot commercials but even acted in a few! [*laughs*] I shot commercials for liquor, suits, cameras, all kinds of things! The whole thing was really quite absurd! [*laughs*]

I'd like to bring your previous film 24 City **back into the conversation. Looking back at your early films—**Xiao Wu, Platform, Unknown Pleasures, The World**—all of them were based on original stories. But starting with** 24 City **and** A Touch of Sin **you began to adapt the real-life stories of subjects. The film** 24 City **was adapted from the interviews with retired factory workers that you conducted, and** A Touch of Sin **was based on four sensational news stories.[1] Could you talk about the process of boiling down such a massive amount of material, much of which is fairly loose in terms of narrative, and structuring it into a complete screenplay?**

When I made *24 City*, the Chinese economy was transitioning from a planned economy to a market economy. During the age of the planned economy in China, workers and factories had a unique relationship. In factories like the one I shot the film at, it wasn't just workers but their entire families who relied on the factory for virtually every aspect of their lives. A big-scale factory like the one in the film had thirty thousand workers and fifty thousand dependents. A factory of this size had its own nursery school, elementary school, middle school, hospital. They even had their own funeral parlor—from birth to death, all of life's major events could be taken care of without even leaving the factory gates! For decades, workers relied on the factory to take care of every aspect of their lives. They were indeed the "masters" of the factory. Once the transition to a market economy started to kick in, they found themselves reduced to nothing more than a labor force. Large numbers of workers were laid off due to their age, and suddenly society was faced with a rising tide of unemployment, and workers were forced to fend for themselves. There were a lot of people still in their thirties who suddenly found themselves without a job. This marked a major shift for society. I am a firm supporter of a market economy system, and yet I am also extremely

CHAPTER FOUR

concerned with the fate of workers when they are faced with this violent, revolutionary, overnight change that suddenly takes away their livelihood and throws them into a very painful state. So I wanted to use this film to express the sudden shift in the fates of so many Chinese workers.

I actually wrote an entirely fictionalized screenplay about workers called *Leaving the Factory*, but I never felt it was good enough, so I never shot it. But I had always had the idea to make a movie about a factory, and later I settled on shooting a documentary film. The first question I faced was which factory to shoot. I started to visit a whole lot of factories. My hometown region of Shanxi is an agricultural area, so there aren't many factories there, so I started to look at factories in Wuhan, Chongqing, and Shanghai. I kept searching for a factory that would draw me in. Each factory has its own personality. Then one day I came across an article in the newspaper about a factory in Chengdu that produced engines for the Chinese air force that was slated for demolition after the land was purchased by a real estate developer. I immediately decided that was the factory I wanted to shoot. The reason I was so certain had to do with the fact that in the age of the market economy the real reason so many of these factories were shutting down and factory workers were being forced to leave had a lot to do with the real estate market. Back during the socialist period, a lot of the factories were set up in the downtown section of major cities, but later, as these cities expanded, the location of these factories didn't make much sense anymore. Once these factories are torn down, these sites that once produced so many memories end up being completely destroyed.

After I started to dig a little deeper, I discovered how massive the scale of this factory truly was. Including dependents, more than fifty thousand people were tied to it. It was a true product of the Cold War era—due to the fear of a coming armed conflict with America, a lot of factories were moved from coastal regions into the mountains. This was a so-called Third Line Construction Project (*sanxian gongcheng*), so the factory was closely tied to Cold War history.[2] At the same time, it was also tied to the capitalist real estate economy of today, so it was a site imbued with different stories. That is what led me to select this factory.

In some sense, searching for this factory was very similar to the process of casting an actor for one of my films. The first thing I had to do was settle on a character—which was the factory itself. Once I had settled on this factory, I needed to approach it from the outside, through interviews with the former workers. That's because I initially couldn't get access to get inside the actual factory. It was a top secret military facility, and now it was on the verge

4.3 Zhao Tao in *24 City*

of being demolished. During that transition period there were two entities overseeing the factory: the managers of the original factory and the real estate development company that purchased the land. With two groups in charge they kept a very tight lid on the site. But they had no control over me if I talked to workers in their dormitories. So I went over there and had them tell me their stories. Whenever I heard something interesting, I would turn the camera on. It was over the course of this rather blind process that I gradually discovered which individuals I wanted to focus on, so I gradually began to get closer to them. After going through this process, I was finally able to settle on just a small handful of people to profile.

But besides these real-life workers, you also designed a few composite characters for professional actors to portray.

That's because over the course of conducting those interviews I discovered the need for fiction as a tool to tell the whole story. The reality of the stories as I understood them wasn't coming through any single individual. Instead, each person had certain elements in their stories, and by combining them I thought I could reveal a kind of truth, a reality that was missing when you just looked at their individual stories. Later, when I was writing the screenplay, I decided to add some fictional elements, so I added Joan Chen's Shanghainese character and a younger worker's story, portrayed by Zhao Tao. Lü Liping's character had an interesting story—virtually everyone I spoke to had told me about her, but she was no longer with us, and I didn't want to rely on secondhand accounts to retell such an important story, so I designed it so Lü Liping could directly convey the story to the audience.

And how did you get access to the factory site?

Well, eventually I did end up getting access to the actual factory site, which was an interesting story. I went directly to the office of that real estate company that had purchased the factory and asked to talk to the boss. The receptionist asked me: "And why would our boss want to see you?" [*laughs*] I said: "Because I'm a very important film director!" [*laughs*] And the boss immediately came out to see me. [*laughs*] I told him that I wanted to shoot a film inside the factory and explained why. Once I had finished my pitch, he responded: "It looks like we are on the same page! I'm actually a poet! I also feel we should shoot a movie to have a record of the people who worked here!" [*laughs*] That's how things got started. Later he asked me: "What do you say about me investing in your film?" [*laughs*] I responded: "Of course that would be fantastic!" [*laughs*] He ended up being the second-biggest investor in the film! He was, after all, a poet! [*laughs*] So we had a good collaboration. But of all my films, this one had the most difficult time getting through the censorship process. It was a most painful experience. In the end, this poet investor wrote an official affidavit on behalf of the factory stating that the factory workers wholeheartedly supported this film, everything depicted in the film was true and accurate, and that the factory approved of the film's release. It was only then that the film was finally approved for official distribution in China.

Speaking of poets, *24 City* also featured one of contemporary China's best poets, Zhai Yongming, as a screenwriter.[3] What role did she play during the screenwriting process?

Zhai Yongming's main contribution was in creating those four composite characters. I sent her all of the raw interview material and told her what my rough ideas were for each of the characters. Since she is from Chengdu, she is quite familiar with the local dialect and was able to capture all of the various details specific to that location and express them in the screenplay.

4.4 Zhao Tao (*left*) and Jia Zhangke (*right*) on location shooting *24 City*

And what about the screenwriting process for *A Touch of Sin*, where you adapted those real-life news stories? How did you approach four completely unrelated stories and tie them together so that they worked as a coherent film narrative? How did you first discover these four stories, and what was the process of piecing them together? It also seems that *A Touch of Sin* is deeply connected to the rise of Weibo and social media in China? Can you also talk about how social media played a role in this film?

Whenever new forms of media come on the scene, I tend to be a year or two behind everyone when it comes to adopting them. I only started using Weibo in 2011 or 2012. At that time, I really had the sense that in the age of Weibo and new media everyone was now a reporter. It was during that time that I started to notice a very large number of reporters coming out from all over China about various random acts of violence. Everyone was reporting these things, with both words and actual images. Amid all of those various reports I was reading, there were seven or eight that really grabbed me and made want to make them into a movie. It was at that point that I started to play with different structures for this film. Why was I so intent on making this film? Part of that reason has to do with the fact that I started to realize that all of the people in these stories reminded me of characters from *The Water Margin*. Actually, *The Water Margin* is in many ways like a Weibo micro-novel. There are 108 characters, and each one is like a short descriptive account you might read on Weibo—it is like 108 short real-life profiles. So I decided to try my hand at making one film that featured multiple characters and stories.

In the end, there were two main social considerations that led me to finally write the screenplay: first off was seeing the inequalities in terms of distribution of wealth, and second was the inability of people to express themselves. What I mean by that latter issue is that there are a whole lot of people who lack the ability to express their frustrations and predicaments with others; even if they are able to, no one listens, no one cares. For them there is no avenue other than to use violence as a means of expressing their predicament in life.

The second segment in the film is a portrait of someone's psychological state. In many cases violence functions as a means for someone to express themselves. For a person like Wang Baoqiang's character in the story, there are very few possibilities in life. But somehow violent acts give him a sense of accomplishment, even a sense of romanticism. This is an alternative reason for committing acts of violence. Zhao Tao's story explores the relationship between violence and dignity; in many cases, sudden acts of violence are the result of someone's dignity being suddenly stripped away. The final segment of the film is the famous Foxconn story, where everyday life in the factory is extremely mechanical and the workers are desperate with no hope for a better tomorrow.[4] In the end, they choose to inflict violence on themselves.

I also hope that, at the very least, Chinese audiences recognize that these stories are all real, which is one of the reasons I decided to shoot each segment at the actual site where the incidents occurred in real life. So we didn't take a story from Shanxi and transpose it to Henan or a Guangzhou story and set it in Hainan; wherever the actual events took place is exactly where we shot the film. The other result of this is that the film is like a cinematic tour of China; it takes the viewer from the northernmost areas of Shaanxi to the southernmost areas in Guangzhou, so it really provides a panoramic perspective on the nation.

Once I sat down to write the actual screenplay, I discovered that the real-life events only provided a very hazy outline, but there were no details, no real content, no logic behind the stories. There were only the incidents themselves, but they weren't connected to anything larger. Let's take Zhao Tao's segment as an example: in the original news report the only information we had was that a woman who worked in a foot massage parlor stabbed a customer to death after he tried to rape her. That's it. But my screenplay requires rich details, so when I wrote the screenplay I needed to rely on my imagination: Why did this thing happen? The news report might be only two hundred words, but from that I have to create an entire character. What is her family life like? Where did this knife come from? Part of the plot concerning the extramarital affair provides a narrative logic to explain where the knife came from, so my imagination often begins with these small details. Later, as I follow that thread, I am able to create a set of relationships for that character. So there is an entire process I follow to develop the story.

By the time of *A Touch of Sin* you had already worked with Zhao Tao on several films, but somehow I feel like *A Touch of Sin* reveals another side of her as a performer; it is truly a breakthrough role for her.

It was over the course of shooting *A Touch of Sin* that I realized just what a remarkable actor Zhao Tao truly is. The way she handled the murder scene at the end was really amazing: that scene was actually shot in three different locations over the course of several months. It was shot alternately in Changyi in Hebei Province, Shennongjia, and Datong in Shanxi. The reason we had spread it out like this was because we found a sauna parlor in Changyi, but it was only suitable for exterior location shots. The shot where Zhao Tao is walking on the street with mountains surrounding her was shot in Shennongjia. And the interior shots from the massage parlor where she is accosted were shot on a soundstage in Datong that we set up. These three locations are separated by several thousand miles, with two or three months between the shoots. Since we couldn't shoot interiors at any of those sauna parlors, we had no choice but to shoot the interiors in a soundstage in Datong. But when we shot each sequence, the rhythm of Zhao Tao's movements, the cadence of her walk, and the power she exerted were all completely in sync and matched up perfectly with the earlier shoots. What is especially hard to match is the precise level of energy she captured in her earlier performance, but it was perfect. This is a real challenge for any actor because you need to perfectly remember little details like exactly how tightly you held the knife during the earlier shots and recapture that same spirit, but she nailed it.

Another special quality about *A Touch of Sin* is the character design and costume designs, which really stand out alongside your earlier films. When

4.5 Zhao Tao in *A Touch of Sin*

Wang Baoqiang's and Jiang Wu's characters first appear, they really jump off the screen.

The first time I saw images of the actual people the four stories were based on, I immediately thought of *The Water Margin*, which made me want to add some elements from Chinese opera. Somehow seeing those images helped me have a renewed understanding of what my job is really about. Generation after generation, China has seen the rise and fall of all kinds of art forms: traditional storytelling, the novel, opera, and today we have cinema. When it comes down to it, all of us as artists are concerned with the fate of man, and violence is a theme that has always been with us.

Actually, all four of those main characters in *A Touch of Sin* have reference points: Dahai's design is based on the Peking opera character Lu Zhishen.[5] Wang Baoqiang's character is inspired by Wu Song.[6] Zhao Tao's character was designed in accordance with the female martial arts heroines in the

4.6 Wang Baoqiang in *A Touch of Sin*

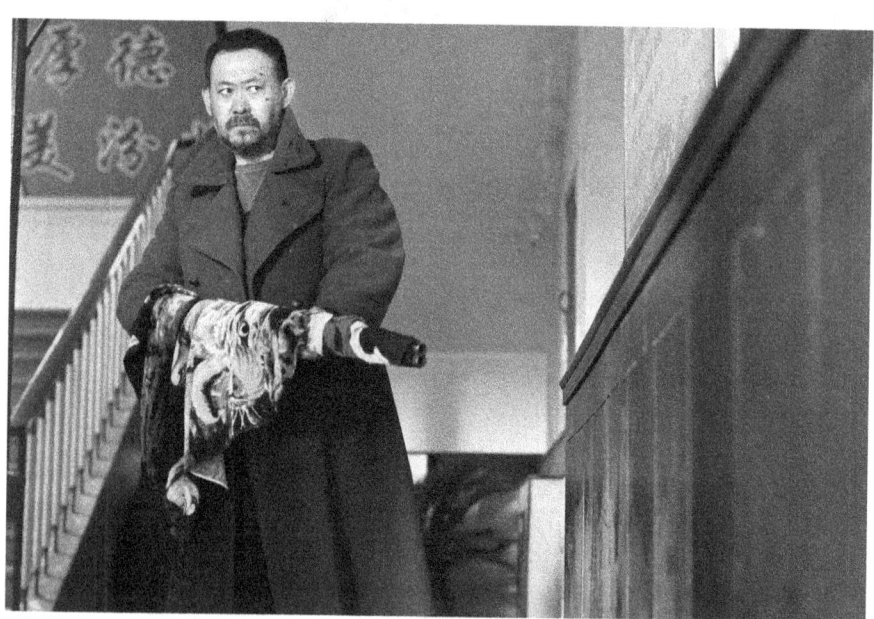

4.7 Jiang Wu in *A Touch of Sin*

4.8 Jia Zhangke on location shooting *A Touch of Sin*

films of King Hu. The final factory worker character was inspired by those bare-chested male leads in Chang Cheh's films.[7] I've been making films for twenty years but have never used other films as reference models for my own work. I haven't even done that with the films I produce. Occasionally a young director will show me someone else's film and say, "This is what I am going for." I always tell them: "That's *not* what you should be going for! Don't ever use someone else's film to tell your own story!" So when I make films, I'm always adamant about not watching reference films, I just start shooting. I also go out of my way not to watch other films from the same genre. But *A Touch of Sin* is the one and only time I made an exception to this rule and watched a film for reference. That was Chen Huai'ai's Peking opera drama *Forest of the Wild Boar* (*Yezhu lin*, 1962).[8] The red pants that Zhao Tao wears are directly taken from that film; in Peking opera those red pants mean that the character is a prisoner. Of course, your average audience doesn't necessarily need to know that the reference here is Lin Chong, the prisoner, but those familiar with Chinese opera will immediately get the reference.[9]

FILM AS SOCIAL JUSTICE

I really love the film *Forest of the Wild Boar*, and genre films play an important role in my work because they are able to build a bridge between traditional narratives and this contemporary moment. At the same time, it takes a story that should be set during the Song dynasty and allows us to see that the same story is still playing out today. It feels like a story that should have come out of *Touch of Zen* (*Xia nü*, 1971) or King Hu's world, but it's happening right now. So by utilizing genre as method, I can tell a story that gets to the heart of human experience removed from time; these are age-old stories that are still playing out before our eyes. So I hope to create a link between these classic literary works or past human experiences to show that we all share the same challenges. So both *A Touch of Sin* and *Ash Is Purest White* share a connection with genre cinema.

You mentioned the importance of Peking opera in *A Touch of Sin*, but elements of Peking opera have actually appeared in several of your films. *Still Life* features a group of Peking opera actors in full makeup and costume appearing amid the ruins of Fengjie, and your short films *The Hedonists* and *Revive* both feature elements from Peking opera. Could you say a bit more about the place of Peking opera in your films?

I'll start with the music I used during the opening sequence of *Still Life*. Once the initial shooting was finished, I sat down with Lim Qiong to discuss the music. During our discussion I mentioned the possibility of using Sichuan opera music because the film is set in the area of Sichuan not far from Chongqing. I told Lim Qiong that the story was in some ways very similar to the traditional story *Lin Chong Feeling by Night* because the two protagonists (Zhao Tao and Han Sanming) had both come from afar to resolve some long-standing issues. In the story of Lin Chong, he had to resolve a problem that impacted his own survival; for my characters they had to resolve an emotional problem with their respective relationships. Lim Qiong tracked down some elderly Sichuan opera actors to sing the melody to *Lin Chong Fleeing by Night* and mixed it with electronic music, which was then used in the film.

Actually, there are a lot of predicaments that we find ourselves facing in our contemporary lives that often make me think about premodern China. In some ways, we really haven't made that much progress and haven't changed that much. [*laughs*] So some of the techniques I use in *A Touch of Sin* and *Still Life*, like the visual references to landscape painting and scroll painting, are all an attempt to express this classical sensibility. These days we may have high-speed railways and iPhones, but in many ways our fate is not that far from what it was for people a long time ago.

In your previous films, you used a lot of long shots and carefully orchestrated setups. Compared with those films, *A Touch of Sin* uses a more conventional approach: you have a lot of close-ups, and the pace of the editing is much quicker. How do you account for this change in film style? Was it purely aesthetic sensibilities driving this, or were there practical challenges you were trying to surmount?

There were no specific issues I needed to surmount; I just wanted to make a film that felt like a *wuxia* martial arts film. All the characters in *A Touch of Sin* are like characters out of a wuxia story. I wanted the audience to also have this association with martial arts cinema. When you see *Ash Is Purest White*, you can see traces of the gangster film genre. [*laughs*] Basically both of these films were not only well suited for a genre film approach, but in some way they *needed* these elements from genre cinema.

Earlier today, one of my film students from China pulled me aside to express a predicament he is facing: he loves films that are critical and introspective like *A Touch of Sin*; at the same time, he is quite concerned that if he goes on to make that type of film in China, they will just end up getting banned. What would your advice be for a student like this? To move forward and make films he is passionate about, even if they are risky, or to make more conservative and "safe" films?

Never take the conservative path. Whatever kind of film you feel like making at this stage in your life is the kind of film you should make. If you have a project you want to film now and you are twenty-five or thirty years old, do it now. If you wait another ten years to shoot it, it will be a different film.

Let me tell you a little story about when I made *Platform*. So *Xiao Wu* somehow ended up being labeled a so-called underground film, and I really wanted to make sure my second film could be commercially released in China. I decided to collaborate with Beijing Film Studio, since it is a state-owned studio. Beijing Film Studio loved my screenplay and assigned Tian Zhuangzhuang as a producer to work with me on the film.[10] After working together for a while to develop the project, we officially applied to the studio for permission to begin shooting. After some deliberations, the censorship department sent us a memo that stated: "This film is a large-scale historical film that spans more than a decade from the 1970s to the 1980s. We looked into the background of the director and discovered that he is only twenty-nine years old and we feel that, in order to achieve the proper results, an older and more experienced director should direct this film." Once we received that memo, I just said: "Thanks anyway, I'll just go ahead and shoot the film myself." That's because *Platform* is a film that only the twenty-nine-year-old me could have made; the forty-nine-year-old me would have shot a different film. [*audience applause*]

Of course you should shoot the kind of film you want to make, but sometimes there is a price to pay for that, especially in China. But, to speak frankly,

4.9 *A Touch of Sin* US film poster

if you are someone with a strong will, you can bear it, you can make the sacrifice. Because I guarantee you that there are a lot of people out there making much bigger sacrifices for all kinds of things every day. After all, compared to those people that are unemployed, those people facing various forms of injustice, those people who have been falsely arrested, what is this thing called film anyway? We can make that sacrifice; we can pay that price. Once you have seen people who are facing true suffering in this world and those facing injustice, the struggles of making a film aren't even worth mentioning.

There were several audience questions about how you design women characters in your films. For the past decade or so, most of your films have been structured around female characters, most notably those portrayed by Zhao Tao. Could you talk about how you think about female characters in your work? Are there common themes that tie these different women together?

All of these characters have a commonality, which is they are all northern girls. And that is because Zhao Tao is a northern girl, and she is good at portraying women from northern China; she knows how they speak, and having grown up in that area, she has a rich imagination to fill out the details of what life is like in those northern cities. Up until this point in my career, all the female lead characters I have written have been from the north, and Zhao Tao provides a lot of help in fleshing them out.

I actually don't make a big distinction between male and female characters; it really all depends on what draws you in during the writing process. Often not even I know what kind of character someone will turn into when I first begin the writing process. For instance, in the beginning of *Ash Is Purest White*, Zhao Tao's character is quite weak, but after she starts hanging out with Bin, he begins to change, as does she. Eventually, Bin grows weaker and she grows stronger. By the end of the film, she has become even more powerful than he was, even in his prime.

What I really want to emphasize is the importance of leaving some elements of your characterizations or the story somewhat hazy; you need to leave room to flesh things out as you complete the film. I have always felt this to be an essential tool. Even up until today, when I write my screenplays I never write an outline, and that's because I need to leave some elements to the unknown. That way, as I am writing the screenplay there is a sense of discovery, and I have room to let my characters grow over the course of the writing process. If I start out with a complete outline, it is like I am using a mold and simply punching my character out according to a predetermined

4.10 Jia Zhangke

pattern. But I never liked that method; instead, I much prefer the process of gradually fleshing out my characters out of a blank canvas. I like to take things step by step, scene by scene, letting whatever mood I happen to be in each day gradually guide the characters in a way that allows them to naturally reveal themselves. The character that eventually emerges is like a tree that has been nurtured to adulthood. When you plant a tree, you have no idea what it will look like once it has grown. It has its own life force. So I am always resistant when it comes to getting too deep under my characters' skin at the very beginning of the writing process; if you set your story in stone too early, you end up losing part of the magic.

MOUNTAINS MAY DEPART (2015)
ASH IS PUREST WHITE (2018)

5 Return to Jianghu

5.1 Jia Zhangke

Those of us in the film industry are also part of a kind of jianghu.

The original Chinese title of *Ash Is Purest White* is actually *Jianghu ernü*, which roughly translates into "sons and daughters from the land of rivers and lakes." The central notion here is *jianghu*, which is a concept you also played with in your earlier films. The world of *Xiao Wu*, in which the pickpocket protagonist operates outside mainstream society according to his own moral code, is very much an example of this kind of jianghu. What is your definition of "jianghu"? Besides the core concept, in both *A Touch of Sin* and *Ash Is Purest White*, we can also see the impact of *wuxia* fiction and film. In what ways has the wuxia genre impacted your work?

I started writing the screenplay for *Ash Is Purest White* in 2015, right after completing *Mountains May Depart*. Part of the reason for writing that film was because I had always wanted to make a film about this underworld of jianghu. I have also always had a strong affinity for those Chinese jianghu films, especially those Hong Kong gangster films from the 1980s. So the primary reason I wanted to make a film like this is because I'm a fan of the genre; besides that, when I was growing up—especially in the late 1970s—even though I was young, I was basically living in a kind of jianghu! [*laughs*] At the time there were a lot of young people who were unemployed and just spent their time hanging around the streets, so somehow seven- or eight-year-old kids like me would end up hanging out with these guys in their twenties! You might wonder, what did we do together? Well, the big kids would fight with each other, and us little ones would help them gather up bricks and stones as weapons. Through that experience, I started to gradually gain some understanding about human nature and human behavior. By the 1980s, when video rooms started to become popular, I discovered that those gang bosses were all starting to imitate those Hong Kong gangster films. All of a sudden, they started to foster a kind of jianghu culture: they would worship Lord Guan, watch out for each other as brothers, and started to talk about things like "fraternity" and "loyalty."[1] This jianghu culture carried on all the way up until the past few years; that's when I started to realize there was a fundamental change in the way jianghu culture functions today.

When I was shooting *Mountains May Depart*, I heard a story about gangs today: as it turns out, if two young guys get into an argument on the street, there is a number they can call to summon some thugs to help them out. These thugs work for a company and charge a fee for their services! [*laughs*] There was one case where both parties called for backup, but they called the same company! [*laughs*] In the past people fought for what they thought was right—perhaps to stick up for a friend who got cheated—but today even the passion of youth is for sale!

At the core of the concept of jianghu is a very complete philosophical system. Loyalty, righteousness, courage, and fraternity are all central concepts around which Chinese people have constructed their relationships for thousands of years. But today those concepts and relationships are gradually breaking down and beginning to disappear. When I was writing the screenplay to *Ash Is Purest White*, the disappearance of those relationships led me to reflect on just what is this thing called jianghu. As far as I am concerned, jianghu represents a place in society filled with danger, such as the chaotic period of the Ming dynasty portrayed in King Hu's films or the social environment of 1980s Hong Kong during the economic boom as seen in the gangster films of John Woo. So I have always thought of the historical backdrop of these jianghu stories as being tied to the dangers lurking amid times of rapid social transformation.

Another dimension of jianghu is the type of complex interpersonal relationships that often appear in those stories. There are more characters that appear on-screen in *Ash Is Purest White* than in any of my other films. That's because jianghu is inherently made up of a mishmash of all kinds of different people from a variety of backgrounds and their complex relationships. When you talk about *chuang jianghu*, or someone who "makes their way amid this jianghu," you are essentially talking about someone who has experiences interacting with a broad cross section of people who have faced different kinds of challenges in life. There is also the saying *sihai weijia*, or "everywhere between the four seas is my home," which describes those jianghu characters who move from place to place throughout their lives without ever settling down. In this sense, most people are all living in a kind of jianghu. They all start out in small country towns and make their way to the cities; from there they go from one city to another, and eventually from China they travel abroad: people are always searching for new possibilities in life. So in the end, we are all part of this jianghu world. Gradually, I began to understand just how attached Chinese culture was to this concept of jianghu. So, in some way, it is through the perspective of jianghu and those people who live amid that world that we are able to get a clearer understanding of how our age has been constructed and what is happening in society.

For me the main takeaway is just how much this concept of jianghu has changed. Classical notions of what is important in a relationship have begun to fall apart and disappear as things move forward.

How did the title of the film evolve?

I realized that whenever the term *jianghu* appeared in various movies, it is usually not translated into English. Usually they just used the Romanized pinyin form of jianghu because there is really no good equivalent in English. When you think of jianghu, you think of someone who has no home and travels the world, someone who lives his life on the road in search of new possibilities. This is a rather general definition of the term. Of course, in Chinese, jianghu can also have a more specialized meaning, referring to those jianghu figures at the bottom of society.

The first time I heard the term *jianghu ernü*, "the sons and daughters of jianghu," which is the Chinese title, was when I was shooting *I Wish I Knew* and interviewed the veteran actress Wei Wei.[2] Wei Wei was the star of Fei Mu's masterpiece from the 1940s, *Spring in a Small Town* (*Xiaocheng zhi chun*, 1948). During our conversation, Wei Wei told me that during Fei Mu's later years he was actually planning to shoot a film called *Sons and Daughters of Jianghu*, which was later completed by Zhu Shilin. As soon as I heard that title, I was immediately drawn in because in traditional Chinese relationships the concept of jianghu was built on emotion, loyalty, and fraternity. So you can see that concept expressed throughout Chinese film and literature, because so much is based on the logic and philosophy of jianghu. People's relationships with one another are built on *qing*, or "emotion." This meant that all of these characters had rich emotional bonds and deep friendships. So I have always liked this term "sons and daughters of jianghu," which like my previous film *Mountains May Depart* also has a certain classical sensibility to it. And both of them explore how these classical layers of meaning that had been with us for so long are now gone.

I remember when we were just getting ready to shoot the film, one of my colleagues complained: "This title sounds like something out of an antique

5.2 *Ash Is Purest White* film poster

store! It's sounds like it's from another era; everyone will think it is a classical costume drama! Can't we change the name?" But I insisted on keeping the name; jianghu is, after all, a very classical-sounding name.

There are some directors who start every film with a clean slate and tell an independent stand-alone story through that film. But there are a handful of film directors who seem more interested in intricately constructed cinematic worlds where each film seems interconnected to the previous one. I am thinking of François Truffaut and Tsai Ming-liang as two clear examples of directors who like to intentionally play with the intertextual lines between their films. You also fall into that category: your films often reveal subtle moments of connection and dialogue with one another. When looking at your entire body of work, different characters, actors, themes, cities, and even camera angles reappear. One of the more obvious examples of this type of an intertextual connection can be seen between *Unknown Pleasures* and *Ash Is Purest White*. As a director, how do you navigate these intertextual relationships?

In 2016, when I first started shooting *Ash Is Purest White*, I discussed some of the problems regarding the historical setting with my art director. We were finding it really difficult to capture all the nuances of those earlier sections of the film because it was a full decade earlier, and a lot of the finer details were already a bit hazy. But as it happens, that was right around the time that digital cameras became available, and I had shot a lot of raw material on my digital camera. So we watched all the material that I shot, and then we also watched *Unknown Pleasures*. As soon as I saw *Unknown Pleasures*, I immediately realized that the male and female protagonists in *Ash Is Purest White* could very well be Qiao Qiao and her boyfriend from *Unknown Pleasures*. After all, I never really developed that particular story line when we were shooting *Unknown Pleasures*. Her boyfriend was certainly a gangster type, and their story was left open. At the time of its release there were even reporters who asked me: "Hey, whatever happened between Qiao Qiao and her boyfriend?" I just replied: "This is what in traditional Chinese brush painting you would call *liubai*, or 'leaving empty space for the imagination'!" It was only many years later when I completed the screenplay for *Ash Is Purest White* that I realized that there perhaps really was something lurking there in that empty space. I decided to change the characters' names in *Ash* to match the two lead characters in *Unknown Pleasures*; I also had them wear the same costumes from the previous film. Of course, those original costumes were long gone, but I had my costume designer make a new set of outfits to match the ones we originally used in *Unknown Pleasures*.

I also realized that we never really cleared up the narrative line in *Still Life* where Shen Hong seeks her husband, so I felt that *Ash* could also explore that thread as well.

You have shot three films that take place against a broad historical timeline. Besides *Platform* as an epic of the everyday depicting 1980s China, *Mountains May Depart* and *Ash Is Purest White* both feature bold timelines that span more than a decade. Perhaps most daring is *Mountains May Depart*, which, besides the past and present, also delves into the future. What kinds of challenges did you face when you needed to imagine a "future tense"?

Back in the 1990s—it was actually in 1995—I completed my very first feature-length screenplay for *Platform*. The film spanned an entire decade, and at the time I had a very powerful sense the 1980s were over. For me it really felt like the end of an era. That was my era—it was the era of my youth—so I felt like I needed to make a film with a broad historical perspective to really deal with that experience. After that point, virtually all of my subsequent films took place over a fairly compact timeline, at least up until *Mountains May Depart*.

By the time I wrote *Mountains May Depart*, I was forty-three years old, so I think it is related to where I was in life during that time. Before that time, I really didn't have a good grasp of time, I was simply too young and didn't have the perspective to understand many facets of life, nor did I want to understand them. But by the time I hit my forties, I had seen a lot of things in my life, and the hand of fate had touched me in different ways. There are certain things we are destined to experience in life; if there was a screenplay for one's life, it would certainly have to include, as the Buddhists say, "birth, aging, illness, and death." I finally got to a point in my own life where I wanted to make a film about these natural challenges we experience over the course of our lives. Young love, marriage, having children, facing the reality of one's parents aging, and all kinds of other things that arise—these are all things that none of us can escape from. At the time, I also started to think about what the future would be like. So for the very first time, *Mountains May Depart* also includes a section of the narrative set in the future.

When it came time to write *Ash Is Purest White*, I suddenly realized that I was still very much interested in placing my characters within a much broader period of time to observe them and reflect on their lives. This is all related to my personal experience. When I was a kid, there was this "Big Brother," a local gangster, who I really admired. Back then he was quite handsome and charming. When I was little my dream was to one day grow up to be just like him! He was really an impressive character. Fast-forward many years later, I was visiting home one summer from college and saw a dejected-looking middle-aged man eating noodles at some street-side stall. I took a closer look and realized it was that Big Brother that I had admired in my youth! I thought to myself, My God! What a toll the years have taken on this guy! How did he end up like this! When I decided to make a film about jianghu, it wasn't just to express the passion and excitement of these

5.3 Sylvia Chang (*left*) and Dong Zijian (*right*) in *Mountains May Depart*

young guys on the streets; it was also to explore what time eventually does to someone who was once so full of vitality and life. So I ended up writing yet another film that spans many years. It is a film that represents where I am in life now, because I have begun to realize that you gain a different understanding of people when you place them in a broader historical framework.

Speaking of the broad time span, when you made *Platform* there were two specific historical markers that served as a framing device for the film—the beginning of Deng Xiaoping's Reform Era in 1978 and the 1989 student protests in Tiananmen Square. *Ash Is Purest White* spans 2001 until 2018. Was there a similar set of historical markers you wanted to explore here?

I have made three films with this broad historical perspective. My second feature film, *Platform*, was set between 1978 and 1990; it was basically a film about the entire decade of the 1980s. When I wrote it I was at the Beijing Film Academy and really felt that that era was gone. That decade represented the happiest childhood memories for a kid like me—my formative years from the ages of ten to twenty all played out during that decade—and it all corresponded to the first decade of the Reform Era.

Ash Is Purest White opens in 2001; that's because that is the year that China's social development went into high gear and entered a new phase. That was the year that China's bid to host the 2008 Olympics was approved, China entered the World Trade Organization, the popularity and accessibility of mobile phones started to really take off, and the influence of the internet

5.4 *Mountains May Depart* film poster

began to spread. As we stood at the crossroads of a new century, we could feel that society was transforming at blinding speed, but none of us knew where things were going. But we were all filled with curiosity and excitement for what was to come. I really wanted to make a film that looked back to reflect on this moment from a decade or two in the future. I wanted to be like a time traveler, returning to that bygone era, and also return to those places where I had previously shot my films—Shanxi, the Three Gorges, and Chongqing—to create a new story in order to reflect on how times have changed and how we have changed.

More than a decade ago I made a film called *Still Life*, which reveals a lot of readily evident social change taking place in China. You can see the Three Gorges Dam construction project, you can see a three-thousand-year-old city being torn down until all that is left are ruins waiting to be submerged, you can see the results of more than a million people being forcibly relocated—all of that is laid out before your eyes, so that type of change is easy to capture on film. But over the course of this past decade or so what has moved me even more is seeing the gradual transformation that is taking place within people and seeing how human emotions have changed. Chinese society has always had a traditional way of navigating interpersonal relationships, which places great emphasis on loyalty and emotional connections. But over time these traditional bonds that tie us together are being gradually revised and dismantled; more and more what ties people together today is profit and money. This kind of internal transformation often leaves me feeling very uneasy. In some way, it is just like that old song by Sally Yeh that you hear in the film.[3] It is like a beautiful voice that is about to disappear, so you need a character like Qiao Qiao to bring that precious beauty from the past back into our present so we remember it.

What was the greatest challenge when it came to portraying such a broad historical period?

The greatest challenge was with the actors because they had to cover seventeen years over the course of the film. The lead actors needed to convincingly portray a character from their twenties all the way up to their forties, which is very difficult for any actor to do. I never liked the method of using two actors to play a single role—that is, getting a twenty-something actor to the play the young version of a character and then a forty-something actor who somewhat resembles him to play the old version. Whenever I see that tactic being used, it always feels fake because you can immediately tell it is a different actor. I much prefer to see the mark left by time imprinted on the characters' faces; that is always much more powerful. So casting for a film like this was a great challenge; I really wasn't sure if there were any actors willing to take on these roles. Finally, I just had to carefully ask Zhao Tao to see if she might be interested. [*laughs*]

Once Zhao Tao read the screenplay, she didn't feel there was any problem in terms of conveying the age of the character; for her the biggest challenge was that she simply couldn't get a good handle on this type of a female character's personality. [*laughs*] I told her that I didn't know any women like her either! [*laughs*] Although I know plenty of men like her! [*laughs*] In order to get a better understanding of the character, Zhao Tao started to do some research; she collected all kinds of documents and read all kinds of court records and police interrogation reports; she also read all kinds of reportage literature about women and oral history accounts. After reading all of these materials, she finally came to me one day and asked if Qiao Qiao reminded me at all of She Ai'zhen.[4] She Ai'zhen was a well-known female gangster active in Republican Shanghai during the 1930s. [*laughs*] She started out working in a casino and later married a notorious gangster named Wu Sibao. She eventually became famous for her gunfights and was labeled as a "traitor to China" during the War of Resistance against Japan. After the war she spent some time in prison before moving to Japan, where she married the writer Hu Lancheng.[5] Zhao Tao asked me: "Isn't she similar?" I could see some similarities, but I was also very surprised by how far she had taken her research. I even said: "Wow, you even dug back as far as the Republican era!" [*laughs*] Not long after that she told me she was done with her research. She said: "I think I finally understand this concept of jianghu, but when it comes down to it and you strip everything else away, I am portraying a woman." That sentence really was a revelation for me.

And once shooting began, were there other practical challenges she had to face? When it came to the actual portrayal? Or capturing the character's personality?

The greatest challenge Zhao Tao faced was actually her "skin problem." The real question was how to create the proper skin effect for the younger iteration of Zhao Tao's character from the 1990s. As a man, I am fairly ignorant about makeup and not particularly sensitive when it comes to how the skin looks, so I had no idea how to handle this. [*laughs*] So we hired a really good makeup artist to help with this issue. I thought what he did was fine, but Zhao Tao insisted that it wasn't good enough. Eventually, I had to turn this task over to Zhao Tao, who hired a French makeup artist and worked closely with the lighting designer and cinematographer to ensure they got the effect they wanted. I jokingly referred to them as the "skin team." So I let her tackle this problem, and I think she did an incredible job because when I looked at the final footage, I really did believe it was the younger version of Zhao Tao that I was seeing on-screen.

Besides that, Zhao Tao also adapted her voice for the role. I remember her one day suddenly asking me: "Do you hear any difference in my voice?" It was indeed different than usual. She told me that this was the voice she had found for the younger version of her character. Her voice was clear and sharp but at the same time felt very natural. She took a long time to find the right voice for that younger version of the character. Then toward the latter portion of the film, she dropped her voice down a bit and the texture became a bit coarser. Her breathing also got a bit heavier during the second half of the film.

But what impressed me most about her performance was when she picked up that bottle of mineral water. In the original screenplay her character never carried a water bottle. But that bottle of mineral water is a carryover from *Still Life*. She asked me: "Since we are going back to the Three Gorges to shoot, how about if I carry a water bottle around with me, just like I did in *Still Life*?" I just casually replied: "Go ahead! It's hot there anyway!" [*laughs*] The first time I really discovered her using that water bottle was when she arrived in Fengjie and went to that office building to look for Bin. When the automatic door was about to close, she suddenly whipped out that bottle and jammed it between the closing doors. As soon as that take was over, my cinematographer Eric Gautier and I looked at each other in awe; we were both blown away by that. [*laughs*] Later when Zhao Tao tracked down that woman in black who had stolen her money, the same bottle suddenly transformed into a kind of weapon. Later still when she met the UFO guy on the train and he wanted to hold her hand, she handed him the bottle to grab hold of, which was yet another brilliant performance. Performance is really the most essential component that holds up this film.

Liao Fan also delivers an incredible performance in *Ash*. Can you talk about your collaboration?

In terms of the aging issues, male actors are a bit easier to deal with because the skin changes are not so noticeable. When I discussed how to manage the physical change of his character for the portions set in 2018, he just said: "Don't worry about it, I'll just grow a beard." So before shooting he grew his beard out, which had a lot of gray in it. I always look at Liao Fan as a handsome leading-man type and have never seen him in any film with a gray beard. It really moved me that he was willing to have the courage to openly display that side of himself.

As for all of the other details in *Ash Is Purest White* that we needed to convey the passage of time, such as costume design or various props like cell phones, we just used a method of historical research and verification. For instance, what model of Nokia cell phone was in popular use in 2001? We

5.5 Zhao Tao (*left*) and Liao Fan (*right*) in *Ash Is Purest White*

had to look all those details up. Actually, these details are all quite easy to get right as long as you are willing to put in the time. A lot of the locations we used were actually sets we had to build because the original locations are all gone. For instance, the teahouse where the gangsters all hang out and play mah-jongg was a set we built.

Besides the lead actors Zhao Tao and Liao Fan, another fascinating aspect of the cast in *Ash Is Purest White* is the cameo appearance of some of China's leading film directors, including Feng Xiaogang, Xu Zheng, Diao Yinan, and Zhang Yibai.[6] You also did something similar in *The World*, which featured cameos from Zhang Yibai and Wang Xiaoshuai. What made you decide to cast so many film directors in these films, and what do they bring to the table?

As I was writing the screenplay, I discovered that there were an especially large number of characters in this film. These other characters are all people the leads encounter during their adventures in jianghu, but I needed to cast all of these roles. Often when I am writing I am already thinking about who I should cast for a particular role. Sometimes that person is an actor I have collaborated with, and sometimes it is just a friend, including some of my director friends. Since these characters only appear on-screen for a very short time and have only a few scenes each, I needed actors with a special quality that would really jump out. I thought all of these directors were quite special! [*laughs*]

For the role of Lin Jiadong, I immediately thought of Diao Yinan, since he is tall, wears glasses, and looks cultured and refined. When Zhang Yibai finished his scenes, he told me: "Now I understand why the film is called *Sons and Daughters of Jianghu* in Chinese. Liao Fan and Zhao Tao and the sons and daughters and the rest of us are collectively portraying jianghu! [*laughs*] You need a lot of people to make up an entire jianghu!"

On another level, I feel that these directors are better able to understand my screenplay because those of us in the film industry are also part of a kind of jianghu. We travel the world with our sworn brothers to make movies, and over the course of our journeys we run into all sorts of crazy situations. So when they read my screenplay, they have an approach that is almost instinctual; after all, we are all part of this same jianghu world!

Normally when we think of the traditional world of jianghu, it is usually positioned as a man's world—from the 108 heroes in *The Water Margin* (also translated as *All Men Are Brothers*) to the masculine martial arts cinema of Chang Cheh. When you made *Ash*, what made you decide to have a female character be our guide into this jianghu world?

That was an unconscious decision because when I first started writing the screenplay I looked at both the male and the female protagonist as equal representations of the jianghu world. But by the time I got to the end of the screenplay, I realized that their transformation was somehow interconnected—as Bin grew increasingly weaker, Qiao Qiao grew stronger. This was perhaps the first time I was writing a screenplay where I found myself unconsciously reflecting on masculinity. In the world of jianghu those elders are always talking to their subordinates about lofty concepts like "loyalty" and "brotherhood," but not even they themselves necessarily believe in any of that. But the younger generation—Qiao Qiao and her generation—absorbed all of those ideas and made them a fundamental part of their belief system. Amid the social order of jianghu, men tend to lose their way more easily

5.6 **Zhao Tao in** *Ash Is Purest White*

because, over time, their values have become overtaken with money and power, which override everything else. Those other values such as friendship and fraternity and loyalty all end up getting tossed by the wayside. But I discovered that women somehow are able to remain more loyal to their own emotional core and remain true to themselves. These are some of the reflections I came to over the course of writing *Ash Is Purest White*.

Earlier you talked about how you used makeup to help accentuate Qiao Qiao's aging process in *Ash*, but another important tool to reveal the passage of time was through the cinematography. Not only did you replace your regular cinematographer Yu Lik-Wai with the French cinematographer Eric Gautier, but you also used a multitude of cameras and formats to shoot the film. Could you talk about this film's unique visual style?

First off, I didn't replace Yu Lik-Wai! Yu Lik-Wai is also a film director, but he has been so tied up shooting my films these past few years that he hasn't had time to shoot his own films! [*laughs*] As I was getting reading to shoot *Ash*, Yu Lik-Wai was also planning his own film, so we decided to bring in someone else to shoot my film. We both simultaneously suggested Eric Gautier;

I have been a big fan of his work. Since Yu Lik-Wai can speak French, he wrote a letter to Eric to see if he might be interested in collaborating with Jia Zhangke. Eric happened to have an open slot in his schedule, and that is how it came together.

Starting in 2001, I developed the habit of shooting documentary footage whenever I had free time. Often I would have no idea what I was going to shoot, but I had just purchased my first digital camera, so I would shoot all kinds of things. When we were working on *Ash*, my art designer and I wanted to refresh our memories about what things looked like back in the early 2000s, so we started to look at all of that old documentary footage I had shot. Once we started digging through those old files, we realized that I had used quite a few different cameras over the course of the previous decade or so: I had shot on Mini DV, HD DV, Betacam, 16mm, 35mm, Red, Red One, Fed 5B, and an Alexa. That was a period when the technology for digital cameras was constantly changing and upgrading. That's when I suddenly got the idea of using different formats to portray different historical periods. Eric loved the idea, so we started to run some tests. He did all kinds of experiments to see what would work, and then we discussed whether or not we wanted each format to stick out and emphasize these shifts. The question was whether or not to have each change in format be marked by a sudden evident shift in the film, or whether we wanted to handle these transitions more subtly and blend them in. I thought we should go for a subtler style with soft transitions between the various formats. I wanted the audience to gradually enter these different visual spaces and textures without even noticing it. In order to see these different subtle shifts, Eric did a lot of tests, including adjustments to the pixelation because the material ranged from low-resolution images all the way up to 6K. Each stage of the film uses a different format; we also used some of the old documentary footage that I had shot on DV. Take, for example, in the scene at the Three Gorges where Zhao Tao is watching a performance: there is a twelve-year lag between the time the footage of the performance onstage was shot and the reaction shots of Zhao Tao sitting in the audience were shot. But with DV we were able to edit these different shots together. So when you look at all the pieces of the cinematography put together, it is really quite impressive. [*laughs*]

The most important thing is that Eric really made sure to fully employ all of that old equipment. He didn't seem to mind that a lot of the old cameras were out-of-date DV cameras; he was really flexible. There were times when we had almost two hundred people in our crew, and we would drive out to a shooting location with nearly four hundred extras, and everyone was performing for a tiny handheld camera the size of a cell phone! [*laughs*] Some of the extras even thought we were a bunch of swindlers. After all, who shoots a movie with a tiny camera like that? [*laughs*]

A UFO first appeared in your 2006 film *Still Life*, but more than a decade later it returned in *Ash Is Purest White*. What is the symbolic meaning of the UFO?

As you mentioned, I also used a UFO in 2006's *Still Life*. That was my first visit to the Three Gorges, and I visited the two ancient towns of Wushan and Fengjie, which were in the final stage of being torn down. As soon as I arrived, I was struck by the surrealist atmosphere there. Since the entire town was basically demolished, walking amid those ruins left me with the impression that what I was seeing wasn't even real. It was as if aliens had come down from space to destroy Earth. I felt there was something magical and monstrous about the changes grappling China. Since the real world was already touched by this surrealist vibe, when I was trying to capture that sensation I had felt, I began to imagine things like UFOs appearing in my screenplay.

By the time I got to *Ash Is Purest White*, there was a scene in which Qiao Qiao was leaving the Three Gorges behind on her way to Xinjiang. Before shooting I had taken a trip out to Xinjiang with my producer for location scouting. I told the local producer that I wanted to find a place where I could see stars and the Milky Way. My producer responded: "You can see the Milky Way everywhere here!" So we drove about ten minutes outside the city, looked up, and there was a sky full of stars and the Milky Way! You can never see those stars in the city—I don't think I have ever seen stars in Beijing. Standing there gazing up at the stars, I thought of all the difficult relationships that Qiao Qiao had to navigate—her relationships with her boyfriend, her father, those hoodlum guys. All she faced was trouble and obstacles, and she was always forced to deal with other people; it was only at that moment standing under the Xinjiang sky that she was finally alone. That was her most solitary and vulnerable moment, and in that moment, I wanted to give her something—so I sent a UFO down to send her a greeting.

Your films often feature performance sequences. In *Ash Is Purest White* there are several, such as Qiao Qiao watching a street performance in Fengjie or attending a small concert. Those performances provide an emotional

outlet for the characters, and at other times they provide an opportunity for a lonely soul to be part of a collective. How do you look at these performance sequences?

My two most recent films both employed disco. [*laughs*] *Mountains May Depart* featured the song "Go West" [by the Pet Shop Boys] in a disco club scene, and *Ash Is Purest White* used "YMCA" by the Village People. The most important part of this is using disco dancing to tell the story of the characters' youth. During our youth, it was actually a very boring era, and besides dancing, playing pool, drinking, and playing mah-jongg there really wasn't anything else to do. When I was writing the screenplay, no matter how I approached it, there was really nothing else for these young people to do in the story! [*laughs*] Those were the only forms of entertainment at that time. Of course, many of my films have these performance scenes, which I really love. According to our traditional education, Chinese people should be reserved and shouldn't reveal their emotions; but those moments when a person is singing karaoke or dancing represent one of the rare moments in which they are able to express their true selves and get some kind of a release, even if only for a short time. That's why I always love shooting scenes of people singing and dancing, because it is only then that they are not hiding behind something.

Ash Is Purest White opens with a song by the Cantopop singer Sally Yeh. Starting with *Xiao Wu* and continuing on through *Touch of Sin*, you have actually used her music several times in your films. Her music can also be heard in the classic John Woo gangster film *The Killer* (*Diexue shuangxiong*, 1989), which immediately brings us back to that world. Could you talk about Sally Yeh's music in the opening sequence?

I made *Ash Is Purest White* because I have wanted to make a film about jianghu for a long, long time—I actually wanted to make a film about the contemporary version of what jianghu is today. But as I was getting close to the film, I decided I also wanted to experiment with genre film because the characters were all quite similar to the kind of characters you find in a typical gangster film, even if they are not exactly the textbook definition of "gangsters." They don't pass on their gang titles to different generations, practice strict rituals, or pass down a strict set of rules to each generation like they do in Hong Kong gangs. They are simply a bunch of guys from a certain street or district who started to get into trouble together! [*laughs*]

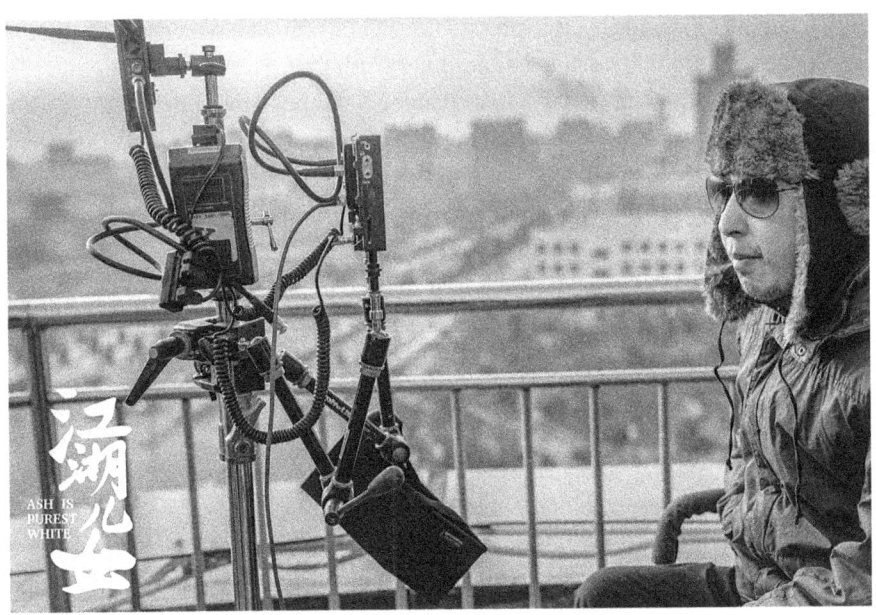

5.7 Jia Zhangke on location shooting *Ash Is Purest White*

Gradually they somehow became defined as part of a jianghu. I just wanted to capture that feeling.

From the perspective of the screenplay, I was hoping that this film would be able to play with certain elements from genre films, especially Hong Kong gangster films. So while I made sure to emphasize that jianghu atmosphere, I also didn't want the film to be typecast as a typical genre film. At the same time, I also wanted the film to be able to explore multiple subjects. I wanted to make a film about the world of jianghu and those gangsters who grew up in mainland China during that era. One of the important cultural factors that led them to foster this self-conception of themselves as gangsters was the video room culture of the 1980s. That is where they first saw those old John Woo gangster films, and then they took to the streets and tried to mimic the attitude and manner of speech of those gangsters they saw on-screen. This was a crucial turning point in how this jianghu culture evolved in the mainland. In the film Bin watches Taylor Wong's film *Tragic Hero* (*Yingxiong haohan*, 1987), so we show a clip of that film. But as for music, I always think of the theme song from John Woo's film *The Killer*, Sally Yeh's "A Lifetime of Intoxication" ("Qianzui yisheng"). I also saw that film in the 1980s, and that song has stayed in my heart ever since. The song has a certain jianghu vibe about it; it expresses the will of someone who dares to explore deep emotions. The song has an inner truth to it. This is what most attracts me about the emotional side of jianghu—the raw emotional truth of what that jianghu world represents. Pop music is always evolving, and these past few years there are quite a few good songs that have come out. The rhythms and melodies are great, but something has changed—people have changed and our emotions have changed. But Sally Yeh's songs carry with them a traditional emotional dimension. If *Ash Is Purest White* is a film about how traditional interpersonal relationships and emotional bonds are falling apart and disappearing—in the end, everyone ends up like Bin—then music too is changing, from something with deep and rich emotional content to something that is pleasing to the ear and relaxing but utterly devoid of meaning on the inside. In some sense, that original truth and genuine emotion are gone, and it is very difficult to ever get them back.

I also faced this situation in 2006 when I was shooting *Still Life*, when the changes there were reaching their tail end. Fast-forward to 2018 when I was shooting *Ash Is Purest White* and I again had that feeling that I was saying goodbye to something. The ways in which we used to interact with one another are gone, and even those lingering vestiges of truth that we find in music can only be found in those old classic songs from the past. Society is ever changing, and though I don't consider myself a nostalgic person, I feel like we don't have that many good things from the past that we have preserved for ourselves today. All of the good things seem to somehow be sealed in the past. Perhaps Qiao Qiao is one of the few people who is hanging on to something from the past for us.

We just talked about Sally Yeh's song "A Lifetime of Intoxication," which opened the film. It has a special warmth that immediately creates a certain mood for the audience. The mood created by the last shot, on the other hand, could not be more different. At the end of *Ash Is Purest White*, our perspective suddenly shifts from that of the detached observer to that of the state. Instead of the filmmaker's perspective, we see Qiao Qiao through the lens of the security camera that has been installed across the street from her teahouse. Once that is paired with Lim Qiong's unsettling music and a series of almost violent jump cuts, we are left with a very dark and uneasy feeling. Can you talk about those final moments in the film?

The final sequence you see in *Ash Is Purest White* is not the original ending I had in mind. According to the original screenplay, Bin left on the first day of the new year, and Qiao Qiao sat down at the table, poured herself a drink, and sat there alone drinking. That was it. But I somehow always felt like this ending was too nostalgic and sentimental. The script even had a line at the end: "'A Lifetime of Intoxication' rings out one last time." [*laughs*] But I just felt that that image of drinking alone while listening to "A Lifetime of Intoxication" just wasn't my style. I'm not so sentimental! So I kept thinking about a better way to end the film.

When it came time to actually shoot the film, we got to the scene where Bin suddenly left and Qiao Qiao ran outside to look for him; then I remembered that we had shot some footage of the police installing security cameras across the street from the teahouse and I wondered if it might work to get a shot from the perspective of the security camera. Once we shot Zhao Tao through the lens of the security camera, she was reduced to a blurry digital image; the image was extremely fuzzy. No exaggeration, at that moment I wanted to cry. I was so moved because I realized that this was the world we are living in today. It is said that by 2020 there will be two surveillance cameras in China for every person, recording our every move. But *this* is how we are being documented, through hazy and blurry pixelated images. You can't see any emotions, nor can you see our lived experience—it is all rendered invisible and ready to be deleted at a moment's notice. It was in that instant that I suddenly realized what my job is. Film is an essential art to record the details of the average person's everyday life. So that is why we need cinema, and not surveillance cameras! [*laughs*]

Music has an important place in your films, but generally speaking you seem to exercise a lot of restraint in terms of using film scores. Could you talk about the place of music in your films? What I am particularly interested in is, what are the factors that help you decide when to include music in a scene and when to leave it out? Do you have a guiding principle when it comes to utilizing music for film?

Film music is one of those subjects that is really hard to talk about! [*laughs*] Usually as I am editing a film, I come to certain portions where I just naturally feel the need to add music! [*laughs*] But it is very difficult to explain *why* I need music at that specific juncture! [*laughs*] Every film has a kind of subtle overtone that lingers, and when you make a good film it needs to have those overtones. The same thing goes for acting. Actors deliver their lines, but at the same time, there is another level of meaning that they can subtly convey. Directors also need to have those overtones in their work. When you get to those moments where you feel the audience needs that little extra something, a subtle overtone, perhaps those are the places where you need to add a little music.

You have been working with the Taiwanese composer Lim Qiong for more than a decade now. What is your collaborative relationship like?

Lim Qiong and I started to work together on *The World* in 2004. He mostly works on electronic music. To be fair, I actually hate electronic music—but I love Lim Qiong's electronic music! [*laughs*] If you use traditional instrumentation, whether it be piano, violin, cello, or Chinese instruments like the *erhu*, the emotions those instruments tend to convey are already familiar to us. But when you incorporate electronic music into the mix, you get new possibilities, and it is particularly suited to the atmosphere in contemporary China today, which is represented by an unprecedented mixture of the fantastic, the surreal, and the sexual. It is at once classical and new; and the new aspects feel as though they represent a stage of human development never before seen! Somehow electronica is able to perfectly capture and express that abstract feeling.

With *Mountains May Depart* and *Ash Is Purest White* we also begin to see more philosophical reflections about the passage of time sneaking into your work, and with that comes a commentary on aging, illness, and death. What were some of your personal takeaways after making these two reflective films?

I think those themes are all connected to things I have experienced in my own life these past few years. When I first started making films I was only twenty-seven years old, and life hadn't yet really opened up. Not only was I still single, but I don't think I even understood what marriage was about. Life was still very fresh and new to me, so mostly I focused on shooting films that recorded my reactions to what was happening in that present moment. By the time I reached my forties, it was as if I had done my homework and had a richer life experience to draw upon, which, in turn, made me want to use a larger historical canvas to convey more of life's complexities. One of my biggest takeaways from this stage in life are the myriad challenges one must face: the environment in which we live is transforming at breakneck speed, and there are a lot of judgment calls we need to make amid this changing environment. With these new situations also come new technologies that

5.8 Production shot from *Mountains May Depart*

appear within this helter-skelter world—the only thing we can do is make the best decision on how to navigate this new environment. For me what is crucial is to look at the world through the perspective of a large cross section of people and only then can we make the best decision on how to proceed.

Let's round out our discussion with a game of free association based around keywords from Jia Zhangke films. Can you talk about what randomly comes to mind when you hear: Sally Yeh.

"A Lifetime of Intoxication," video rooms.

Realism.

I can't think of anything! [*laughs*] I think of truth. Truth in art. Why did so many Chinese directors during the 1990s stubbornly pursue realism? Because they had a real hope that Chinese cinema could represent a kind of truth. I'm not sure if there are other national cinemas that have this same fixation, but my generation of film directors in China certainly did, and that's because the films we were watching growing up were all so artificial! [*laughs*]

Fenyang.

Fenyang alcohol! [*laughs*] As I get older, all I want to drink is alcohol from my hometown! [*laughs*]

Independent.

Freedom. Without freedom you can never be independent.

The here and now.

I think of 1905 because I have always wanted to shoot a traditional Chinese costume drama. It's been eight years, and I still haven't begun shooting. But when you say the here and now, I think of that film, which is set in 1905! [*laughs*] That was the year China abolished the official examination system.

On location.

Box lunches! [*laughs*]

Break dancing.

I still secretly break out some moves every now and then! [*laughs*] Sometimes at the office I find myself dancing without even realizing it! But my colleagues always notice, and they immediately whip out their cell phones to record me! [*laughs*] But I'm not as good as I used to be! I used to be able to do all kinds of twists and flips. The other day I suddenly had the urge to pull one off, but I decided I better not, I'd probably break my neck! [*laughs*]

UFO.

I think of those times when I am all alone. Everyone seems to think I am always so busy, juggling all kinds of different projects. Actually, every day there is always a lot of time that I spend by myself. From my twenties until now, I always make sure to carve out some alone time for myself. I recently moved back to my childhood home, and at night you can see the moon and stars, and I can imagine UFOs. So these days I am spending more and more time longing for outer space. A few years ago I even wrote an essay on astrophysics. After I wrote it, I showed it to a friend of mine who is a sci-fi fan, and he said: "Director, this is what you call 'trash sci-fi'!"

STUDENT YEARS
XIAO SHAN GOING HOME (1995)
THE AESTHETICS OF AN OPENING SHOT
MASTER CLASS

6 Toward an Accented Cinema

6.1 Jia Zhangke

Actually, if we use the metaphor of language to analyze film, you can look at a filmmaker's style as an "accent." One of the most fundamental questions for a filmmaker is: Does your film have an accent?

Over the course of the more than two decades that you have been making films, in what ways has your notion of cinema been transformed?

It is hard for me to clearly describe in exactly what ways my understanding of film has changed because it is a process of transformation that is forever unfolding. I think each film I shoot unconsciously incorporates new ideas into a new form. Film is an art form that relies on the summation of a lot of different elements: there are screenplay elements, location issues that need to be resolved, timeline issues you need to figure out, as well as performance components with actors. All of these certainly change over time, but for me perhaps one of the biggest changes occurred around the time I made *A Touch of Sin* when I began to incorporate elements from genre cinema into my work. For me that was a really addictive process that gave me a lot of satisfaction.

I increasingly feel that the most important thing you can do in a film is to innovate or develop something new. Besides innovations in cinematic language, perhaps even more important is to discover a new type of character to be seen on-screen. I am thinking of iconic characters like Charlie Chaplin's Tramp, or Lu Xun's Ah Q. I think we need to invent these types of archetypal characters in order to articulate the new challenges, situations, and problems that face us. These past few years I keep asking myself whether we are able to create a unique new character like that. Are we able to create a type of character unlike any we have ever seen before on-screen, yet one that reminds us of someone around us that we see every day in our normal lives? That's the kind of character I want to create.

As a director, you need to synthesize a broad knowledge of many areas, including cinematography, editing, lighting, and screenwriting. However, besides those technical skills you also need experience, vision, interpersonal skills, communication skills, et cetera. What area of knowledge do you feel is most essential for young film students to spend their time on? Back when you were a film student, what areas did you focus on the most?

I began my studies at the Beijing Film Academy in 1993, and my major was film theory, which was focused on training talent in film theory, film history, and cultural criticism. But there is something quite unique about the curriculum at the Beijing Film Academy because there is a common curriculum for all freshmen and sophomore students. Those core common classes include cinematography, performance, screenwriting, and film history, and students from all different majors take these courses together. Even though my major was film theory, during those first two years I was able to get a solid education in all the various basic aspects of filmmaking, including producing and directing.

As I was pursuing my studies, I also took advantage of my time outside of class to do some things for myself, like write screenplays. When I first applied to the Beijing Film Academy, I applied to the school of literature, which included theory and critical studies, because it was much easier to get into—back then there weren't that many people interested in studying film history or film theory. Moreover, back when I applied, I really didn't have a strong foundation in film studies—the only thing I knew how to do was write. At the time, there were very few film publications that were readily available. There was also the fact that most of those classic films that are always cited in film history books were completely unavailable; there was simply no outlet where I could see them. So, at the time, I felt like I really didn't have much of a choice because I didn't have the specialized knowledge to apply for any other major. So I ended up getting into the film theory track, since that major required strong writing skills. But at the same time, I had a very strong urge to explore my creative side. Starting from my freshman year, I was already writing screenplays, and I maintained that habit all the way through college.

Another thing I started to do was to create an environment in which I could actually produce short films. We studied a lot of different areas such as theory, sound design, and art design, but making short films was essential in terms of applying that knowledge to my own real-life experience and understanding of things. Making shorts really helped me with that process. It was only when I ran into curious creative problems when I was a director shooting those short films that I truly understood the value of the knowledge I was acquiring.

Because I was a film theory major, I actually only had two five-minute short film homework assignments that I was required to produce over the course of my college years. That meant that I really didn't have a lot of opportunities to make films through my classes—two five-minute shorts really weren't enough. In order to create more opportunities for us to make films on our own, my classmates and I organized a club which we called the Beijing Film Academy Youth Experimental Filmmaker Group. Although the club was made up of students from various departments, it wasn't officially sponsored by the academy. We had students majoring in literature, cinematography, sound design, and various majors who would get together to shoot short films. I made two films with this group, *Xiao Shan Going Home* and *Du Du*.

And how important was that experience of making short films during your student years for your overall growth as a filmmaker?

I would like to discuss *Xiao Shan Going Home* in more detail because that was a film that was really important for my growth. At the time, there were twenty-odd members of our film club, and we decided that we would make a short film together. Each of us wrote our own screenplays and then we selected the script that we most wanted to shoot. I wrote *Xiao Shan Going Home*, and everyone seemed to feel that was the best one, so we went ahead with me as director. Because this project was not directly connected to any of our coursework, it was very hard to get access to equipment through our school. Somehow our cinematographer was able to get his hands on a Betacam, and the sound designer managed to pull some strings to borrow a microphone and some old Nagra recording equipment from that era. We all pooled together whatever resources we had to make that film. At the time, I was doing some "hired gun" freelance work, basically writing uncredited scripts for television, and used that cash to cover whatever production costs we had.

Back when we shot *Xiao Shan Going Home*, there was actually one narrative line that I never shot. In the original screenplay, there was one more character that Xiao Shan was supposed to seek out. That character was a nanny working for a rich family, and she was having an affair with the head of the household that she was working for. But because we ran out of money and needed to return all the equipment that we borrowed, we were never able to shoot that sequence. I was really disappointed by that, and without that narrative thread I always felt the film was somehow not quite finished. But I eventually pushed forward and decided to try and edit it together anyway—I had to force myself to finish the editing. Besides the regret that the film was somehow incomplete, I also felt really bad for the actress we had cast in that role that got cut. That role had already been cast, and one of my classmates who was an acting major was scheduled to portray that role; she had already done all the prep work! The editing process ended up being extremely drawn out because we didn't have any money; we had to keep hustling to find a way to finish it. We would find some editing rooms that would allow us to use their space for free, but only for an hour here or three hours there. Sometimes we would just settle down to start editing and be chased away by a paying client. So it took quite a while to finally complete the editing.

You might wonder if anyone actually saw this film once it was done. Well, one of my classmates made a poster advertising a screening in one of our dormitories. A lot of our classmates all came out to see the film; the dorm where we held the screening was packed. *Xiao Shan Going Home* has a run time of approximately fifty minutes; within ten minutes the room was empty—everyone had walked out! [*laughs*] That was a crushing blow to me at the time. [*laughs*] Editing that film was a truly torturous experience. I was so self-critical of that film and felt like it was so poorly shot: there were also a lot of shots that were missing. But all that chaos was a result of our inexperience. Sometimes there was no narrative logic to tie certain shots together; there were all kinds of problems. But through this prolonged process of editing I gradually came to understand where these problems were, and when I was able to finally piece everything together into a coherent whole it really felt like a miracle. [*laughs*] When you look at the film, there are still all kinds of problems with the subtitles and various materials, but what inspired me to keep going was that famous quote from Jean-Luc Godard: "All films can be saved during the editing process." I felt that if Godard can do it, then I can do it! [*laughs*] Yet deep down I knew there were a lot of problems with the film.

Once all my classmates left, I started to harbor deep suspicions about my own abilities. But then I started to think back to those moments during the shoot that really moved me; although I knew we hadn't executed them well from a technical perspective, there were a lot of elements that stuck out during the writing and later shooting process. For instance, we used real locations to shoot the film and selected authentic locations appropriate for the story, which really opened up the space; we also had the characters speaking dialects, which was forbidden at the time. In order to promote standard Mandarin spoken Chinese, you weren't supposed to use dialects in film. This really frustrated me when I was writing the screenplay because I knew that my character, who was a migrant worker in Beijing, would not be using Mandarin in real life; he would certainly be speaking some local dialect. So in the end I simply couldn't accept the fact that he would be speaking Mandarin; it just wouldn't make sense and would not feel authentic. So when it came time to actually shoot the film, we used local dialects and nonprofessional actors, which when used together created an effect that was, on the one hand, very gritty but also very unadorned and true to the real world; this process really moved me.

In the end, I found myself arguing with myself—perhaps it's because I'm a Gemini—but part of me felt like the film was a piece of garbage that was never even complete, and the other side of me felt like there were still some good qualities about the film. In the end, one of my classmates suggested getting out there and showing the film to students at other schools. So we went on the road with the film and exhibited it on videotape to students at Peking University, Renmin University of China, and Central Academy of Fine Arts along with a bunch of schools outside of Beijing, including Shanxi University. That was really an unforgettable journey. For each screening we sought out other students our age from the class that entered in 1993 and asked around to find students majoring in Chinese, film, journalism, or other related fields who might be interested; then we found an empty classroom and played the movie. After each screening we held Q&A sessions, just like what we're doing now. Through that process of interacting with audiences, I gradually came to understand what it was I was doing with that film. For instance, when we were at Peking University, there were a lot of students who brought up questions concerning China's peasant population and other sociological questions that the film touched upon. They weren't film students, so they didn't pay too much attention to those sloppy shots or the choppy editing, but they were drawn in by the main character, which gradually gave me more confidence in the work.

6.2 Wang Hongwei in *Xiao Shan Going Home*

Sometime later another classmate told me about a short film festival in Hong Kong, and we submitted *Xiao Shan Going Home*. Then one day I heard that it had been selected, so I went to Hong Kong, and *Xiao Shan Going Home* won an award for Best Short Fiction Film! It was at that same festival that I met two of my most important collaborators—my cinematographer Yu Lik-Wai and my producer Lee Kit-Ming. We decided we wanted to work together, and that led to my first full-length feature, *Xiao Wu*.

Looking back on *Xiao Shan Going Home* after all these years, what is your biggest takeaway from that early filmmaking experience?

Reflecting on the process of making *Xiao Shan Going Home* fills me with all kinds of emotions: back then I had all kinds of doubts about my abilities, and that process was so painful since I really felt it was a lousy film at the time. But there is one crucial aspect of all this I want to emphasize: I saw it through. I stuck it out and made sure that this film was able to go through all the various stages that a film needs to go through: planning, drafting a script, casting, shooting, editing, exhibition, discussions about the film, all the way up to submission to film festivals. I am very thankful for this film because it made me hunker down and experience all of the various stages of a film's production process, so it was an extremely important experience for me. When you think about it, even though the principal photography was never finished, I insisted on editing the film. If I hadn't done that, I would have never gotten that crucial editing experience, and none of those other things that came later would have happened. After editing the film, I screened it for my classmates. I was crushed by their reaction, but if I hadn't insisted on taking it to other schools, I would have never had the opportunity to have those deep exchanges about the film with other students, nor would I have ever submitted it to that film festival. In some sense, the most important thing about a short film isn't necessarily the film itself but the entire process of making the film and being conscious of what we can learn from that process.

People often ask me what the greatest thing I learned from making those short films was. Actually, a lot of the knowledge used during production—knowledge about various aspects of the aesthetics of film, including art design, cinematography, and lighting—were all topics we learned about in class. The most important thing I learned when making those short films was how to make a decision. You might have a single scene, but according to the way it is written in the screenplay, you could shoot it a variety of ways: you could shoot it this way or that way; you could choose this actor or that actor. Making a film is actually the process of continually making various decisions. Once I had started actually working in the industry, I realized that my previous experience making short films had already helped me grow accustomed to making decisions and committing to them. It also helped me grow accustomed to understanding myself; actually, when it comes down to it, making a decision is the same thing as understanding yourself. You might have a scene that you want to shoot as one long take, but why didn't you chop it up into shorter shots? In what context do you need to use a long take? Sometimes the reason boils down to intuition, but at other times there is a concrete rationale. But, in the end, you as the director have to make a call; so with the job of film director comes the responsibility of making clear decisions and committing to them.

While at the Beijing Film Academy, what classes did you gravitate to? What was the greatest thing you learned from those classes?

Back when I was still in school, there were two classes that I enjoyed most, those were my film history classes and classes in my own major of film theory. That was back during the early 1990s, which was the age of theory: feminism, new historicism, postmodernism, postcolonialism were all the rage, yet a lot of those film theories had yet to be translated into Chinese. Then there was linguistics, phenomenology, and all kinds of other forms of philosophy that were often interwoven together. We had quite a few teachers who had studied abroad, and they were trying their best to understand all of these new theories, but things were still quite chaotic back then. We would study one theory today and another one tomorrow. Only later would I realize that that experience would become a very important step for my later creative work.

Since I have been labeled as a Sixth Generation director, people often ask me how my generation differs from previous generations. Naturally, one big difference is our personal experience: the previous generation all lived through the Cultural Revolution and only after that began to study film and direct films in the 1980s. My generation all experienced 1989 and started making movies amid the height of the Reform Era. But I think that the main difference actually comes down to a fundamentally different understanding of people and society. While we were so starved for knowledge that we were just swallowing everything whole and forcing all those things down, the result was a very different way of looking at the world, a new perspective on things. Film was new, the characters were new, and in the end, our method of understanding the world was new. The "newness" came from what we were reading and studying at that time. So even after all these years of making movies, I am still very thankful that I was exposed to all those philosophical works in college.

Some people ask me why I made my first feature film about a pickpocket. Why did I make my second film about a group of touring performers? Why do I make films about coal miners and people like that? A lot of this of course comes down to an emotional connection, but another side of that is simply from the fact that I have never had any interest in making films about heroes or icons of any kind. This is something I feel quite strongly about. So you never see heroes in my films, and I have no interest in shooting any films about those idols most people look up to. If you see my film *A Touch of Sin*, there are four characters and four stories about violence. Why did I put them together? It all boils down to structure. None of those individual stories was able to fully describe my complex feelings about violence in China today. That film was shot just as social media and Weibo were gaining popularity and everyone suddenly had the power to be a reporter. Every day I was seeing all kinds of shocking new events being reported on Weibo. But how do you capture that in a film? I decided I needed to use a format that allowed me to tell multiple stories and really try to portray their power and density in the film. But none of these are stories about idols or icons, and none of them are complete stories. Actually, any one of those four stories could have been made into a more classical form and expanded into a feature-length film: you could easily make four independent stand-alone films out of that content. But that wouldn't have represented the sense of the world that I was getting from this era of new media; instead, I needed a new structure to interpret this era. This new structure called for multiple stories taking place in different locations separated by thousands of miles, like Shanxi, Hubei, Guangdong, and Chongqing, but playing out simultaneously in our lives. So I used the structure of four shorts to bring them together—I needed this particular structure to express my understanding and feelings about my reality and the atmosphere of violence pervading our reality during this particular time period. So the structure was essential to this project, and I very much relied on that structure. As far as I'm concerned, a closed narrative structure simply does not have the ability to express my feelings about the contemporary world; instead, I needed this new structure to tell the story.

When it comes to film history, as someone who works in this industry, I feel we need to understand the various stages the art form has gone through over the course of its development. This is essential because as we search for new possibilities for film, those explorations are built on the foundations of previous chapters in film history. When studying film history, there are two components I focus on: besides the history of world cinema, as a Chinese, I also feel it is essential for me to have a solid understanding of Chinese film history as well.

Since we are talking about film history, I wanted to jump in. In 2013 you made a short film for the Venice International Film Festival entitled *Future Reloaded*. That short functioned as an homage to some of the great classics in Chinese film history: Wu Yonggang's *The Goddess* (*Shennü*, 1934), Xie Fei's *Black Snow* (*Benmingnian*, 1990), Chen Kaige's *Yellow Earth* (*Huang tudi*, 1984), and Fei Mu's *Spring in a Small Town* (*Xiaocheng zhichun*, 1948). Earlier you spoke of the impact *Yellow Earth* had on you when you first saw it. When thinking about Chinese film history, are these the films that have had the greatest influence on you?

That's right. I made this short in celebration of the seventieth anniversary of the Venice International Film Festival. The festival invited a few directors to make shorts about their own conception of film history. I selected these four films that I was fond of to pay tribute to. I should say that studying film history is not just a means of understanding how films are made; it is also a powerful method to understand your own local audiences.

Even up until today, when we refer to Chinese cinema in Chinese, we often use terminology borrowed from theater. For instance, when we are making a film, we say we are "shooting a drama" (*pai xi*); this use of the term *xi* reflects audiences' expectations about film ever since the art form first entered China. What it means is that when audiences go to the cinema, they hope to see a drama. The earliest Chinese films were all adaptations of Peking opera stories or stage dramas. More realistic, documentary, or experimental forms of cinema have a much weaker tradition in China. So in this context, when audiences go to the cinema, what most of them want to see is theatricality, which is a result of what has gradually evolved over time. With a strong background in film history, I can make documentaries or more experimental films and have a much clearer idea of the role they play in our culture and the challenges they face. Film history can teach us why [Chinese audiences] are not fond of documentary films or experimental films. Back when I made *Xiao Wu*, I appropriated a lot of documentary film techniques, and a lot of people, including some film directors, reacted by saying: "This isn't a film! Since everything in it is real, it cannot qualify as a real film!" [*laughs*] That's why it is so essential to understand film history. By studying film history, we can understand our bloodline, our lineage.

Our film students often have short film projects they have to make for their classes, which is not dissimilar from the kind of project you took on for the Venice Film Festival. Getting back to *Future Reloaded*, how did that project come about, and what led you to select those four films that were featured?

When I was invited to take part in this project, I started to think about what Chinese films had the biggest impact on me. I started from the silent film era and Wu Yonggang's *The Goddess,* which is my favorite Chinese film from the silent period. Chinese film was quite modern back then, and I also felt the lead, Ruan Lingyu, is the single greatest actress in Chinese cinema; I really love all of those close-up shots of her in the film. Since it is a silent film, the emotion that she is able to convey through her eyes is so very powerful and moving. It is actually really important to study those old silent films because back then the art form was still in its infancy and there were still all kinds of possibilities that were open. It is like a child: when they are very young there are infinite possibilities for their future, but once they grow up those possibilities start to narrow. Once sound film came into being and the literary dimension of cinema came to be emphasized, the medium became less malleable, its vitality diminished, and it became less experimental. I have always paid close attention to the silent film era in China, and *The Goddess* is really a masterpiece.

Yellow Earth is a film very deeply connected to me personally because I have always loved that film. It was back when I was a student that I saw *Yellow Earth* and decided that I wanted to become a filmmaker.

When I was in film school, there were two directors that I studied in depth: Eisenstein and Charlie Chaplin. I actually spent very little time studying art films with long takes. The reason I was so enthralled by Eisenstein was that his research expanded the possibilities of film language. I may never make a film like him, but the method he used to understand film is an incredible tool. For instance, he was the one who first argued that by juxtaposing two different images you can create new meaning. He represents an extremely subjective approach to images, which is very different from the more objective approach I tried to reveal in my later films. But it is only because I spent time researching Eisenstein that I was able to understand what subjectivity in film meant, so when I set out to make films that were more objective and observational in style, I knew what I had to do. Charlie Chaplin is a film director who can never be duplicated, and there will never be another actor like him. His films always serve as a reminder of where we came from, a reminder of our film lineage. That's because film was born out of a sleight of hand, a trick. When film was invented, it was very closely related to magic and acrobatics. That is a reminder for me to continually adjust my own mode of making films, because embedded in the very DNA of cinema itself are these populist genres; Charlie Chaplin helps us understand that film is a popular art form. Whether you make art house films or commercial films, I feel like all filmmakers need to reflect on this issue.

Spring in a Small Town is a film that I feel represents the absolute pinnacle in artistic achievement in Chinese film history. It is very hard to articulate in words what that film accomplished, but I strongly recommend anyone who is a student of cinema to watch *Spring in a Small Town*.

Black Snow is a rather unique case because it is a film that I feel has been tremendously underappreciated in China. It is a film by Xie Fei, who is usually categorized as a Fourth Generation director; however, in many ways this film has a deep connection to the work that the so-called Sixth Generation would later make. Jiang Wen's portrayal of Li Huiquan in *Black Snow* presented the image of a marginalized urbanite, which would later inspire a lot of Sixth Generation directors to portray dispossessed individuals who were living on the margins of society. That film opened up a space for portraying the malaise of modernity in China. Before that time, virtually no one in China was making films that explored loneliness, which is essentially a symptom of modernity. We never saw that expressed in earlier films, not even in the work of the Fifth Generation, but Xie Fei's film had it. That was the very beginning of the Reform Era, and we were just starting to have a new urban culture and adopt modern lifestyles, so that really was the first film to use these types of characters to express one's reflections on modernity.

I just mentioned the generational concept in categorizing Chinese film directors. Actually, even I am not entirely clear on the difference between the First, Second, and Third Generations of Chinese filmmakers! [*laughs*] My understanding of the so-called Fourth Generation is that is the generation that studied film before the outbreak of the Cultural Revolution. They had their careers interrupted by the political turmoil of the Cultural Revolution and only began to actually make films during the Reform Era. The Fifth Generation refers to the group that went to film school around 1978 and started making films in the 1980s. But the Sixth Generation is a large and strange category. It refers to the group that studied film in the 1980s and 1990s, and even some filmmakers who went to school during the 2000s are included—all of them are lumped together as the Sixth Generation. For a filmmaker, none of this really matters; I frankly don't care what generation you want to label me as. But this issue brings up a problem: when you are still at a very active stage in your creative career, and suddenly critics and historians refer to you as part of a collective or slap a clear label on you, how are you supposed to respond? Even if they don't lump you into a certain movement, critics always try to summarize the unique qualities of your work. I feel that this is the moment that a director needs to really summon up his spirit of resistance. You need to resist the labels that other people are assigning to you. For instance, after I finished my second film, *Platform*, one critic wrote a really glowing review; it was really flattering, but there was one line where the critic stated he hoped I would go on to continue making more films about these types of provincial towns throughout my career. He felt that my film helped him discover the existence of these provincial cities in China, but I don't want to be labeled as a director who only makes films about provincial cities; I want to make movies about the moon! [*laughs*]

When it comes down to it, the most important thing is to have an understanding of who you really are. Every time you make a movie, write a screenplay, or commit to an artistic act, you have to ask yourself if it is something you are truly interested in and committed to. It doesn't matter what the outside world says about your work; even if some aspect of your work has become a marketable asset, you need to resist. This spirit of resistance needs to be built on the foundation of loyalty to yourself. If you want to make this film today, do it! If you want to make that film tomorrow, do it! I remember when I was just starting out, a veteran director recommended that I prepare a bunch of different scripts. Once you are ready to start shooting, you should weigh which one is best suited for the critics and the market at that specific time; that way you will have a smoother career. But I never liked that kind of approach. As far as I am concerned, film is not like gambling. Just because martial arts films are hot at the box office right now doesn't mean I should run off and shoot a martial arts film! At the same time, if I am set on making a martial arts film, you better believe that I am going to make it, even if no one is interested in that genre! That's because I am making films out of a spiritual necessity; you need to always respect yourself and never lose sight of that.

The opening shot of a film is extremely crucial. In just a few minutes you need to provide so much information: introduce the main character, announce the setting of the film, and provide some clues about the larger historical background. Even more important is capturing the audience's attention by setting up a conflict or plot details for the action to follow. Your filmography is filled with several brilliant opening sequences, from *Xiao Wu* to *The World*. Could you walk us through the design and ideas behind the first few minutes of one of my favorite opening sequences, the first few minutes of *Still Life*?

Actually, whenever I am writing a screenplay and first start conceptualizing the opening sequence, it is usually an unconscious process, and the opening usually evolves by chance. As I see things, opening sequences usually fall into one of two categories. The first is a dramatic opening where you quickly get into the story and plotline; something happens, or a character faces some kind of predicament and needs to figure out what to do. This a classic dramatic opening. But I much prefer the second category, which is more experiential in nature; that is, there are no dramatic elements, but instead you get a portrait of a person and learn what kind of environment he is from. The opening sequence establishes the atmosphere as the most important component. This approach is devoid of drama and plot, but it is experiential and atmospheric. *Still Life* is an example of this latter, antidramatic approach; instead, it is immersive and experiential; it brings the audience into the environment in a way that makes them feel as if they too are sitting on that boat.

A crucial aspect to setting up an opening sequence is the type of film language you want to use and how you set the shot up. For those opening shots I used a set of dolly tracks that we put the camera on. We laid the tracks down on the boat and slowly shot portrait-style images of the passengers' faces. Because of the topography of the Three Gorges region, whenever I am there either walking along the river or on a boat, I am always reminded of the visual sense you get from looking at a traditional Chinese landscape scroll painting. I am thinking of those horizontal scroll paintings that gradually reveal a landscape. As you roll the painting open, the scenery constantly changes and you see different characters in the painting being revealed. The natural landscape of the Three Gorges region is very similar to what you see in those paintings. If you are sitting on a boat and look out in one direction, it is really just like a scroll painting! If you ride on a motorcycle along the river's edge, you get the same effect. So that led me to use a lot of dolly tracks in this film so I could capture the visual style of a scroll painting. This was completely inspired by my gut reaction to the environment there.

Later in postproduction we emphasized the green tints in the landscape because that is the color you always see in those landscape scrolls. We wanted to capture that classical feeling on film. If you ask me why, it is because the Three Gorges always left a very strong impression on me. Those mountains and that river have been there for thousands of years, and what we see are the same vistas that the great poet Li Bai saw back in the Tang dynasty. Thousands of years later, that scenery is still there unchanged, yet humankind has changed so much. I wanted to use this method to tie a contemporary story together with a classical sensibility. The way we decided to execute that was by using a slow-moving camera on dolly rails to mimic the effect of looking at a traditional scroll painting.

Once we had settled on the method, the next challenge had to do with the performances. We cast all of those people who appear on the boat right there at the dock! Some of them are dockworkers while others are local residents; we selected them based on their faces and led them aboard—but then there was the problem of performance. A lot of people think I just picked a few nonprofessional actors, led them aboard, shot the scene, and that's it. That would be impossible. If you don't design the shot, if you don't coach those performers, all you will end up with is a bunch of blank faces staring at you in confusion! [*laughs*] The first thing to do was to imagine a task for each one of them to be doing: it might be playing cards, drinking a beer, fortune-telling, talking on a cell phone, eating a snack, but you need to design all of that carefully. You have to imagine what the various possibilities are for them as passengers on that boat. We ended up breaking up into different units to tackle this: I was responsible for one group, and my two assistant directors were responsible for two other groups. Each of them did some rehearsals with their groups, and then we started shooting. When you are working with extras or nonprofessional actors, you need to provide them with crystal clear instructions; you need to tell them exactly what to do, otherwise they just end up staring at you. [*laughs*]

Then there was the problem when it came to executing the scroll effect—I wanted to re-create the effect of opening a long horizontal scroll, but our boat wasn't long enough to achieve that effect! After discussing the problem with my cinematographer, we decided to begin the shot out of focus, then as the camera moves along the track gradually come into focus, then just as we are almost out of track, transition back to out of focus. Then we set the shot up again with the next group of extras. Later in postproduction we were able to edit these shots together by overlapping those out-of-focus portions, which gave the illusion that the boat was much longer than it really was and captured the scroll-like effect I was looking for. But you have to plan all of this out before you start shooting so you have the right material when it comes time for editing; that way the series of shots you capture are able to produce the feeling you are looking for. Since I was really insistent on capturing that scroll painting effect, we had to use those out-of-focus fades and reconstitute the sequence in order to make the scene flow as if it was a single shot.

6.3 Production shot from the opening sequence of *Still Life*

AUDIENCE: I just shot a short film and discovered that sometimes there would be a lag between the instructions I gave the actors and their ability to match that with the practical reality on set. Your films always feel so genuine and real to me, so I am wondering, what techniques do you use to communicate with actors on set?

The first thing to note when explaining acting issues with performers is the fact that no two actors are alike, so there is no one-size-fits-all approach. Every actor requires a different approach. For instance, I have worked with Zhao Tao longer than any other actor, and whenever we collaborate, she has a method for approaching her role that involves writing a short biography for her character. She will write out all the biographical details that didn't appear in the film: for instance, what street the character grew up on, where she went to elementary school, what happens to her after the film—she builds up a detailed biography based on her imagination. Once she is done, she always discusses it with me to figure out which aspects match with my own conception of the character and which aspects feel off. The reason for this kind of deep character discussion is because when the character appears in the film, it is just a cross section of one aspect of that character's life, but there are a lot of elements that go into deciding which possibility to pursue for any given character. As an actor, Zhao Tao needs to imagine her character as being three-dimensional. When I work with Zhao Tao, she explores a lot of different ideas, but in the end, it all comes down to the question of making the right call for that particular character. So when working with an actor like Zhao Tao, clear communication is essential. As long as I am able to clearly express what I want, she is able to deliver it.

Another example is the actor who played Xiao Wu's father in *Xiao Wu*. He is a nonprofessional actor, so at first his performance was very much influenced by the overly dramatic acting style he was accustomed to seeing in films. I loved the way he looked and he had a great presence, but as soon as he started acting, you could see he was obviously *acting*! When he walked, he took these exaggerated steps like he was an actor in a Peking opera performance! [*laughs*] Let me demonstrate it for you. [*Jia Zhangke gets up and takes several giant, exaggerated steps and speaks in a loud theatrical voice*] "Xiao Wu, you're back!" [*laughs*] So that's what I had to work with! But I still really liked him, and since I didn't have that much time to work with him, I thought of a way to guide him in the right direction: I decided to demonstrate the scene to him using an even *more* exaggerated style. I told him his acting was off, and I repeated the scene in a manner that really was right out of a Peking opera performance. When he saw it he said: "Huh, I guess that's not quite how we look in real life." So I asked him: "Well, what do you think a more real-life version would look like?" And then he did much better. During that first take his approach was completely unconscious. He never imagined that when he walked he was taking huge steps like that, whereas he should have been performing in a much more natural manner. So I functioned as a mirror so he could see what he was doing, and he immediately saw what he had been doing was wrong.

I worked with Joan Chen on *24 City*; she is an incredible actor, but our scene was set in a hair salon inside a workers' apartment building. It was a real-life environment, and when we started shooting, she couldn't get through the scene because all the noise was distracting her. She was accustomed to working on a soundstage or a closed set, and all the city noise made it difficult for her to focus. But that was precisely the kind of environment that I like. So in situations like that I have to just sit down and explain to the actors why we need to shoot in this type of environment. I called for a break; then I patiently explained to Joan where all those noises were coming from. For instance, when we heard the sound of a motorcycle, I told her that might be a father dropping his son off at school; when we heard the piercing voice of two old ladies talking, I told her that they were at the market haggling over prices. So I just took my time and explained all these noises to her. And she immediately adapted and nailed the scene; all she needed was a sense of security in what was a new shooting environment for her. This is where Joan Chen's genius really shone through for me: she immediately understood what I was trying to do and why we needed to shoot the scene in a real-life location—it all just clicked.

And then there are cases when you try everything, but nothing seems to be working—you just aren't getting the performance you want. I also have experience with those types of situations, and I usually just stop shooting and go back to the screenplay. Sometimes the problem is at the level of the script. If there is something wrong with the screenplay, there is no way the actors will feel comfortable. So sometimes you need to go back and check the screenplay, and often the problem is that the actors don't feel the dialogue is believable or the logic of the screenplay doesn't conform to the logic of real life or the internal logic of that character. Once you revise the screenplay and make another attempt to reshoot the scene, the results are usually much better.

AUDIENCE: You have mentioned that Lee Chang-dong and others have talked about the need for Chinese art house movies to take the box office into

6.4 Joan Chen in *24 City*

consideration and think of ways to interest audiences in art films. I am wondering, what kind of elements can attract more mainstream audiences to art house films?

I don't look at this as a problem with the box office; the question is really how films can win over the audiences that they should be winning over. I feel that every individual must face his own market environment, or you could say that the audience environment is different for each filmmaker. I'm quite certain that Lee Chang-dong's comments were directed at the Korean market, which has some fundamental differences with the Chinese environment. The film environment in China is extremely complex. The first problem is that there is a group of directors who are not willing to let their films enter into circulation, which I don't think is a good idea. Societies rely heavily on business structures to make various connections. The creative process can remain independent, but the most effective methods for promoting your films and establishing a bridge to your audience are commercial networks. So in order for this commercial bridge to flow freely, we need directors to take part in this process.

Another issue is related to the methods we use to make our films and how we promote content we care about. Speaking frankly, Chinese art film, especially during the 1990s, passively became extremely elitist. Why do I say that? Well, when you think about it, by the time the Film Bureau held that conference in 2003 there were more than fifty directors who had been banned from making films. With so many directors' work cut off from Chinese audiences for so many years, you end up with a situation where those types of films are completely unfamiliar to mainstream Chinese viewers. Over the course of these past few years, whenever I release a new film I travel all around China giving lectures and doing interviews—this is a necessary step because most audiences are completely unfamiliar with art films. If we as directors don't take our work out there and introduce it to the people, in some sense, it is like rejecting our audience. And I think that it is starting to have an impact because *Mountains May Depart* sold 1.2 million tickets at the Chinese box office, but just a few years later that number increased to 2.5 million for *Ash Is Purest White*.

As for actual production of art films, it is somewhat awkward to explain this, but I feel that there are some directors who intentionally try to make arty films in a very calculated way that feels very inauthentic. [*laughs*] They do things like bundling up their emotions, making their films unnecessarily complicated, and deliberately mystifying, and employing art film tactics in a calculated way. But when they do this, you can tell the films are missing genuine emotional weight and the films end up just having a superficial artsy-fartsy tone. [*laughs*] With a film like that there is no way you can attract an audience. I think we should do our best to rid ourselves of these types of obstacles, which inhibit your independent perspective and observations or ability to explore new film techniques. There is a phenomenon in China where directors often get nervous before their film is distributed and say: "I tried to make a commercial film this time. I hope it gets the commercial distribution it deserves!" Then when it flops they say: "See what happens when you make an art film and try to get it distributed commercially!" [*laughs*] So I think we should all be more consistent about what kind of films we really want to make.

AUDIENCE: I wonder if you can introduce your working method, especially when it comes to screenwriting. For film students, much of our training is focused on more commercial films, whereas your films are more observational and realistic. Could you talk about what methods you use to capture that more true-to-life aesthetic?

6.5 Michael Berry (*left*) and Jia Zhangke (*right*) during a film master class with UCLA students

You might not believe me if I tell you, but when I was studying screenwriting in college, I started with a strict Soviet-style screenwriting education, which was then quickly followed by a strict Hollywood-style screenwriting course! Our professor required us to think of one hundred different twists of fate someone could experience in their life: being admitted to the hospital, getting in a car accident, et cetera. We studied all of these different prescriptive methods. One exercise we did was to follow a narrative thread. We had to basically provide the rationale for someone to buy a ticket to this movie and sit there for the entire ninety minutes, so we had to explain where the narrative direction was going. For instance, when the story feels like it is starting to hit a dead end, what do you do? Each classmate was required to provide a plotline to push the narrative forward. Some would yell out, "The character moves to a new house!" and teacher would say: "Great answer! One hundred percent!" [*laughs*] We did these kinds of exercises for an entire year.

Honestly, these kinds of exercises were extremely important for me, even if I never used those methods in my own screenplays. Take, for instance, the first section from *Xiao Wu*, which focuses on Xiao Wu and his friendship with Xiao Yong. The narrative keeps pushing forward until the point where Xiao Wu confronts Xiao Yong about not being invited to his wedding. According to the rules of drama, I knew all too well that that scene should be emotionally packed, filled with brilliant dialogue and heated exchange, and both characters should really open up to each other! [*laughs*] But it was only because I knew about those principles of dramatic tension that I was able to step outside of that during the writing process and ask myself: What would the logic of realism dictate for a scene like this? What would logic dictate a native of Shanxi do in a situation like this? Well, my answer was that a lot people from Shanxi would remain silent during an awkward moment like that. [*laughs*] But he was able to express what he felt without words. In the end, that is what I wanted—I wanted the actors to express their feelings without words; instead they just kind of beat around the bush. I knew all too well that this was a crucial dramatic moment in the film, but I didn't play it as a typical dramatic confrontation. That's what I wanted for that scene. But when you are writing a screenplay, the ability to take liberties like that is based on the foundation of those more conventional approaches—you have to understand what this thing called drama is and how it functions.

Normally when I write screenplays, I have two golden rules that I stick to, which have always proved useful to me. The first rule applies to what in traditional Chinese narratives is referred to as *qi cheng zhuan he*, or "introduction, elucidation, transition, summing up." After my first draft I always analyze what I have written according to this principle. I dissect the screenplay to figure out which section serves as the "introduction," which section is the "elucidation," where is the "transition," and how I "sum everything up." I am really fond of this theory of *qi cheng zhuan he*. The second rule is that in almost all of my films I always make sure to put the most emotionally impactful scenes in those "golden sections" of the film that create a balance in terms of the physics of the film. This is rather hard to explain, but I really believe in maintaining this inner balance within the film. It is similar to how you think of the eyeline in a particular shot or the axis of a shot; the physics of film has its own internal aesthetics, as does a screenplay.

Among all the various screenwriting theories out there, the most popular one in China today is: *Tell me what your screenplay is about in one sentence.* You hear directors being asked this question all the time by investors, producers, and studio heads. People have also asked me that question, and I just say: I'm sorry, but I don't make the kind of films that can be summed up in one sentence. Life is complicated and messy; how can you sum it up in one sentence? So in the end you have to rely on the logic of life and your own internal sense of what makes sense.

What advice do you have for young filmmakers just starting out in the industry?

There have been several occasions when young filmmakers have asked me that question, and I was never good at responding. But in 2017 the Pingyao International Film Festival invited Johnnie To (Du Qifeng) for a workshop with young filmmakers, and I really liked the answer he gave to that question, so I will share that with you now. Johnnie To summed his advice up in two words: passion and vision.

Over the course of your career, your style has continually transformed. It is as if you are eternally searching for new methods of expression and new ways to tell your stories. At the same time, it only takes two minutes of watching one of your films to immediately recognize it as a "Jia Zhangke film." What do you feel are the most important elements that are there in all of your work? And as your style continually changes, what is that one thing that never changes? Is there a core element that is always there?

[*laughs*] It is very hard to respond to this question by citing any specific details, but I'll instead say a little bit about what I hope to achieve through my films. In China there are many languages we hear in our daily lives: the Mandarin Chinese that most people speak in everyday situations and the kind of Mandarin Chinese you hear the newscaster speaking on the CCTV evening news. [*laughs*] I think the type of Chinese I speak is more infectious than what you hear on CCTV because it is coming from me. [*laughs*] But if I were to speak Fenyang dialect, that would be much more colorful than my Mandarin. You sometimes hear people speaking extremely eloquently, but it doesn't necessarily have that infectious quality that grabs you and brings you in. On the other hand, there are some people who have something to say, but all that comes out are stutters; they are unable to articulate their thoughts, yet I am able to completely understand the emotions they are conveying behind the words.

Actually, if we use the metaphor of language to analyze film, you can look at a filmmaker's style as an "accent." One of the most fundamental questions

6.6 Michael Berry (*left*) and Jia Zhangke (*right*) during a film master class with UCLA students

for a filmmaker is: Does your film have an accent? A film's accent can be revealed through things like how you deal with the passage of time, how you render space, how you confront the rhythm of your narrative, This accent is actually very hard to define because it is made up of a lot of things combined.

Sometimes I watch mainstream Hollywood films and fall asleep. [*laughs*] That's because the language is bland, boring—I can't hear the filmmaker's accent, nor can I feel their passion. And when that happens I don't have the interest to keep up with the story. After ten minutes of watching a car chase sequence, I feel exhausted! [*laughs*] Why does it have to go on for ten minutes? [*laughs*] Of course, there are a lot of truly outstanding Hollywood films, but there are a lot of lousy ones as well. Many of those lousy ones are typical industrial products, completely devoid of any individual accent. Sometimes I'll go to a Hollywood film and step out in the middle; then I will just stand there outside the theater and listen for a while. After a few minutes I usually think to myself: I'm glad I left. That's because if you watch a hundred Hollywood films and listen to the sound design, they are all the same! Most of it is dominated by the sound of race cars and motorcycles: *Vroom! Vroom! Vroom!* [*laughs*] They are all noises created by sound effect designers, and they all sound the same!

What kind of sound do I like to hear in film? In *Still Life* I mixed a variety of sounds: we recorded the sound of the river flowing, the sounds coming from the boats docked at the harbor, and once we recorded all of these different noises from the environment, we edited them together like we were composing a song, rearranging the structure and order as we went. Eventually, this process creates the environment for my films. When you use this kind of a method to make a film, it ends up having an accent. It is as if you are inside the film itself, and that is when a film starts to come alive.

Coda
To the Sea

At what year, what time, what place are we relaying this history? This is just as important as the history being conveyed.

Swimming Out Till the Sea Turns Blue is very much a film about literature. When your generation of filmmakers—the so-called Sixth Generation—came to prominence, one thing that set you and other filmmakers of that movement apart was the drive to tell original stories. That marked a stark break from earlier generations of filmmakers. From 1949 all the way up until the heyday of the Fifth Generation, most Chinese films were adapted from literary works. What were the novels and short stories that had a strong impact on you during your teenage and young-adult years in the 1980s and early 1990s?

During the 1980s when I was going to middle school and high school, it was mostly contemporary Chinese literary works that had the biggest impact on me. The 1980s was an extremely lively period in the Chinese literary scene; average people were all avid readers, and there was a wide assortment of literary journals available. But among the numerous writers active during that time, the ones who were most important to me on a personal level were writers like Jia Pingwa, who is featured in *Swimming Out Till the Sea Turns Blue* and was known for setting many of his stories in his home village.[1] Another writer who had a big impact on me was Lu Yao, the author of *Life*. Those were works that depicted Chinese society against the backdrop of the early Reform Era and the tremendous changes taking place during that period. The themes these works explored were especially attractive to young readers of my generation at the time.

Then in the 1990s, during my studies at the Beijing Film Academy, I rediscovered the work of those writers from earlier generations. At the time, I was most interested in the writings of Shen Congwen and Eileen Chang.[2] They were both writers who did not receive much attention in China after 1949, but by the early 1990s we suddenly rediscovered this incredible page in Chinese literary history that had been largely overlooked. I was especially drawn to Shen Congwen since his personal experience was quite similar to my own. We both came from backwater rural villages and went on to try to make it in the big city. That shared experience of going from a native place to an urban center led me to have a kind of spiritual identification with Shen Congwen's writing, which was immensely important to me.

Another branch of literature that I was drawn to during the mid-1990s was the Chinese avant-garde movement. Gradually, a group of writers like Su Tong, Yu Hua, and Sun Ganlu began to appear on the scene.[3] Their literary style represented a major break with the earlier generations of writers who had preceded them. Of course, many of their works were also adapted for film, such as Su Tong's novella *Wives and Concubines* (*Qiqie chengqun*), which became the source material for Zhang Yimou's *Raise the Red Lantern* (*Dahong denglong gaogao gua*, 1991), and *To Live* (*Huozhe*, 1994), which was also adapted by Zhang Yimou into a film of the same name. I feel like on a spiritual level, my starting-off point and approach to creativity is perhaps closest to this generation of writers. But many film directors of my generation didn't go out of their way to adapt literary works by these writers for the screen. Instead, we used those literary works as a portal to find our own film language; those were works that helped us discover a brand new way of understanding Chinese society. Some directors my age still like to adapt literary works, but most prefer to write original screenplays as a means of becoming an auteur-style director.

How did *Swimming Out Till the Sea Turns Blue* evolve?

When it comes to the origin of this film, it actually goes back to a series of films I have been making over the past fifteen years. In 2006, I made a documentary film about a painter named Liu Xiaodong titled *Dong*; in 2007, I made a another documentary about a fashion designer named Ma Ke titled *Useless*. After those films, I continued to explore my interest in contemporary Chinese literature and art. I really wanted to make a film about another artist, and at the time, I had a lot of different choices. At one point I wanted to make a film about an architect, then there was a project about an urban planner I was considering, but in the end none of those projects panned out because I couldn't find the right subject to shoot. But a few years ago I moved back to my family's ancestral village. This village actually has a deep connection with Chinese literary history. This was where the veteran writer Ma Feng lived, worked, and wrote; during the 1950s and 1960s, his novels were also adapted into numerous films.[4] So it is the kind of place that has deep literary roots.

There were essentially two things that led me to make this film. On the one hand, it was tied to the experience of living in the countryside: Chinese society has been evolving quickly, and the economic development has been extremely fast paced, which led to a process of rapid urbanization. Waves of young people left behind their rural homes to migrate to those big cities. That marks a major break with thousands of years of Chinese history, which has always been dominated by a more rural lifestyle for most people. It is that rural lifestyle that has created our personalities; it has created who we are as a people and how we interact with the world. You can even say that if you truly want to understand city life in China today, you need to go back to the countryside. But there are many young people in China today who have absolutely no direct experience with what rural China is like. At the same time, you can see that there is also a large group of writers who have kept that connection with rural China alive through their work. Generation after generation, writers have used their work to observe, bear witness, and record the rural experience. As far as literary works are concerned, this tradition has never been broken.

I wanted to use this film to record the experience of rural life in China from 1949 to the present; there was a drive to capture an experience that is disappearing right before our eyes. There are a lot of people in China today whose parents came from the countryside to the city, and although they are separated by just a single generation, the countryside is already a very distant place. Take, for example, Liang Hong's son: his mother has such a deep connection with the Chinese countryside, but when we get down to his generation, so much is already forgotten.[5] He can barely speak his mother's local dialect. So those are the two reasons that led me to make this film.

There are quite a few writers who appear on-screen in *Swimming*—Mo Yan, Su Tong, Li Jingze, Alai, et cetera. Why did you ultimately decide to home in on Jia Pingwa, Yu Hua, and Liang Hong? Could you talk about what drew you in to their work? Was it more about their body of work or their on-camera presence?

Once I decided to make a film like this, the first task was to select characters that I wanted to feature. I didn't want to restrict my film to just one specific period; I knew I wanted something with a much more expansive historical canvas. The Chinese people have experienced different challenges during different historical eras. So I wanted to explore what we have experienced during these past several decades. That is what lies at the heart of this film. So when it came to selecting subjects to be featured, I knew I wanted to highlight a group of writers instead of a single figure. In China we sometimes also categorize writers according to their generation, with each of their formative years representing a different historical era. So the first individual we selected was Ma Feng. He represents the period from 1949 through the 1950s and 1960s; that was a period of socialist construction and collectivism. There are questions from that era that we are implored to ask: Why collectivism? What were the historical factors that led to collectivism? What problems did collectivism attempt to solve? That's what led to my curiosity about Ma Feng. But since Ma Feng is no longer with us, I had to interview his daughter and other villagers who knew him to tell the story about what life was like during that era. The two elderly figures who are featured at the beginning of the film are both in their nineties, and they are the survivors, they are the witnesses to that history.

Jia Pingwa was born in the 1950s, so his memory begins with the late 1950s and early 1960s. By the time we get to Yu Hua, he is a writer born in the 1960s, and Liang Hong comes a generation later, as she was born in the 1970s. So when you put their experiences together, we can collectively create a relatively complete snapshot of social development during this period.

Another consideration has to do with location and space. Ma Feng and Jia Pingwa are both from Northwest China; Liang Hong is from Henan, which is in Central China; and Yu Hua is from a coastal region in Zhejiang Province called Haiyan. So from the perspective of the geographic mapping of China, we traverse a course that goes from Northwest China to Southeast China. In terms of time, we are covering seventy years of contemporary social change. But even more important is the fact that all of these writers share the experience of living in the countryside and have continued to observe and write about the rural experience over the course of their careers. Of course, many of them also live in the city now; for instance, Liang Hong was educated at Beijing Normal University and has been teaching at Renmin University for many years, but she has maintained her connection to the countryside. She has continued to write about rural China and is able to use this dual experience to express social change in China through her work.

Besides the different locations the film explores—Fenyang, Xi'an, Yellow River, and Haiyan—and the writers whose stories structure the film, you also use images of traditional Chinese arts, including opera, calligraphy, and poetry as a structuring device. Can you talk about how the structure of *Swimming Out Till the Sea Turns Blue* came together?

As you mentioned, the film highlights different regional opera performances. When the project began, I actually didn't plan to include any local opera; however, as the shoot continued I discovered that all of the writers featured were real opera fans! [*laughs*] Jia Pingwa is a true aficionado when it comes to Shaanxi opera; during the literary festival held in Fenyang I discovered that Mo Yan really wanted to hear Shanxi-style Peking opera. One unique characteristic about China is that every location has its own local opera tradition, which is marked primarily by the local dialect used to sing. I later decided to feature these local opera performances in the film because it is, after all, a film about writers, and these writers—Jia Pingwa, Liang Hong, et cetera—all feature a strong local color in terms of their use of language. Liang Hong always writes about Henan, and you can see a lot of elements from the Henan dialect in both her fiction and her nonfiction writings. Jia Pingwa also uses a quite a few elements unique to Shaanxi dialect in his fiction. Since the use of local dialect is a trait common to all of the writers featured, it opened the door to this question of language, which can also be extended through those opera sequences. So that is what led us to shoot those local opera performances, which represent the unique characteristics of those different regions and dialects.

I talked about how *Swimming Out Till the Sea Turns Blue* features multiple characters, a broad historical canvas, and traverses different locations, but those are elements that are not limited to this film alone. In fact, for the past few years I have been repeatedly pondering just what it is that keeps me coming back to films that appropriate this kind of a structure. For instance, both *Mountains May Depart* and *Ash Is Purest White* employ a similar approach that spans many years. I think it is partly due to the fact that we are now in the age of the internet, where we are inundated with different voices and different perspectives; in order to truly understand Chinese society, we need a more comprehensive perspective. I don't want to spend too much time on a tightly constrained time period or a specific problem; instead, I think we need to look at things from a macro perspective to really understand the inner structures. We need a *longue durée*-style perspective to observe, to feel, to understand, especially if we want to get deep enough to reveal the true cause-and-effect relationships that have brought us to where we are. I think this is important if we really want to understand Chinese society. That's why *Swimming Out Till the Sea Turns Blue* also employs this broad historical perspective. We could have chosen to focus on any one of several historical periods. For example, we could have just homed in on Yu Hua's generation or Liang Hong's generation; but if we really want to understand the era that Liang Hong is living in, I'm afraid we must still go back to Ma Feng's generation. Liang Hong's very personal, individual, and private style of writing can be truly appreciated only if you understand the philosophy of collectivism that dominated Chinese literature and society during the 1950s and 1960s. So this is a film that includes four individuals—Ma Feng, Jia Pingwa, Yu Hua, and Liang Hong—and spans seven decades; for me right now, I feel that in order to properly think through real issues concerning contemporary China, this kind of an overarching approach and comprehensive perspective is necessary.

Many of your documentary films have an interesting intertextual relationship with your feature films. For instance, *In Public* is tied to many of the locations used in *Unknown Pleasures*; *Dong* and *Still Life* are also very much campaign pieces that are deeply linked. Does *Swimming* also fit into the logic of your recent narrative films?

Swimming Out Till the Sea Turns Blue doesn't have a direct connection to my feature films in the same way that *In Public* was linked to *Unknown Pleasures* or *Dong* was connected to *Still Life*. But I suspect that some of the approach and experiments that I tried to put forth in *Swimming* may very well impact some future narrative films as I move forward. We just discussed the structure of the film in terms of space and time, but as I was editing *Swimming*, I realized that this is the single most subjective film I have ever made in terms of the content. In the end, we divided the film into eighteen chapters. This method of chapter division is, of course, a traditional structuring device used in Chinese literature, but these chapters follow a linear narrative that evolves from the stories of the writers featured. We quickly discover that each era and each generation are facing the problems of their respective eras. They are facing the challenges presented by the period in which they live. Their process of coming of age is also a process of trying to figure out how to solve these challenges. Each generation faces its own set of unique problems. In the end, we boiled these down to a set of eighteen keywords. For instance, at the beginning of the film we open with "Eating" (*chifan*); that is the foundation of our existence, and during the 1950s and 1960s, it was also the single greatest challenge faced by so many Chinese people who struggled with famine. It was the greatest hurdle that so many people needed to face. From there, we gradually begin to encounter other issues such as people's right to choose their own romantic partners [instead of arranged marriage], issues of illness and disease, and ultimately family problems. By the time the film gets to the story of Liang Hong, we end up confronting much more personal problems concerning her family, her father, her mother, and her sister. From this perspective, it is not a purely linear narrative; those eighteen chapters are like eighteen monuments. Each one of those monuments is a record of the pain we have experienced, like your own book, *A History of Pain*, documenting the challenges we have lived through. *Swimming Out Till the Sea Turns Blue* was the first time I attempted this kind of a subjective perspective and structure, but I suspect it will impact how I approach future projects as I move forward.

Fairly early in the film we start to see images of young people staring at their cell phones, and we hear the sound of cell phones ringing. . . . These images seem to mark a stark contrast with the older writers featured, who are usually portrayed in connection to traditional arts such as opera and calligraphy. Do you worry about the young generation's ability to enter into more complex narratives like feature films, opera, and novels? Do you feel we are facing a kind of crisis in terms of the state of traditional arts, culture, and literature in the face of tweets, texts, and the internet?

When I first started shooting those scenes of people on their cell phones, I was just thinking about the fact that this was a film about language, which is the tool for these writers. They employ language in their speech and through their writing, but everything they do is tied to language. In some sense, you can look at these writers as documenting an oral history, using their individual perspective to tell these stories. So it is only natural for the film to be filled with language. But I wanted the film to have two sides: filled with language on the one hand and silence on the other. I need something outside of language to balance the film. All the sections of the film dominated by language point us toward history, but all those stories are being related from our contemporary perspective, and that is also a very important vantage point. What is our contemporary economic and social reality from which we are telling this story? At what year, what time, what place are we relaying this history? This is just as important as the history being conveyed. So although most of the film is about history, there are also a lot of images of our current contemporary moment, the here and now, from which our perspective emerges.

There is also a private component to this film, the sections where people are retelling their personal stories, which runs alongside the public component. For the contemporary elements of the film, I mostly shot public spaces like train stations, people riding on trains, and street scenes. Collectively, these shots serve as a complement to the interview content with the featured writers, which reveals a more private and personal dimension. You could even look at them as creating a kind of yin-yang structure to the film.

In our everyday lives, if you shoot what is happening in public spaces like trains or train stations, you will see most young people staring down at their cell phones. But it's not just young people: you can see people from all age groups staring at their phones. The internet is quite well developed in China, and most people today spend much of their lives hunched over staring at their phones—it is a portal through which people get their news and information about the world. I'm not sure about the United States, but in China short videos are extremely popular. We used to get our information from text sources, but now news comes to us primarily through short videos, which is a completely different medium. This brings me back to an old question I keep returning to: for the past few years, I have continued to make films that span broad historical time frames. Every medium has its benefits and unique characteristics: for the internet, the benefits are the speed with which it can transmit information and its broad popularity. But that comes with a price: it is also fractured and provides only a partial glimpse of the whole story; it has no ability to give you the kind of comprehensive narrative description that literature is able to provide. It doesn't have the structure that literary works can provide. So in terms of the method we use to ponder the world, at least in terms of structure and comprehensiveness, we are gradually beginning to lose our historical perspective. If we look at film as a traditional art form, that's the reason why we insist on making full-length feature films instead of one- or two-minute-long short videos.

AUDIENCE: You talked about the broad historical canvas you have used in recent films like *Mountains May Depart* and *Ash Is Purest White*, but how did your historical perspective shift for a documentary film like *Swimming Out Till the Sea Turns Blue*?

The biggest difference comes from the fact that *Ash Is Purest White* begins in the 1990s, which was just before the economic development went into high gear and moved forward into the period of rapid urbanization; that film explores how the characters' traditional views of morality and relationships undergo changes over the course of this process. So in some sense, a film like *Ash* explores fate and the forces that tear people apart and separate them over the course of this unprecedented economic transformation. But *Swimming* begins in 1949, so it covers a much broader period of time during which Chinese society encountered many different challenges, including many waves of economic and political change. So here I am putting people within a much longer historical framework to observe. For a film like *Ash*, set in the 1990s, I myself am a witness to that history, so my attitude when I approach that era is very different from how I would approach the 1940s or 1950s. I was born in the 1970s; I have absolutely no personal experience when it comes to the 1950s or the 1960s, and that calls for me to use a historical approach where careful listening [*lingting*] is the most important trait. When making a film like this, we don't make too many judgments about history; we just try to understand why those things in the past happened. How did those historical actors solve the problems they faced? In order to convey and portray the reality of history, unlike *Ash*, this film required us to be more objective and to have a sense of distance in our approach.

Another reason we decided to structure the film along the lines of those eighteen chapters was that we wanted to trace the transition from a Chinese context to a more global perspective. Whether you are discussing themes like having enough food to eat; having the dignity to choose your own romantic partner; issues of aging, illness, and death; or family problems, these are all told from a Chinese perspective. But when you really think about it from a human perspective, these are common issues faced by all humanity.

It's not about Chinese people, but all of us. These are problems we all must face in life. We may come from different political systems, economic realities, and locations, our countries are all at different stages of development, but we all face these same issues. Sure, you could look at the stories in *Swimming* as collectively telling the story of the Chinese nation, but for me, it is really a history of humanity. It is the story of what we all experience. It is a film that emerges from a very local, nativist experience but opens up much broader avenues for reflecting on more universal questions.

AUDIENCE: A unique facet to your work is the notion of genre crossing, where you employ elements from different genres (martial arts, science fiction, gangster films, et cetera) and forms (narrative film, documentary film) in your work. Can you talk about this approach?

As an art form that is more than a hundred years old, film is a fairly closed medium in some respects. It may be a massive industry, but I feel it still needs to build bridges with other mediums and take its place as a part of contemporary art and culture. It shouldn't just continue to exist as it always has; it needs to be in dialogue with other arts. That's why I spend so much time interacting with artists, designers, and writers; that's why I explore the line between documentary and narrative film, and why I use my work to respond to real-life events that occur in the world. If we study film history, we will see that as early as the 1920s, whenever a major event in the world occurred, cameras would almost immediately appear on the scene to document what was happening. So film has always been about creating dialogue with the world around us. I have always held on to the hope that film as a medium can retain its flexibility, which I think we need more of in terms of what is coming out of the mainstream film industry today.

I also feel that interacting with artists from other mediums can open up new possibilities for film. We all come from the same humanistic society, but each medium has its own language: the language of painting, the language of design, the language of film. Each language represents its own unique method for observing the world. Film is a medium that has the benefit of being able to easily incorporate elements from these other worlds into its own language. I think that is one of the main reasons I am drawn to these genre-crossing and discipline-crossing explorations.

AUDIENCE: The title of the film comes from a quote from Yu Hua, but that wasn't the original title. Could you talk about the film's title?

The original title was not *Swimming Out Till the Sea Turns Blue*; it was actually *So Close to My Land* (*Yige cunzhuang de wenxue*). It was only after shooting the segment of the film involving Yu Hua that we decided to change the name of the film. Of the four main subjects featured in the film, Yu Hua was the last one we shot, and it was actually on the final day of shooting, when we went to the ocean near his hometown, that he told the story about swimming in the ocean when he was a child. [He was always told that the ocean was blue, but when he saw the water was green, he decided to swim out as far as he could until the water turned blue.] Since we had already shot all the other interviews by that time, when Yu Hua told that story, I immediately felt like it encapsulated so much of the spirit of what the other writers had talked about, so that is when we changed the title to *Swimming Out Till the Sea Turns Blue*. All four of the subjects featured have experienced so many challenges and difficulties in life, they have all lived through so much pain, and yet they keep pushing forward. There is an old Chinese parable about a foolish old man who tries to move a mountain; it tells the story of an old man who insists that he can move a mountain, and even if he fails, his son will carry on the work, so generation after generation, they will eventually move the mountain. It is essentially a parable about the Chinese people's willpower, perseverance, and lust for life. I thought that Yu Hua's story not only perfectly resonated with the stories of the other writers but also was an ocean version of the "old man who moves a mountain" parable. No matter what we may experience, we always strive to get to that beautiful place. So that place where the sea turns blue is the place of our hopes and our ideals.

And what is next for you? How has COVID-19 impacted your approach to filmmaking?

In 2020, before the outbreak of COVID-19, I had two completed screenplays; then, during the pandemic, I wrote two new screenplays. So I now have four screenplays in hand. But I still haven't decided which project I will shoot next; they span a lot of different subjects, including historical subjects and contemporary stories about young people today. After the experience of COVID-19, the world seems to have changed so much, and there are a lot of things that I need to rethink. I am still in the process of working through all of this. I feel as if something brand new has arrived, but I still don't know what that is. So I decided that, at this point, it is best to wait and take some time to understand myself.

Afterword

DAI JINHUA
Translated by Michael Berry

JIA ZHANGKE ON JIA ZHANGKE might surprisingly expose something quite deep about Chinese cinema as we are situated here in 2020, a year still playing out, that is destined to be recorded in history and remembered.

This is a narrative carried out through conversation, and over the course of the memories recalled, the story of a film director is told: his personal story—which everyone seems to have heard about, yet no one truly knows; his creative life—from what is nakedly displayed before the camera to what is hidden behind the scenes. Beginning during the final years of the twentieth century and running through the first two decades of the twenty-first century, Jia Zhangke's films have unfolded and provided a consistent thread through which to tie these two eras together, from the youthful and unyielding spirit of "independent cinema" where he first built his reputation to the point when his career ran parallel with the rise of the Chinese film industry. This is also a story whose form and meaning are revealed through dialogue: a story about film, art, artistic creation, and the choices that artists make. At the same time, it is a story about the river of life, tracing its movement through the rapids and winding corridors and its encounters with the shore.

Over the course of the past few decades, Jia Zhangke's films have left a record of the key threads running through some of contemporary China's most unusual stories. Initially he was unable to show his work in Chinese theaters and official screening venues; instead, he was met only with challenges.

Thus, he was forced to go through the "narrow gate" of the European film festival circuit, eventually succeeding Zhang Yimou and Zhang Yuan as a name synonymous with "Chinese film" in the world of international art house cinema. From there, as the Chinese film industry witnessed its own resurgence and process of rejuvenation, Jia Zhangke would experience all kinds of interactions (and sometimes clashes) with the commercial side of the industry up until the present day in which he is now regarded as one of the shining stars of Chinese cinema. However, the meaning of Jia Zhangke lies not in identifying a different culture or a different phase in film history, nor in describing or clarifying those binary symbols that had for so long been projected on the coordinates of Chinese cinema: art versus commerce, international film festivals versus the local Chinese market, the city versus the country, the super metropolis versus the small inland town, "Mandarin Chinese" versus local dialects, independent versus official, "auteur" film versus genre film, or documentary film versus fiction film. Through it all, Jia Zhangke has persistently held true to his ideals, flexibly adapting to changes along the way. Rather than saying he has described or clarified these binaries, it would be more fitting to understand Jia's films as continually clashing with, and sometimes cutting through, those mutually opposing binaries and seemingly fixed dividing lines. There seems to be an established consensus on Jia Zhangke's identity as a "Chinese auteur," and yet he himself does not seem at all attached or committed to a single "signature style." Instead, he repeatedly translates his interactions with China and the world into film and, in the process, quietly extends the very boundaries of what cinema can be. Jia Zhangke's "Fenyang" thus becomes a site that is highly distinctive and brimming with rich details. All this makes *Jia Zhangke on Jia Zhangke* all the more interesting.

In these interviews that Michael Berry has conducted and recorded, our attention is drawn from the outside to the inside as we gaze toward China, film, art, and ultimately Jia Zhangke as he responds and reflects. Along the way, Berry intently listens as he tries to capture and identify the various "accents" that are spoken. Is this a Chinese accent or a Fenyang accent from Shanxi? But he seems to be more interested in the accent of the individual, the accent of art, the accent of film, and the accent of style. He is interested in hearing Jia Zhangke's voice, hearing his "accent." Pushing the interviewer forward and supporting the conversation is a rich genealogy of knowledge concerning film art, art house cinema, and film auteurs or, as we might call them, film artists. Through these interviews, Jia Zhangke responds to questions and thinks back, reflecting on moments on set and moments in life, artistic decisions and happenstance occurrences, his understanding of things and various misreadings. And through the questions and answers contained within this book you can also see the "faith" and "suspicions" lingering when it comes to art/film art; the deep respect a scholar holds for the artist/auteur/director; the artist's willingness to answer the questions of the researcher; and the humor, informal comfort, and deep connection between a filmmaker and his friend. Undoubtedly, there is also a sense of dislocation and fluctuation as we move from "inside" to "outside." To gaze at Jia Zhangke's films is to gaze not only into the small city of Fenyang but also into one part of contemporary China. On the margins of those international metropolises, you find these small provincial cities where you will discover nameless individuals and floating laborers, but these were never really ever "alien places" or "somewhere else." Ever since the time that Jia Zhangke's films first appeared, the movement behind China's radical transformation and "great migration" toward globalization has begun to spill "inward," beginning in places like Fenyang and extending outward, unfolding like a scroll of moving images. Perhaps in some ways this book represents overlapping conversations and perspectives about "inside" and "outside." The book is not simply an American scholar of Chinese literature's focus on a Chinese film director; it also represents the expression of an overlap between "the external side of what's inside" and "the internal side of what's outside." It is just like the UFO lingering in the sky in *Still Life* or the "worldly" bullets loaded into a theme park. During that unique period of transition between centuries, between the rush hour of China's hundred years of modernization and the period of intermission as they prepared to change the stage; it was during this period that "the West" was suddenly no longer regarded as some distant, faraway place; it had already taken its place deep in our cultural self-consciousness. At the same time, China was no longer an "Other" space to be controlled by Europe and America; it was now at the cutting edge of the modern world. In the form of the dialogue contained here, through these interlocking perspectives, the story of Fenyang is always the story of China, as it is also the story of the world under globalization. We set out from the platform and, strolling through the crowds of people, look down from the cliffs in Fengjie and see the "Shanxi" mines and those sons and daughters of *jianghu* wandering about the modern cities, and though it is hanging right there on a string around their very necks, they still can't find the key to get home . . .

Perhaps at the turn of the century, during this moment in Chinese cinematic and cultural history, Jia Zhangke, his classmates, and people from his generation consciously or unconsciously began to transform how Chinese films tell their story. We began with the Fifth Generation, for whom space, ritual aesthetics of historical commemoration, and wandering lives were caught in time; what came later was a process of transformation through which people came to distinguish between their frozen imagination about China and the hyperfast, ultramodern reality of what China had become. Of course, Jia Zhangke also attempts to traverse time itself in order to capture remnants of a quickly fading past, yet as his films race toward the river of time, it is perhaps only from the future that we can capture a true still life image of what we have seen. Jia Zhangke may not be an old-fashioned storyteller, yet in this book he offers us the story of his films' stories. In responding to Michael Berry's questions, he recounts, reflects, and states his views. Sometimes, he sidesteps, offering subtle counterstatements or self-defensive comments. It is through these moments that we can catch a glimpse of the continuities and fissures between film time, narrative time, and world time.

It is 2020, and as the demonic shadow of COVID-19 continues to haunt the world, we attempt to restart the clock of modernity. And here arrives a book of conversations about cinema, situating itself amid a fissure whose lines and scope are still not yet clear; a book of memories about cinema, which is, after all, "an installation of memories."

SEPTEMBER 20, 2020
BEIJING

Notes

INTRODUCTION

1. Dai Jinhua, *After the Post–Cold War: The Future of Chinese History* (Durham, NC: Duke University Press, 2018), 75.
2. Corey Kai Nelson Schultz, *Moving Figures: Class and Feeling in the Films of Jia Zhangke* (Edinburgh: Edinburgh University Press, 2018), 34.
3. For more on representations of marginalized figures in the film of Jia Zhangke, see Xie Xiaoxia, *Research on the Image of the Lower Class in Contemporary Cinema* [当代电影底层形象研究] (Kunming: Yunnan People's Publishing House, 2009), 264–317.
4. Li Yang, *The Formation of Chinese Art Cinema, 1990–2003* (London: Palgrave Macmillan, 2018), 162–63.
5. Shaoyi Sun and Li Xun, *Lights! Camera! Kai Shi! In Depth Interviews with China's New Generation of Movie Directors* (Norwalk, CT: Eastbridge Books, 2008), 94.
6. Cecilia Mello, *The Cinema of Jia Zhangke: Realism and Memory in Chinese Film* (London: I. B. Tauris, 2019), 5.
7. Qi Wang, *Memory, Subjectivity and Independent Chinese Cinema* (Edinburgh: Edinburgh University Press, 2014), 96.
8. See Jason McGrath, "The Independent Cinema of Jia Zhangke: From Postsocialist Realism to a Transnational Aesthetic," in *The Urban Generation: Chinese Cinema and Society at the Turn of the Twenty-First Century*, ed. Zhen Zhang (Durham, NC: Duke University Press, 2007), 81–114; Yang, *Formation of Chinese Art Cinema*.
9. Yang, *Formation of Chinese Art Cinema*, 161.
10. When Jia Zhangke announced he was stepping down from the film festival, he made a widely quoted public statement: "I should've left [the festival] earlier and

begun to groom a new team to take over the festival, so that this festival can get rid of 'Jia Zhangke's shadow.'" This version is from an October 19, 2020, report in *Variety* by Vivienne Chow titled "Jia Zhangke Unexpectedly Quits the Pingyao Film Festival." The ambiguous nature of Jia's statement led to widespread rumors and conjecture about political meddling in the festival. On June 1, 2021, just over six months after he left the Pingyao International Film Festival, it was announced that Jia would return to the festival for its fifth edition in 2021, although his new role remains unclear.

ONE. A PORTRAIT OF AN ARTIST AS A YOUNG MAN

Chapter 1 includes some content excerpted from my 2002 interview with Jia Zhangke, originally published in *Speaking in Images: Interviews with Contemporary Chinese Filmmakers* (New York: Columbia University Press, 2005).

1. Ulan Bator would later become an important site for the film *The World*, which not only references the city but also prominently features the Mongolian folk song "Ulan Bator Night" ("Wulan Batuo de ye").

2. Teresa Teng (Deng Lijun, 1953–95) was one of the most popular Chinese singers and performers during the second half of the twentieth century. Teng was the first Taiwanese singer to gain widespread popularity in mainland China during the early Reform Era. Best known for her love ballads, such as "The Moon Represents My Heart" and "My Sweetie," Teng released albums in Mandarin, Taiwanese, Cantonese, Japanese, and English.

3. Chang Ti (Zhang Di, 1942–) is a popular Taiwan singer and talk show host. Sometimes referred to as the "quick-witted pop star" (*jizhi gewang*) for his ability to respond in real time to audience questions with humorous lines of song, Chang is best known for the songs "The Hair Song" ("Mao mao ge") and "The Nation" ("Guojia"), the latter being a patriotic song that became very popular in mainland China.

4. "Go with Your Feelings" ("Gen zhe ganjue zuo," 1988) is a popular song from Taiwan written and composed by Chen Zhiyuan and originally sung by Taiwan pop star Su Rui and included on the album *Taipei Tokyo*. An excerpt of the lyrics reads: "Follow your feelings, let them take me away / I hope you will be not far away waiting for me / Follow your feelings, let them take me away / Those things we dream about will be everywhere." This was one of the most popular songs in late 1980s China.

5. Cui Jian (1961–) is one of the earliest innovators of pop and rock music in mainland China during the early Reform Era and is generally referred to as the "father of Chinese rock and roll." His representative albums include *Rock Along the New Long March* (*Xin changzheng lushang de yaogun*), *Solution* (*Jiejue*), and *Eggs under the Red Flag* (*Hongqi xia de dan*). Cui Jian is best known for his rock anthems from the 1980s, including "I Have Nothing to My Name" ("Yiwu suoyou"), "It's Not That I Don't Understand" ("Bushi wo bumingbai"), "The Fake Monk" ("Jia xingzeng"), and "Greenhouse Girl" ("Huafang guniang"), which were extremely influential. Cui Jian is also active in film circles and directed the feature film *Blue Sky Bones* (*Lanse gutou*, 2013).

NOTES TO INTRODUCTION

6. *Garrison's Gorillas* was a twenty-six-episode miniseries originally broadcast on ABC in 1967. It tells the story of First Lieutenant Garrison and the daring suicide squad he led in Europe during World War II, focusing on a series of their missions. After the reestablishment of Sino-US relations in 1979, *Garrison's Gorillas* was one of the first American television miniseries to be broadcast in China. The Chinese version was dubbed by the Shanghai Film Dubbing Studio and broadcast on CCTV in 1980, and it was warmly received by Chinese audiences. *Man from Atlantis* was a thirteen-episode science fiction–fantasy miniseries originally broadcast on NBC between 1977 and 1978. It was one of the earliest American television shows to be broadcast in China during the early stages of the Reform Era.

7. *Breakin'* was a mainstream 1984 film documenting the challenges faced by a group of young break-dancers. The film was extremely popular in China and even inspired Tian Zhuangzhuang's film *Rock Kids* (*Yaogun qingnian*, 1988).

8. *Life* (*Rensheng*), a novella written by Lu Yao (1949–92), was originally published in 1982 and was awarded the National Prize for Most Outstanding Novella of that year. The story follows Gao Jialin, who travels back and forth between the city and the countryside as he finds himself caught in a love triangle that included the peasant girl Liu Qiaozhan and the city girl Huang Yaping. The story was widely acclaimed and in 1984 was adapted into an award-winning film under the same title by Wu Tianming.

9. The film *Old Well* (*Lao jing*, 1986), which was adapted from a novel by Zheng Yi, was produced by the Xi'an Film Studio and directed by Wu Tianming. The film starred Zhang Yimou, in his first role as an actor, and Lu Liping. It depicted the difficult lives of peasants in an impoverished village in northwest China and their struggle to dig a well.

10. Misty Poetry was a poetry movement that took place during the late 1970s and early 1980s in large part as an artistic response against the Cultural Revolution. The movement was criticized by officials who described it as "misty," "murky," or "hazy," which the movement's founders eventually took on as a point of pride, standing in opposition to the black-and-white directives of Maoist art. The representative figures of the movement included Han Lu, Shu Ying, Bei Dao, Gu Cheng, Liang Xiaobin, Ouyang Jianghe, Mang Ke, and Shi Zhi. Many of these poets published in the journal *Today* (*Jintian*), which became one of the most progressive and influential portals for intellectuals and artists during the early Reform Era.

11. Bei Dao's poem "The Answer" (1976) is one of the most important representative works from this early period of his writing. Originally published in the 1976 issue of *Today*, it was an attempt to interrogate what happened during the Cultural Revolution and bring out the absurdity of that era. An excerpt of the poem reads: "Let me tell you, world / I—do—not—believe! / If a thousand challengers lie beneath your feet, / Count me as number thousand and one. / I don't believe the sky is blue; / I don't believe in thunder's echoes; / I don't believe that dreams are false; / I don't believe that death has no revenge" (translated by Bonnie S. McDougall from *The August Sleepwalker*).

12. Chen Kaige's *Yellow Earth* (*Huang tudi*, 1984) is considered one of the most important early representative films of the Fifth Generation. Besides Chen Kaige, the

film featured several other important figures from the Fifth Generation, including cinematographer Zhang Yimou, art designer He Ping, and composer Zhao Jiping. *Yellow Earth* was adapted from an essay entitled "Echoes from Deep in the Valley" ("Shengu huisheng") by Ke Lan. The story is about a soldier named Gu Qing (Wang Xueqi) who travels to a remote village in northern Shaanxi Province to collect folk songs. While he is there, he witnesses great poverty and encounters an adolescent girl named Cuiqiao (Xue Bai), who is desperate to escape from an impending arranged marriage and join the Eight Route Army. But in the end Gu Qing is unable to save her from her circumstances. The film received numerous international awards but proved controversial at home, becoming a key work of the "Culture Fever" that swept China during the 1980s.

13. *The Story of Qiuju* was awarded the Golden Lion and the Volpi Cup at the 1992 Venice Film Festival; *To Live* was awarded the prize for Best Actor and the Grand Prix at the 1994 Cannes Film Festival; and *Farewell My Concubine* was awarded the Palme d'Or at the 1993 Cannes Film Festival and the Best Foreign Language Film at the 1994 Golden Globe Awards and also was a nominee for Best Foreign Language Film at the Academy Awards.

14. *Dingjun Shan*, sometimes translated as *Taking Army Mountain*, was the first Chinese film ever produced. First exhibited on December 28, 1905, it was directed by Ren Qingtai and starred Peking opera star Tan Xinpei. The content of the film was adapted from a Peking opera of the same name, which in turn was derived from a story in *Romance of the Three Kingdoms* (*Sanguo yanyi*).

15. Besides being an established cinematographer who has shot such features as Ann Hui's *Ordinary Heroes* (*Qianyan wanyu*, 1999) and William Kwok's *In the Dumps* (*Laji niantou*, 1997), Nelson Yu Lik-Wai (1966–) is also an established director in his own right. His 1999 feature *Love Will Tear Us Apart* (*Tian shang renjian*) was an official selection at Cannes the year of its release and is also playfully referenced in *Unknown Pleasures*. Yu has served as cinematographer for almost all of Jia Zhangke's feature films.

16. Robert Bresson (1901–99) was a painter and film director who became a key figure in French cinema. After beginning to make films in 1934, Bresson directed thirteen feature films over the course of more than four decades. His major works include *A Man Escaped* (1956), *Pickpocket* (1959), *Diary of a Country Priest* (1951), and *The Trial of Joan of Arc* (1962).

17. Eric Gautier (1961–) is an award-winning French cinematographer who has worked on films by Agnès Varda, Olivier Assayas, Walter Salles, Sean Penn, Alain Resnais, Ang Lee, and Hirokazu Koreeda.

TWO. THE HOMETOWN TRILOGY

Chapter 2 includes some content excerpted from my 2002 interview with Jia Zhangke, originally published in *Speaking in Images: Interviews with Contemporary Chinese Filmmakers* (New York: Columbia University Press, 2005).

1. After the success of his work with Jia Zhangke, Wang Hongwei has been increasingly in demand as an actor and was featured in Dai Sijie's production of his novel

Balzac and the Little Chinese Seamstress (2002). He later eased into film production and has produced several independent Chinese films.

2. *The Human Condition* has been made into a film by producer-director Michael Cimino under the title *Man's Fate* (2003).

3. Lu Xun (1881–1936), the father of modern Chinese literature, gave up a career in medicine and began writing after seeing a slide of a Chinese man being executed surrounded by a crowd of his compatriots, who looked on numbly as the sentence was carried out. Images of apathetic crowds would be featured prominently in several of Lu Xun's later literary works, such as *The True Story of Ah Q* (*Ah Q zhengzhuan*, 1921).

4. Kent Jones, *Physical Evidence: Selected Film Criticism* (Middletown: Wesleyan University Press, 2007), 24.

THREE. DOCUMENTING DESTRUCTION AND BUILDING WORLDS

1. Liu Xiaodong (1963–) is a contemporary Chinese artist. He studied at the Central Academy of Fine Arts, earning both a BA and an MFA in oil painting, and later furthered his study in Madrid. His work has been exhibited in major exhibitions, museums, and galleries around the world. He has also had numerous ties with the independent Chinese cinema movement, starring in one of the first Chinese independent films, *The Days* (*Dongchun de rizi*, 1990), serving as art director for *Beijing Bastards* (*Beijing zazong*, 1993), and even becoming the subject of documentary films by Jia Zhangke and also Yao Hung-I's *Hometown Boy* (*Jincheng xiaozi*, 2011).

2. Takeshi Kitano (1947–) is a prolific Japanese actor, director, comedian, television personality, and film producer. Sometimes referred to as Beat Takeshi, he has directed more than eighteen films and starred in more than fifty; his major works include *Sonatine* (1993), *Hana-bi* (1997), *Brother* (2000), and *Zatoichi* (2003).

3. Shozo Ichiyama (1963–) is a Japanese film producer who has produced films such as *Violent Cop* (1989), *Lovers on Borders* (2017), and *Chasuke's Journey* (2015). He has worked on several Chinese-language films, including Hou Hsiao-hsien's *Flowers of Shanghai* (1998), *Good Men, Good Women* (1995), and *Goodbye South, Goodbye* (1996) and Edward Yang's *Yi Yi* (2000). He has collaborated with Jia Zhangke on numerous films, including *Platform*, *Unknown Pleasures*, and *The World*.

4. Jean-Pierre Melville (1917–73) was a French filmmaker best known for classic films like *Le Doulos* (1962), *Le Samouraï* (1967), *Army of Shadows* (*L'armée des ombres*, 1969), and *Le cercle rouge* (1970). His work had a major influence on the French New Wave and later influenced a new generation of East Asian filmmakers, including Johnnie To, John Woo, and Takeshi Kitano.

FOUR. FILM AS SOCIAL JUSTICE

1. The raw interviews upon which Jia Zhangke structured *24 City* were published in a full-length collection, *Interviews with Chinese Workers: 24 City* [*Zhongguo gongren fangtanlu: Ershisi chengji*] (Jinan: Shandong Pictorial Publishing, 2009).

2. The Third Line Construction Project (*sanxian gongcheng* or *sanxian jianshe*) was a national government plan implemented in 1964 in response to escalating tensions brought on by the Vietnam War, American military activities near the South China Sea, and a small-scale armed skirmish with the Soviet Union. The Third Line Construction Project was aimed at expanding the infrastructure in China's less populated inland regions to bolster national defense, science and technology, industry, power, and transportation. It originated with the Chinese military and ended up impacting thirteen provinces and autonomous regions in central and western China from 1964 until 1980, resulting in the creation of thousands of factories, the relocation of millions of people, and a fundamental shift in the priorities of national development.

3. Zhai Yongming (1955–) is a poet from Chengdu who began publishing her work in 1981. She has published more than a dozen collections of essays and poetry; one representative work is the twenty-poem cycle "Woman" ("Nüren").

4. This is reference to a series of suicides that took place at a Foxconn factory in southern China in 2010. The suicides led to a large number of news stories about the working conditions of Foxconn employees.

5. Lu Zhishen is a character from the novel *The Water Margin*. He is one of the 108 heroes of Liangshan who is known for his short temper, unmatched strength, and uncompromising sense of justice. Originally named Lu Da, he was once an army officer, but after being charged with murder during a battle, he deserted his post and became a monk, assuming the Buddhist name Lu Zhishen.

6. Wu Song is another character from the novel *The Water Margin* who also appears in the classic novel *The Golden Lotus* (*Jinping mei*). An orphan raised by his elder brother Wu Dalang, Wu Song was renowned for his uncanny strength and became known for killing a tiger with his bare hands. Later, when his brother became the victim of adultery and the target of a murder plot, Wu Song killed his brother's unfaithful wife, Pan Jinlian, along with her lover, Ximen Qing.

7. The wuxia films of King Hu (Hu Jinquan) frequently featured strong female protagonists, such as Golden Swallow (Cheng Pei-pei) in *Come Drink with Me* (1966) and Yang Hui-zhen (Hsu Feng) in *A Touch of Zen* (1971). The English title of *A Touch of Sin* is also clearly inspired by the latter film. In a direct reaction against the dominance of female stars in Hong Kong cinema from the 1960s, Chang Cheh's (Zhang Che's) martial arts kung fu films like *The Heroic Ones* (*Shisan taibao*, 1970) and *The Blood Brothers* (*Ci ma*, 1973) featured male-dominated casts and highlighted a new notion of masculinity.

8. *Forest of the Wild Boar* (*Yezhu lin*, 1962) was an opera film produced by the Beijing Film Studio. It was codirected by Cui Wei and Chen Huai'ai and starred Li Shaochun, Du Jinfang, and Yuan Shihai.

9. Lin Chong is a fictional character from the classic Chinese novel *The Water Margin*. Lin was a skilled martial artist and an instructor of the Chinese imperial guards when the son of a powerful official attempted to steal his wife. This plot led to Lin Chong's false arrest and exile. Eventually, Lin joined the 108 outlaws of Liangshan

and became one of their leaders. Lin Chong's story has been popular in numerous forms, also appearing in several traditional Chinese operas, including *Record of the Precious Sword* (*Baojian ji*) and *Lin Chong Fleeing by Night* (*Lin Chong yeben*).

10. Tian Zhuangzhuang (1952–) is a representative figure from the Fifth Generation. While best known for his fifteen feature films as director, including *On the Hunting Ground* (*Liechang zhasa*, 1985), *The Horse Thief* (*Daomazei*, 1986), and *The Blue Kite* (*Lanfeng zheng*, 1993), Tian has also served as producer for several independent Chinese filmmakers. He has also won acclaim for his acting in films like *Love Education* (*Xiangai xiangqin*, 2017) and *Us and Them* (*Houlaide women*, 2018).

FIVE. RETURN TO JIANGHU

1. Lord Guan (Guan gong), or Guan Yu, was a historical figure who served as a general under the warlord Liu Bei during the Eastern Han dynasty. He was renowned for his loyalty and military prowess. After his death, his achievements were glorified through literature (like the novel *Romance of the Three Kingdoms*) and through various dramas and stories. Over time, he came to be worshipped as a deity by various Chinese folk religions, with shrines and statues found all over the Chinese-speaking world.

2. Wei Wei (1922–) is best known for her role in *Spring in a Small Town*. She was most active between 1948 and 1964, during which time she starred in more than fifteen films.

3. Sally Yeh (Ye Qianwen, 1961–) was born in Taipei and immigrated to Canada at a young age before starting her singing career in Hong Kong in the early 1980s. She was one of the most popular Mandopop and Cantopop singers of the 1980s and 1990s and has released more than thirty albums. Yeh also starred in more than twenty-five films from 1980 through the early 1990s.

4. She Ai'zhen first became involved with the Shanghai underworld during the Republican period. She was the goddaughter of Li Yunqing and later married the notorious gangster Wu Sibao. After Wu Sibao's death, She began a relationship with Hu Lancheng, who was serving in the Ministry of Propaganda for the Wang Jingwei puppet regime. In 1945, She was arrested and served a seven-year sentence; on her release, she moved to Hong Kong and later settled in Japan.

5. Hu Lancheng (1906–81) was a writer, intellectual, and politician who served in the Ministry of Propaganda under Wang Jingwei during the Japanese occupation of Shanghai. His major works include *China through Time* (*Shanhe suiyue*, 1954) and *This Life, This World* (*Jinsheng jinshi*, 1959). He was married to the noted writer Eileen Chang from 1944 to 1946 and later served as a mentor to Taiwan writers Chu Tien-wen and Chu Tien-hsin.

6. In the wake of the tax scandal that shook the Chinese film industry in 2018, Feng Xiaogang's scenes from *Ash Is Purest White* were cut from the domestically released version of the film, although his scenes were still shown in versions screened at various international film festivals.

CODA

1. Jia Pingwa (1952–) is a prolific and popular writer best known for the novels *Happy Dreams* (*Gaoxing*), *Broken Wings* (*Jihua*), *The Lantern Bearer* (*Dai deng*), *The Mountain Whisperer* (*Laosheng*), and *Ruined City* (*Feidu*). He is the winner of the 2009 Mao Dun Literature Prize and is generally considered one the greatest Chinese writers of his generation.

2. Shen Congwen (1902–88) was a leading Chinese writer active during the Republican period, when he wrote such classic works as *The Border Town* (*Biancheng*) and a series of acclaimed short stories. After 1949, he turned away from fiction and spent the second half of his life conducting research on traditional Chinese costumes and clothing. Eileen Chang (Zhang Ailing, 1920–95) was a novelist, screenwriter, translator, and essayist best known for her works of classic fiction like *Half a Lifelong Romance* (*Bansheng yuan*), *Love in a Fallen City* (*Qingcheng zhi lian*), and *Lust, Caution* (*Se jie*). Her work has been adapted into numerous films and has been widely influential across the Chinese-speaking world.

3. Su Tong (1963–) is a contemporary Chinese writer best known for the books *Raise the Red Lantern* (*Qiqie chengqun*), *Rice* (*Mi*), *My Life as Emperor* (*Wo de diwang shengya*), and *Petulia's Rouge Tin* (*Hongfen*). Yu Hua (1960–) is a contemporary Chinese writer whose major works include the novels *To Live* (*Huozhe*), *Chronicle of a Blood Merchant* (*Xu Sanguan maixue ji*), and *Brothers* (*Xiongdi*) and the collection of nonfiction essays *China in Ten Words* (*Shige cihui li de Zhongguo*). Sun Ganlu (1959–) is an influential writer who came to prominence in the 1980s and was closely associated with the Chinese avant-garde movement. His major works include the novel *Breathing* (*Huxi*) and *The Messenger's Letter* (*Xinshi zhi han*).

4. Ma Feng (1922–2004) was a veteran writer of numerous novels, essays, and short stories including *The First Investigation* (*Diyici zhencha*) and *Vendetta* (*Cun chou*). He fought against the Japanese during the War of Resistance and joined the Chinese Communist Party in 1938, later doing cultural work, education, and propaganda in Yan'an. He also wrote the screenplay to several films, including *Marriage* (*Jiehun*, 1953).

5. Liang Hong (1973–) is a professor of Chinese literature at Renmin University. She is also the author of several books of literary criticism, essays, and fiction. She is best known for the book *China in One Village* (*Zhongguo zai Liangzhuang*).

Jia Zhangke Filmography

FEATURE-LENGTH FILMS

1997 *Xiao Wu* aka *Pickpocket* [小武]
2000 *Platform* [站台]
2002 *Unknown Pleasures* [任逍遥]
2004 *The World* [世界]
2006 *Dong* [东] (documentary)
2006 *Still Life* [三峡好人]
2007 *Useless* [无用] (documentary)
2008 *24 City* [二十四城记]
2010 *I Wish I Knew* [海上传奇] (documentary)
2013 *A Touch of Sin* [天注定]
2015 *Mountains May Depart* [山河故人]
2018 *Ash Is Purest White* [江湖儿女]
2020 *Swimming Out Till the Sea Turns Blue* [一直游到海水变蓝] (documentary)

SHORT FILMS

1994 *One Day in Beijing* [有一天，在北京]
1995 *Xiao Shan Going Home* [小山回家]
1996 *Du Du* [嘟嘟]
2001 *In Public* [公共场所]
2001 *La condition canine* [狗的状况]
2006 *This Moment* [这一刻]

2007	*Our Ten Years*	[我们的十年]	
2008	*Black Breakfast*	[黑色早餐]	
2008	*Cry Me a River*	[河上的爱情]	
2009	*Remembrance*	[十年]	
2011	*Cao Fei*	[曹斐]	
2011	*Pan Shiyi*	[潘石屹]	
2011	*3:11 Sense of Home*	[3:11 家的感觉]	
2013	*Future Reloaded*	[重启未来]	
2015	*Smog Journeys*	[人在雾途]	
2016	*The Hedonists*	[营生]	
2017	*Revive*	[逢春]	
2019	*The Bucket*	[一个桶]	
2020	*Visit*	[来访]	
2021	*My Little Wish*	[有一个小店叫童年]	

OTHER CREDITS

2002	*Overloaded Peking* (actor)		
2003	*All Tomorrow's Parties* [明日天涯] (producer)		
2003	*My Camera Doesn't Lie* [我的摄影机不撒谎] (actor)		
2006	*Karmic Mahjong* [血战到底] (actor)		
2006	*A Walk on the Wild Side* [赖小子] (producer)		
2008	*Perfect Life* [完美生活] (producer)		
2013	*Boundless* [无涯：杜琪峰的电影世界] (actor)		
2013	*Forgetting to Know You* [忘了去懂你] (producer)		
2014	*The Continent* [后会无期] (actor)		
2014	*Jia Zhang-ke, A Guy from Fenyang* [汾阳小子贾樟柯] (actor/subject)		
2015	*Chen Jialeng* [陈家冷] (producer)		
2016	*Everybody's Fine* [一切都好] (actor)		
2020	*Pseudo Idealist* [不浪漫] (actor)		

Bibliography

WESTERN SOURCES

Berry, Michael. "Cultural Fallout." *Film Comment*, March/April 2003, 61–64.

Berry, Michael. "Jia Zhangke: Capturing a Transforming Reality" (interview). In *Speaking in Images: Interviews with Contemporary Chinese Filmmakers*, edited by Michael Berry, 182–207. New York: Columbia University Press, 2005.

Berry, Michael. *Jia Zhangke's Hometown Trilogy: Xiao Wu, Platform, Unknown Pleasures*. New York: Palgrave Macmillan, 2009.

Dai Jinhua. *After the Post–Cold War: The Future of Chinese History*. Durham, NC: Duke University Press, 2018.

Edwards, Dan. *Independent Chinese Documentary: Alternative Visions, Alternative Publics*. Edinburgh: Edinburgh University Press, 2015.

Frodon, Jean Michel. *Le Monde de Jia Zhang-ke*. Crisnée: Editions Yellow Now, 2016.

Hui, Calvin. "Dirty Fashion: Ma Ke's Fashion 'Useless,' Jia Zhangke's Documentary *Useless* and Cognitive Mapping." *Journal of Chinese Cinemas* 9, no. 3 (2015): 253–70.

Jaffee, Valerie. "Bringing the World to the Nation: Jia Zhangke and the Legitimation of Chinese Underground Film." *Senses of Cinema*, no. 32 (July 2004). https://www.sensesofcinema.com/2004/feature-articles/chinese_underground_film/.

Jia Zhangke. *Jia Zhangke Speaks Out: The Chinese Director's Texts on Films*. Translated by Claire Huot, Tony Rayns, Alice Shih, and Sebastian Veg. Piscataway, NJ: Transaction Publishers, 2014.

Jones, Kent. "Out of Time." *Film Comment*, September/October 2002, 43–47.

Jones, Kent. *Physical Evidence: Selected Film Criticism*. Middletown, CT: Wesleyan University Press, 2007.

Kaufman, Mariana, and Jo Serfaty. *Jia Zhangke, a cidade em quadro*. Rio de Janeiro: Fagulha Films, 2014.

Kraicer, Shelly. "Interview with Jia Zhangke." *Cineaction* 60 (2003): 30–33.

Li, David Leiwei. *Economy, Emotion, and Ethics in Chinese Cinema: Globalization on Speed*. New York: Routledge, 2016.

Lin, Xiaoping. "Jia Zhangke's Cinematic Trilogy: A Journey across the Ruins of Post-Mao China." In *Chinese-Language Film: Historiography, Poetics, Politics*, edited by Sheldon H. Lu and Emilie Yueh-yu Yeh, 186–209. Honolulu: University of Hawai'i Press, 2005.

McGrath, Jason. "The Independent Cinema of Jia Zhangke: From Postsocialist Realism to a Transnational Aesthetic." In *The Urban Generation: Chinese Cinema and Society at the Turn of the Twenty-First Century*, edited by Zhen Zhang, 81–114. Durham, NC: Duke University Press, 2007.

McGrath, Jason. *Postsocialist Modernity: Chinese Cinema, Literature, and Criticism in the Market Age*. Stanford, CA: Stanford University Press, 2010.

Mello, Cecília. *The Cinema of Jia Zhangke: Realism and Memory in Chinese Film*. London: I. B. Tauris, 2019.

Schultz, Corey Kai Nelson. *Moving Figures: Class and Feeling in the Films of Jia Zhangke*. Edinburgh: Edinburgh University Press, 2018.

Sun, Shaoyi, and Li Xun. *Lights! Camera! Kai Shi! In Depth Interviews with China's New Generation of Movie Directors*. Norwalk, CT: Eastbridge Books, 2008.

Wang, Qi. *Memory, Subjectivity and Independent Chinese Cinema*. Edinburgh: Edinburgh University Press, 2014.

Xiao, Ying. *China in the Mix: Cinema, Sound, and Popular Culture in the Age of Globalization*. Jackson: University Press of Mississippi, 2017.

Yang, Li. *The Formation of Chinese Art Cinema, 1990–2003*. London: Palgrave Macmillan, 2018.

CHINESE SOURCES

Bai Ruiwen (Michael Berry). *An Accented Cinema: Jia Zhangke on Jia Zhangke* [电影的口音：贾樟柯谈贾樟柯]. Guilin: Guangxi Normal University Press, 2021.

Cheng Qingsong and Huang Ou. "Jia Zhangke: Waiting on the Platform" [贾樟柯：在站台等待]. In *My Camera Doesn't Lie: Files on Avant-Garde Filmmakers Born between 1961–1970* [我的摄影机不撒谎：先锋电影人档案——生于1961–1970]. Beijing: China Friendship Press, 2002.

Jia Zhangke. *Interviews with Chinese Workers: 24 City* [中国工人访谈录：二十四城记]. Jinan: Shandong Pictorial Publishing, 2009.

Jia Zhangke. *Jia's Thoughts on Film I: Jia Zhangke's Film Notebook, 1996–2008* [贾想I：贾樟柯电影手记1996–2008]. Edited by Wan Jiahuan. Beijing: Taihai Publishing, 2017.

Jia Zhangke. *Jia's Thoughts on Film II: Jia Zhangke's Film Notebook, 2008–2016* [贾想II：贾樟柯电影手记2008-2016]. Edited by Wan Jiahuan. Beijing: Taihai Publishing, 2018.

Jia Zhangke. "My Perspective" [我的焦点], *Avant-Garde Today* [今日先锋], no. 5 (1997): 197–201.

Jia Zhangke. *A Touch of Sin* [天注定]. Edited by Ren Zhonglun. Jinan: Shangdong Pictorial Publishing, 2014.

Jia Zhangke and Zhao Jing. *Asking the Way: Twelve Portraits of Dreamers* [问道：十二种追逐梦想的人生]. Guilin: Guangxi Normal University Press, 2013.

Jia Zhangke and Zhao Jing. *The Road of Language* [语路]. Taipei: Freedom Village–Wooden Horse Culture Publishing, 2012.

Li Xun. "Chinese Independent Filmmaker" [中国独立电影人]. In *Cinematic Kitchen: Film in China* [电影厨房：电影在中国], edited by Wang Shuo, 147–64. Shanghai: Shanghai wenyi Publishing, 2001.

Lin Xudong. "Jia Zhangke: A Director for the People from China's Lower Class" [贾樟柯：来自中国底层的民间导演]. In *Dialogues with Contemporary Chinese Artists* [有事没事：与当代艺术对话], edited by Song Xiaoxia, 55–82. Chongqing: Chongqing Publishing, 2002.

Lin Xudong, Zhang Yaxuan, and Gu Zheng. *Jia Zhangke's Hometown Trilogy: Platform* [贾樟柯故乡三部曲之站台]. Beijing: Zhongguo mangwen chubanshe, 2003.

Lin Xudong, Zhang Yaxuan, and Gu Zheng. *Jia Zhangke's Hometown Trilogy: Unknown Pleasures* [贾樟柯故乡三部曲之任逍遥]. Beijing: Zhongguo mangwen chubanshe, 2003.

Lin Xudong, Zhang Yaxuan, and Gu Zheng. *Jia Zhangke's Hometown Trilogy: Xiao Wu* [贾樟柯故乡三部曲之小武]. Beijing: Zhongguo mangwen chubanshe, 2003.

Luo Yinsheng. *Jia Zhangke: From Artist to New Generation Director* [贾樟柯：From 文艺范儿 to 新生代导演]. Shanghai: Shanghai Jiaotong chubanshe, 2013.

Miao Ye. "I Only Make One Kind of Film" [我只拍一种电影]. In *Removing Celebrities' Makeup* [为名人卸妆], edited by Miao Ye, 156–69. Beijing: Dongfang Publishing, 2001.

Ouyang Jianghe, ed. *Chinese Independent Cinema* [中国独立电影]. Oxford: Oxford University Press, 2007.

Sun Jianmin, Yu Aiyuan, and Jia Zhangke. "Experiencing Different Visual Choices in the World" [经验世界中的影像选择], "Breaking Out, Escaping, Caught in the Net" [突围、逃离、落网], "Fragmented Decisions" [片段的决定], "*Platform*: Excerpts from the Screenplay" [〈站台〉电影剧本节选]. *Avant-Garde Today* [今日先锋], no. 12 (2002): 18–72.

Wu Wenguang, ed. *On Location* [现场]. Issue 1. Tianjin: Tianjin Social Science Publishing, 2000.

Xie Xiaoxia. *Research on the Image of the Lower Class in Contemporary Cinema* [当代电影底层形象研究]. Kunming: Yunnan People's Publishing House, 2009.

Yuan Yuan. *Jia Zhangke: A Cinematic Poet for His Generation* [贾樟柯：记录时代的电影诗人]. Shenzhen: Shenzhen Haitian Publishing, 2016.

Zhang Li. *Jia Zhangke Film Research* [贾樟柯电影研究]. Hefei: Anhui wenyi Publishing, 2016.

Zhang Xianmin. "Xiao Wu and Lao Liu" [小武与老六]. In *Invisible Images* [看不见的影像], 39–48. Shanghai: Shanghai sanlian, 2005.

Index

"accent," in filmmaking, 179–81
acting. *See* nonprofessional actors; performance
Alai, 185
alienation, 4, 6, 10, 13, 50
Anna Karenina, ix
"Answer, The" ("Huida"), 31–32, 199n11
Antonioni, Michelangelo, 14
Apocalypse Now, 34
art house cinema, 4, 13–15, 110, 111, 168, 174–76, 194
Ash Is Purest White (*Jianghu ernü*), xiii, 7, 10, 16, 17, 108, 128, 131–54, 176, 203n6; actors, 63, 104, 131, 145, 146; cinematography, 45; dialect, 61; and gangster films, 8, 11, 69, 129; jianghu, 8, 29, 134; music, 150, 152, 154; performance, 149, 150; screenplay, 134, 135, 138, 147; time span, 139, 140, 187, 190; UFO, 149; and *Unknown Pleasures*, 138; *wuxia*, 134

Bazin, Andre, 34
Bei Dao, 31–32, 199nn10–11

Beijing Film Academy, x, xi, 2–4, 17, 33–35, 40, 42, 48, 57, 64, 65, 67, 84, 88, 89, 109, 140, 159, 160, 164, 183
Beijing Film Academy Youth Experimental Filmmaker Group, 160
Beijing Film Studio, 129
Berlin International Film Festival, 14, 88, 108
Black Snow (*Benmingnian*), 166, 168
Boiling the Sea: Hou Hsiao-hsien's Memories of Shadows and Light, 16
bootleg film, 58, 90, 115–17
Boys from Fengkui (*Fenggui laide ren*), 79
break-dancing, xi, 3, 55
Breakin', xi, 3, 28, 55, 199n7
Bresson, Robert, 14, 42, 200n16
Buddhism, 2, 139, 202n5
budget, x, 4, 70–73, 118

calligraphy, 186, 188
Cannes International Film Festival, 14, 116, 200n13, 200n15
Cantopop, 24, 150, 203n3

Cao Guoxiong, 12
censorship, x, 15, 34, 116, 121, 129
Chang Cheh (Zhang Che), 28, 127, 146, 202n7
Chang, Eileen (Zhang Ailing), 110, 183, 203n5, 204n2
Chang, Sylvia (Zhang Aijia), 63
Chaplin, Charlie, 158, 168
Chen Daoming, 102
Chen Huai'ai, 127, 202n8
Chen Jianbin, 63, 107
Chen, Joan (Chen Chong), 7, 63, 107, 120, 174
Chen Kaige, x, 11, 33, 48, 199n12
Cheng Taishen, 6,
Chengdu, 10, 107, 119, 121
China Film Bureau, xi, 89–90, 176
Chinese painting, 3, 30, 44, 96, 128, 138, 171, 172, 191
Chow Keung (Zhou Qiang), 4, 16, 35
Chow Yun-fat (Zhou Runfa), 104
cinematography, 41, 42, 45, 68, 147–48, 159, 160, 164
City of Sadness (*Beiqing chengshi*), 110
Cold War, 119
collective, the, 25–27, 51, 66, 110, 150, 169
collectivism, 185, 187
commercial cinema, 1, 2, 8, 9, 11, 13–16, 111, 112, 176, 194
composite character, 107, 120, 121
Confucianism, 2
Coppola, Francis Ford, 34
costume design, 70–72, 101, 124, 128, 138, 144
COVID-19, 192
Cui Jian, 2, 26, 198n5
Cultural Revolution, x, 1–3, 21, 26, 29, 30, 49, 165, 169, 199nn10–11
Culture Fever, 1–2, 200n12

Dai Jinhua, 6, 13
dance, 6, 8, 28, 44, 45, 60, 72, 92, 100, 101
Daoism, 2
Dark Water, 14
Datong, 10, 78, 124
Deng Xiaoping, 1, 140

destruction. *See* ruins
dialect, 61, 100, 121, 162, 179, 185, 186, 194
Diao Yinan, 12, 145, 146
digital film, 4, 5, 11, 74–77, 98, 99, 138, 148, 153
Dingjun Shan, 37, 200n14
Ding Ling, 49
disco, 150, 158
documentary film: aesthetics, 4–5, 12, 13, 49, 58, 68–69, 75; influence on Jia, 22, 41; about Jia, 14; by Jia, 7, 12, 14, 16–18, 35, 37, 96, 98–99, 105–7, 119, 148, 184, 190; vs. narrative/fiction film, 6, 7, 11, 37, 105–7, 167, 187, 190–91, 194
Dong, 7, 10, 18, 96, 98, 99, 106, 184, 187
Dong Zijian, 63
Dongguan, 10
Doyle, Christopher, 41
Du Du, 3, 35, 37, 39–40, 160

Eco, Umberto, 2
Eisenstein, Sergei, 34, 168
extras, 69, 148, 149, 172

Fabula Entertainment (Shanghai nuanliu wenhua chuanmei), 12
famine, 188
Farewell My Concubine (*Bawang bieji*), 34, 200n13
Faulkner, William, 10
Feng Xiaogang, 145, 203n6
Fengjie, 7, 10, 96–99, 128, 144, 149, 195
Fenyang, x, 3, 5, 12–15, 18, 32, 155, 195; companies based in, 12, 111; dialect, 61, 100, 179, 194; growing up in, 20, 21, 28, 33; literary festival, 186; and *Platform*, 60, 66, 73; presence in Jia Zhangke's films, 10; stillness, 73; transformation, 47, 50, 51, 54; and *Xiao Wu*, 47, 50, 51, 58
Fenyang dialect. *See* dialect
Fifth Generation, x, 2, 6, 8, 34, 42, 48, 78–79, 169, 182, 196, 199n12
film format, 4, 11, 74, 75, 148. *See also* digital film
Flash animation, 6, 90, 99

Flowers of Shanghai (*Haishanghua*), 55, 108, 201n3
Forest of the Wild Boar (*Yezhu lin*), 127, 128, 202n8
Four Modernizations (*Sige xiandaihua*), 26
Freud, Sigmund, 27, 28, 31, 54
"Für Elise," 81
Future Reloaded, 166, 167

gangster film, 8, 11, 28, 69, 129, 134–35, 150, 151, 191
Garrison's Gorillas, 27, 199n6
Gautier, Eric, 14, 45, 144, 147, 200n17
genre cinema, 63, 69, 128, 129, 158
globalism, 6, 95, 96
Godard, Jean-Luc, 161
Goddess, The (*Shennü*), 166, 167
Godfather, The, 34
Golden Lion, 6, 14, 200n13
Goodbye South, Goodbye (*Nanguo zaijian, nanguo*), 55, 108, 201n3
"Go West," 150
"Go with Your Feelings" ("Gen zhe ganjue zou"), 26, 198n4
Guangzhou, 60, 61, 73, 123

Han Dong, 12
Han Han, 12
Han Jie, 12, 35
Han Sanming, 9, 97, 98, 102, 103, 128
He Ping, 49, 200n12
Hedonists, The, 102
Hero (*Yingxiong*), 8
Hometown Trilogy (*Guxiang sanbuqu*), 4, 5, 16, 17, 20, 74, 77, 88
Hong Kong, 4, 11, 24, 27, 28, 34, 35, 39, 41, 47, 50, 55, 135, 150, 151, 163, 202n7, 203nn3–4
Hong Kong Independent Short Film and Video Awards, 4, 35, 39
Hou Hsiao-hsien, 14, 16, 34, 41, 55, 79, 108–10
House of Flying Daggers (*Shimian maifu*), 8
Huang Jianxin, 48

hukou, 31
Human Condition, The, 79, 201n2
hunger, sensation of, 22
Huo Yuanjia, 27
Hu Tong Productions, 4

Ichiyama, Shozo, 14, 108
"I Have Nothing to My Name" ("Yiwu suoyou"), 26, 198n5
"I Love You" ("Wo ai ni"), 25
individualism, 25, 115
In Public (*Gongong changsuo*), 106, 187
internet, 51, 90–91, 140, 187–89
intertextuality, 11, 18, 137, 138, 187
I Wish I Knew (*Haishang chuanqi*), 7, 14, 18, 109, 136

Jia Pingwa, 183–87, 204n1
Jiang Wu, 63, 125
jianghu, 8, 17, 29, 30, 134–37, 139, 143, 146, 150–52, 195
Jia Xiang (*Jia Zhangke Speaks Out*), 12
Jia Zhang-ke, A Guy from Fenyang, 14
Jia Zhangke's Hometown Trilogy: Xiao Wu, Platform, Unknown Pleasures, 16
Jones, Kent, 82
Joyce, James, 10

karaoke, 24, 48, 51, 62, 79, 85, 150
Kentucky Fried Chicken, 96
Killer, The (*Diexue shuangxiong*), 150, 151
King Hu (Hu Jinquan), 28, 127, 128, 135, 202n7
Kitano, Takeshi, 108, 201n2
Kong Jinlei, 40, 45
Kundera, Milan, 1
Kurosawa, Akira, 35

Laclau, Matthieu, 14
Lau, Andy (Liu Dehua), 102
Lee Chang-dong, 112, 174, 175
Lee Kit-Ming (Li Jieming), 4, 163
Li Bai, 96
Li Jingze, 185
Liang Hong, 185–88, 204n5

Liao Fan, 63, 64, 144–46
Life (*Rensheng*), 29, 31, 183, 199n8
"Lifetime of Intoxication, A" ("Qianzui yisheng"), 151–53, 155
Lim Qiong (Lin Qiang), 6, 14, 109, 128, 152, 154
Lin Chong, 63, 127, 128, 202n9
Lin Chong Feeling by Night, 128, 203n9
literature, 2, 17, 30–33, 54, 73, 110, 114, 115, 143, 182–89, 195; literary adaptation, 3, 78, 79, 118, 182, 183
Liu Xiaodong, 7, 96, 106, 184, 201n1, 203n9
location shooting, 10, 43–45, 47, 65, 75, 118, 119, 121, 145, 156, 162, 166, 174; controlling locations, 69; scouting, 44, 85, 86, 149; *Still Life*, 7; *Swimming Out Till the Sea Turns Blue*, 185–87; *Touch of Sin*, 124
Lü Liping, 63, 107, 121
Lu Xun, 81, 158, 201n3
Lu Yao, 31, 183, 199n8
Lu Zhishen, 63, 125, 202n5

Ma Feng, 184, 185, 187, 204n4
Ma Ke, 184,
magic realism, 1–2, 6
makeup, 101, 143, 144, 147
Malraux, André, 79
Manchester by the Sea, 110
Man from Atlantis, 27, 199n6
Mao Zedong, ix, 1, 6, 30, 80, 114, 115
martial arts cinema, 8, 11, 28, 69, 125, 127, 129, 146, 170, 191
McDonald's, 95
McGrath, Jason, 13
Mello, Cecilia, 10, 197n6
Melville, Jean-Pierre, 112, 201n4
Mermaid, The (*Meirenyu*), 8
migrant workers, 3, 5, 93, 103, 162
Misty Poetry (Menglong shi), 2, 31, 32, 199n10
modernism, 36, 98, 164
modernity, 6, 10, 168, 169, 196
Monster Hunt (*Zhuoyao ji*), 8
montage, 2, 80

"Moon Represents My Heart, The" ("Yueliang daibiao wo de xin"), 25, 198n2
Motorcycle Diaries, The, 14
Mountains May Depart (*Shanhe guren*), 7, 12, 17, 20, 63, 108, 112, 134–39, 150, 154, 187, 190
Mo Yan, 10, 185, 186
"My Sweetie" ("Tian mimi"), 25, 198n2

Neon Goddesses (*Meili de hunpo*), 41, 42
New Face of the Nation (*Zuguo xinmao*), 22
New Wave cinema, 1–3, 13
New York Film Festival, 14, 16, 116
Nietzsche, Friedrich, 1, 27, 31, 54
noise, 41, 174, 181
nonprofessional actors, x, 4, 7, 58–64, 162, 171–73

Office Kitano, 108, 109
"old man who moves a mountain" (Yugong yishan), 192
Olympics (2008), 93, 140
One and Eight (*Yige he bage*), 2
One Day in Beijing, 3, 35, 37, 38
On the Road, 14
Open Door Policy, 26
opening shot, 17, 170–72
Ozu, Yasujiro, 14, 35

Peking opera, 6, 37, 125, 127, 128, 167, 173, 174, 186, 200n14
People's Congress, 13
performance, 7, 56, 60–62, 64, 68, 71, 102, 103, 124, 144, 150, 158, 159, 171, 173, 174
Pingyao Crouching Tiger Hidden Dragon International Film Festival, 12, 15, 110–12, 179, 198n10
Platform (*Zhantai*), x, xi, 4, 14–17, 20, 38, 40, 79, 81, 89, 108, 118, 169, 195, 201n3; actors, 56–60; autobiographical, 56; cinematography, 67–69; collaboration with Beijing Film Studio, 129–30; costume design, 70–72; ending, 82–83;

format, 75; funding and budget, 55, 72; green tint, 43; music, 25–27, 29; radio, 21; screenplay, 53–55, 64–67, 86; setting, 10, 73; time span, 5, 7, 74, 138–40; video rooms, 28; Zhao Tao, 100–102
poetry, 2, 31–33, 73, 96, 186
popular music, 2, 24–27, 41, 152
Promise, The (*Wuji*), 8
provincial town/city (*xiancheng*), 10, 20, 21, 25, 28, 31–33, 55, 169, 195
public spaces, 76, 77, 106, 189

qi cheng zhuan he ("introduction, elucidation, transition, summing up"), 178
qigong, 2

Raise the Red Lantern (*Dahong denglong gaogao gua*), 183
realism, ix, 12, 13, 69, 99, 155, 178
Red Firecracker, Green Firecracker (*Pao da Shuang deng*), 48
Reform Era, x, 2, 5, 7, 13, 22, 27, 30, 54, 73, 74, 103, 115, 140, 165, 169, 183, 198n2, 198nn5–6, 199n10
rehearsal, 62, 68, 71, 72
Renoir, Jean, 35
repetition, 79
Revive (*Fengchun*), 16, 44, 128
rock and roll, 1, 24, 27, 29, 198n5
ruins, 6, 10, 77, 78, 96–98, 128, 142

Salles, Walter, 14
Sandwich Man, The (*Erzi de da wan'ou*), 110, 111
SARS, 90, 94
Sartre, Jean-Paul, 27
Scar (*Shanghen*) movement, 2
Schopenhauer, Arthur, 1, 27
Schultz, Corey Kai Nelson, 7, 197n2
science fiction, 11, 191
Scorsese, Martin, 14, 16, 34
Scorsese on Scorsese, 34
screenwriting, 35, 49, 64, 84, 121, 122, 159, 176–78
scroll effect. *See* opening shot

Sculpting in Time: Reflections on the Cinema, 34
Shanghai Expo, 7
Shanghai Film Group, 89
Shanxi University, 33, 162
Shaw Brothers, 44
Shen Congwen, 110, 183, 204n2
Shenzhen, 92
Sixth Generation, x, 2, 3, 8, 12, 79, 165, 168, 169, 182
social change, 4, 5, 7, 115, 119, 141, 171; *Ash Is Purest White*, 152, 190; during childhood, 22–26, 32; and costume design, 70–72; film industry, 64, 90; Han Sanming, 103; Liang Hong, 186; *Platform*, 65–67, 74; *Still Life*, 97, 142, 149; *Swimming Out Till the Sea Turns Blue*, 183, 186, 190; *The World*, 90–93; *Xiao Wu*, 47–55
socialist realism, ix, 1, 3
song-and-dance troupe (*wengongtuan*), x, 5, 27, 28, 55, 66, 74
sound design, 40, 41, 160, 174, 181
Soviet style of screenwriting, 35, 36, 84, 177
Speaking in Images: Interviews with Contemporary Chinese Filmmakers, 16, 198, 200
Spring in a Small Town (*Xiaocheng zhi chun*), 136, 166, 168, 203n2
Stars collective (Xingxing huahui), 2
Still Life (*Sanxia haoren*), 4, 6–7, 10, 11, 14, 16, 17, 56, 86, 96–104, 106, 114, 128, 138, 142, 144, 149, 152, 170, 181, 187, 195
storyboard, 44, 86
Story of Qiuju, The (*Qiuhu da guansi*), 34, 200n13
structuralism, 36
Su Tong, 183, 185, 204n3
Sun Ganlu, 183, 204n3
Swimming Out Till the Sea Turns Blue (*Yizhi youdao haishui bianlan*), xiii, 16–18, 182–92

tai chi, 2
Taiwan, x, 3, 14, 24, 25, 27, 28, 34, 154, 198nn2–4

Taiyuan, 3, 20, 21, 33, 61
Tarkovsky, Andrei, 34
television, 12, 20, 22, 27, 28, 51, 54, 160, 199n6
Teng, Teresa (Deng Lijun), x, 3, 25, 198n2
Third Line Construction Project (*sanxian gongcheng*), 119, 202n2
Three Gorges Dam, 6, 96–99, 141, 142, 144, 148, 149, 171
Tian Zhuangzhuang, x, 129, 203n10
Tiananmen Square, 5, 35, 38, 140
Tiananmen Student Movement (1989), 5, 29, 54, 65, 74, 140
tightrope walker, 6, 99
Tiny Times (*Xiao shidai*), 8
To, Johnnie (Du Qifeng), 179
Today (*Jintian*), 2, 199n10
To Live (*Huozhe*), 34, 183, 204n3
Tolstoy, Leo, ix
Touch of Sin, A (*Tianzhuding*), 7, 10, 15–17, 56, 112, 114, 115, 204n7; acclaim, 14; actors, 63, 69; censorship, 116–18, 129; costume design, 124–28; film style, 129; genre cinema, 158; jianghu, 29, 134; martial arts/*wuxia*, 11, 44; music, 150; Peking opera, 127–29; revenge, 30; screenplay, 122–24; social media, 122; structure, 165; Zhao Tao, 124
Touch of Zen (*Xia nü*), 128, 202n7
Tragic Hero (*Yingxiong haohan*), 151
Truffaut, François, 137
Tsai Ming-liang (Cai Mingliang), 137
Turn East Media (Yihui chuanmei), 12
24 City (*Ershisi cheng ji*), 4, 7, 10, 12, 17, 63, 106, 107, 114, 117–21, 174, 201n1

UCLA, 16, 17
UFOs, 6, 144, 149, 156, 195
Ulan Bator, 20, 21, 198n1
Unknown Pleasures (*Ren xiaoyao*), 4, 14, 16, 17, 51, 56, 58, 89, 118, 200n15, 201n3; *Ash Is Purest White*, 138; destruction, 77–78; digital filmmaking, 74–77; *In Public*, 106, 187; motorcycle breaking down, 84; remnants of socialism, 10; repetition, 79; transformation, 5
Useless (*Wuyong*), 17, 18, 184

Venice Film Festival, 6, 14, 166, 167, 200n13
video rooms, 17, 28, 134, 155
violence, 11, 115, 116, 122, 123, 125, 165, 166

Wang Baoqiang, 63, 69, 123, 125
Wang, Faye (Wang Fei/Wang Jingwen), 80, 81
Wang Hong, 12
Wang Hongwei, 3, 4, 5, 56–58, 62, 67, 68, 82, 100
Wang, Qi, 11
Wang Xiaoshuai, 2, 3, 145
war film, 1
washing machine, 20, 22, 24
Water Margin, The (*Shuihu zhuan*), 8, 31, 63, 123, 125, 146, 202nn5–6, 202n9
"We Are the New Generation of the Eighties" ("Women shi bashi niandai de xin yidai"), 25
"We Are the Successors of Communism" ("Women shi gongchanzhuyi de jiebanren"), 25
Wei Wei, 136, 203n2
"We the Workers Have the Power" ("Zamen gongren you Liliang"), 25
Wham!, 1
"Wine with Coffee" ("Meijiu jia kafei"), 25
Wives and Concubines (*Qiqie chengqun*), 183
Wolf Warrior II (*Zhanlang II*), 8
woman characters, 131–32, 142, 143
Wong, Taylor, 151
Woo, John (Wu Yusen), 8, 14, 28, 125, 150, 151, 201n4
Wooden Man's Bride, The (*Wukui*), 48
working with actors. *See* nonprofessional actors
World, The (*Shijie*), xi, 5, 6, 16, 17, 56, 88–96, 100, 102, 108, 114, 118, 154, 170, 201n3

World Park, 5, 91–93, 95
World Trade Organization, 140
Wu Song, 63, 125, 202n6
Wu Xiaobo, 12
Wu Yonggang, 166, 167
wuxia, 28, 44, 63, 129, 134, 202n7. See also martial arts cinema

Xiao Shan Going Home, 3, 4, 16, 17, 35, 37, 38, 56, 57, 64, 93, 160, 161, 163
Xiao Wu, 4, 9, 10, 14–17, 22, 38, 39, 40, 41, 45, 59, 62, 65, 108, 118, 134, 163, 170; actors, 56–64, 173; approval, 88, 89, 129; destruction, 6, 77, 78; documentary techniques, 167; ending, 81; Fenyang, 12, 20; format, 74, 75; jianghu, 29, 134; karaoke, 24, 48; music, 150; opening scene, 80; origin of film, 47, 48; relationships, 5, 51–53, 80, 81, 178; screenplay, 53–55; sound design, 41; structure, 49; title, 49, 50; *Unknown Pleasures*, 77, 78; Wang Hongwei, 56–58
Xie Fei, 166, 168, 169
XStream Pictures, 12, 110
Xu Zheng, 145

"Yan'an Talks on Art and Literature," 114
Yang, Li, 13
Yangtze River, 6, 28, 96, 97
Yeh, Sally (Ye Qianwen), 142, 150–52, 155, 203n3

Yellow Earth (*Huang tudi*), x, 2, 3, 11, 14, 33, 166, 168, 199–200n12
Yellow River, 28, 47, 186
"YMCA," 150
"Young Friends Come Together" ("Nianqing de pengyou lai xianghui"), 26
Yu Hua, 183, 185, 187, 191, 192, 204n3
Yu Lik-wai, Nelson (Yu Liwei), 4, 17, 35, 40–45, 47, 76, 85, 102, 147, 148, 200n15

Zatoichi, 108
Zhai Yongming, 121, 202n3
Zhang Yang, 40, 41, 45
Zhang Yibai, 145, 146
Zhang Yimou, x, 29, 34, 42, 48, 183, 194, 200n12
Zhang Yuan, 2, 3, 54, 194
Zhao Tao, 5–7, 107, 121, 131, 148, 153; character in *Platform*, 66–69; character in *Still Life*, 97, 98; character in *Touch of Sin*, 123–25; collaborative relationship with Jia Zhangke, 100–102, 173; comments on dance performance, 44, 45; contributions to *The World* screenplay, 92; costumes, 72, 127, 128; dialect, 61; female characters, 131, 142–46; makeup, 143–44; smoking scene in *Platform*, 60
Zhong Dafeng, 37
Zhu Shilin, 136

www.ingramcontent.com/pod-product-compliance
Lightning Source LLC
Chambersburg PA
CBHW070842160426
43192CB00012B/2275